Sign Up Online

SBAC

Grade 8 ELA Practice

Get Digital Access To

2 SBAC Practice Tests

3 ELA Strands

Register Now

Url: www.lumoslearning.com/a/tedbooks

Access Code: SBACG8E-43990-P

W9-AVS-614

SBAC Test Prep: Grade 8 English Language Arts Literacy (ELA) Common Core Practice Book and Full-length Online Assessments: Smarter Balanced Study Guide

Contributing Editor   -   **Erin Schollaert**
Contributing Editor   -   **Nina Anderson**
Contributing Editor   -   **George Smith**
Executive Producer   -   **Mukunda Krishnaswamy**
Designer and Illustrator -   **Harini N.**

COPYRIGHT ©2015 by Lumos Information Services, LLC. **ALL RIGHTS RESERVED.** No portion of this book may be reproduced mechanically, electronically or by any other means, including photocopying, recording, taping, Web Distribution or Information Storage and Retrieval systems, without prior written permission of the Publisher, Lumos Information Services, LLC.

First Edition - 2020

NGA Center/CCSSO are the sole owners and developers of the Common Core State Standards, which does not sponsor or endorse this product. © Copyright 2010. National Governors Association Center for Best Practices and Council of Chief State School Officers.

SBAC is a copyright of The Regents of the University of California – Smarter Balanced Assessment Consortium., which does not sponsor or endorse this product.

ISBN-10: 1940484804

ISBN-13: 978-1-940484-80-8

Printed in the United States of America

Last updated - July 2022

For permissions and additional information contact us

Lumos Information Services, LLC
PO Box 1575, Piscataway, NJ 08855-1575
http://www.LumosLearning.com

Email: support@lumoslearning.com
Tel: (732) 384-0146
Fax: (866) 283-6471

Lumos Learning
Developed by Expert Teachers

INTRODUCTION

This book is specifically designed to improve student achievement on the Smarter Balanced Assessment Consortium (SBAC) Test. With over a decade of expertise in developing practice resources for standardized tests, Lumos Learning has designed the most efficient methodology to help students succeed on the state assessments (See Figure 1).

Lumos Smart Test Practice provides students SBAC assessment rehearsal along with an efficient pathway to overcome any standards proficiency gaps. Students perform at their best on standardized tests when they feel comfortable with the test content as well as the test format. Lumos online practice tests are meticulously designed to mirror the SBAC assessment. It adheres to the guidelines provided by the SBAC for the number of questions, standards, difficulty level, sessions, question types, and duration.

The process starts with students taking the online diagnostic assessment. This online diagnostic test will help assess students' proficiency levels in various standards.

After completion of the diagnostic assessment, students can take note of standards where they are not proficient. This step will help parents and educators in developing a targeted remedial study plan based on a student's proficiency gaps.

Once the targeted remedial study plan is in place, students can start practicing the lessons in this workbook that are focused on specific standards.

After the student completes the targeted remedial practice, the student should attempt the second online SBAC practice test. Record the proficiency levels in the second practice test to measure the student progress and identify any additional learning gaps. Further targeted practice can be planned to help students gain comprehensive skills mastery needed to ensure success on the state assessment.

Lumos Smart Test Prep Methodology

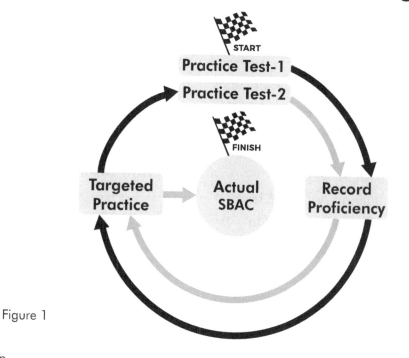

Figure 1

Table of Contents

Introduction 1

Chapter 1 Lumos Smart Test Prep Methodology 4

Chapter 2 Reading: Literature 9
Lesson 1   RL.8.1   Textual Evidence 10
Lesson 2   RL.8.1   Inferences 19
Lesson 3   RL.8.2   Theme 28
Lesson 4   RL.8.2   Objective Summary 37
Lesson 5   RL.8.2   Plot 47
Lesson 6   RL.8.2   Setting 52
Lesson 7   RL.8.2   Character 58
Lesson 8   RL 8.3   Analyzing Literature 64
Lesson 9   RL.8.4   Meaning and Tone 71
Lesson 10 RL.8.5   Compare and Contrast 81
Lesson 11 RL.8.6   Producing Suspense and Humor 88
Lesson 12 RL.8.7   Media and Literature 93
Lesson 13 RL 8.9   Modern Fictions and Traditional Stories 100
           Answer Key & Detailed Explanations 106

Chapter 3 Reading: Informational Text 130
Lesson 1   RI.8.1   Making Inferences Based on Textual Evidence 131
Lesson 2   RI.8.2   Central Idea 138
Lesson 3   RI 8.3   Connections and Distinctions 146
Lesson 4   RI.8.4   Determining Meaning of Words 152
Lesson 5   RI 8.5   Analyzing Structures in Text 158
Lesson 6   RI.8.6   Author's Point of View 167
Lesson 7   RI.8.7   Publishing Mediums 173
Lesson 8   RI.8.8   Evaluating Authors Claims 179
Lesson 9   RI.8.9   Conflicting Information 184
           Answer Key & Detailed Explanations 189

Chapter 4	**Language**	⋯⋯⋯⋯⋯⋯⋯⋯⋯⋯⋯⋯⋯⋯⋯⋯⋯⋯⋯⋯	**202**
Lesson 1	L.8.1.A	Adjectives and Adverbs	⋯⋯⋯⋯⋯⋯⋯⋯⋯	203
Lesson 2	L.8.1.B	Subject-Verb Agreement	⋯⋯⋯⋯⋯⋯⋯	208
Lesson 3	L.8.1.C	Pronouns	⋯⋯⋯⋯⋯⋯⋯⋯⋯⋯⋯⋯⋯⋯⋯	212
Lesson 4	L.8.1.C	Phrases and Clauses	⋯⋯⋯⋯⋯⋯⋯⋯⋯⋯	216
Lesson 5	L.8.1.D	Verbals	⋯⋯⋯⋯⋯⋯⋯⋯⋯⋯⋯⋯⋯⋯⋯⋯	219
Lesson 6	L.8.2	Capitalization	⋯⋯⋯⋯⋯⋯⋯⋯⋯⋯⋯⋯⋯	223
Lesson 7	L.8.2.A	Punctuation	⋯⋯⋯⋯⋯⋯⋯⋯⋯⋯⋯⋯⋯⋯	227
Lesson 8	L.8.2.B	Ellipsis	⋯⋯⋯⋯⋯⋯⋯⋯⋯⋯⋯⋯⋯⋯⋯⋯	230
Lesson 9	L.8.2.C	Spelling	⋯⋯⋯⋯⋯⋯⋯⋯⋯⋯⋯⋯⋯⋯⋯⋯	233
Lesson 10	L.8.3.A	Mood in Verbs	⋯⋯⋯⋯⋯⋯⋯⋯⋯⋯⋯⋯	237
Lesson 11	L.8.3.A	Active and Passive Voice	⋯⋯⋯⋯⋯⋯⋯	240
Lesson 12	L.8.4.A	Context Clues	⋯⋯⋯⋯⋯⋯⋯⋯⋯⋯⋯⋯	244
Lesson 13	L.8.4.B	Multiple Meaning Words	⋯⋯⋯⋯⋯⋯⋯	248
Lesson 14	L.8.4.B	Roots, Affixes, and Syllables	⋯⋯⋯⋯	252
Lesson 15	L.8.4.C	Reference Materials	⋯⋯⋯⋯⋯⋯⋯⋯⋯⋯	256
Lesson 16	L.8.4.D	Using Context to Verify Meaning	⋯⋯	260
Lesson 17	L.8.5.A	Interpreting Figures of Speech	⋯⋯⋯	264
Lesson 18	L.8.5.B	Relationships Between Words	⋯⋯⋯	268
Lesson 19	L.8.5.C	Denotations and Connotations	⋯⋯⋯	273
Lesson 20	L.8.6	Domain Specific Words	⋯⋯⋯⋯⋯⋯⋯⋯	277
		Answer Key & Detailed Explanations	⋯⋯⋯⋯	**281**

Additional Information	⋯⋯⋯⋯⋯⋯⋯⋯⋯⋯⋯⋯⋯⋯⋯	**309**
SBAC FAQ	⋯⋯⋯⋯⋯⋯⋯⋯⋯⋯⋯⋯⋯⋯⋯⋯⋯⋯⋯⋯⋯	309
Progress Chart	⋯⋯⋯⋯⋯⋯⋯⋯⋯⋯⋯⋯⋯⋯⋯⋯⋯⋯	312

Chapter 1

Lumos Smart Test Prep Methodology

Step 1: Access Online SBAC Practice Test

Use the URL and access code provided below or scan the QR code to access the first SBAC practice test to get started. The online SBAC practice test mirrors the actual Smarter Balanced assessments in number of questions, item types, test duration, test tools and more.

After completing the test, your student will receive immediate feedback with detailed reports on standards mastery. With this report, use the next section of the book to design a practice plan for your student.

URL	QR Code
Visit the URL below and place the book access code **www.lumoslearning.com/a/tedbooks** **Access Code: SBACG8E-43990-P**	

Step 2: Review the Personalized Study Plan Online

After student complete the online Practice Test 1, student can access their individualized study plan from the table of contents (Figure 2).

Parents and Teachers can also review the study plan through their Lumos account.

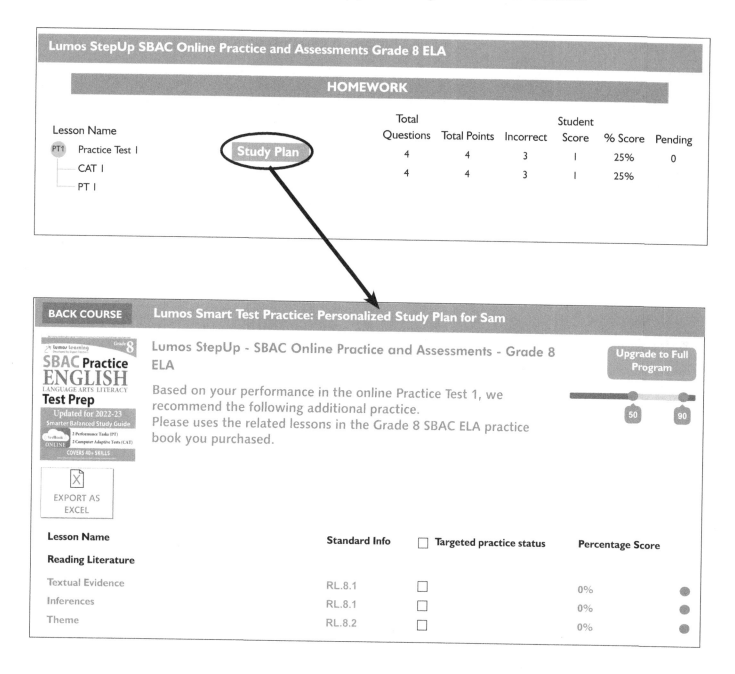

Step 3: Complete Targeted Practice

Using the information provided in the study plan report, complete the targeted practice using the appropriate lessons to overcome proficiency gaps. With lesson names included in the study plan, find the appropriate topics in this workbook and answer the questions provided. Students can refer to the answer key and detailed answers provided for each lesson to gain further understanding of the learning objective. Marking the completed lessons in the study plan after each practice session is recommended.(See Figure 3)

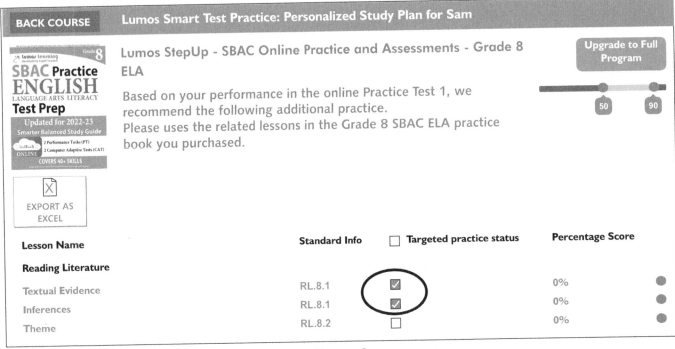

Figure 3

Step 4: Access the Practice Test 2 Online

After completing the targeted practice in this workbook, students should attempt the second SBAC practice test online. Using the student login name and password, login to the Lumos website to complete the second practice test.

Step 5: Repeat Targeted Practice

Repeat the targeted practice as per Step 3 using the second study plan report for Practice test 2 after completion of the second SBAC rehearsal.

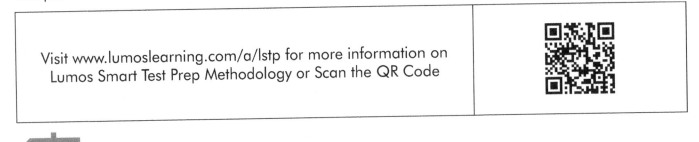

Visit www.lumoslearning.com/a/lstp for more information on Lumos Smart Test Prep Methodology or Scan the QR Code

What if I buy more than one Lumos Study Program?

Step 1 ⟶ Visit the URL given below and login to your account

www.lumoslearning.com

Step 2 ⟶ Click on 'My tedBooks' under the "Account" tab

Place the Book Access Code and submit.

🚀 Get Started		**Access Lumos Tedbook Online Resourse**	
◄ Assign Practice		**BOOK CODE**	
Account ⌄		Enter Access Code	Submit
💲 Billing			
👥 My Students		No.	Name	Access Code
🎥 My Lessons		1	Sam Jones	★★★★★★★★★★★★★★★★
📖 My tedBooks		2	John Doe	★★★★★★★★★★★★★★★★
♥ My Stickies		3	Ron Miller	★★★★★★★★★★★★★★★★

Step 3 ⟶ Add the new book

To add the new book for a registered student, choose the '**Existing Student**' button, select the student and submit.

Assign To ⓘ

⦿ Existing Student   ○ Add New student

○ Sam Jones

○ John Doe

○ Ron Miller

Submit

To add the new book for a new student, choose the '**Add New Student**' button and complete the student registration.

Assign To ⓘ

○ Existing Student   ⦿ Add New student

Register Your TedBook

Student Name:*   Enter First Name   Enter Last Name

Student Login*

Password*

Submit

7

1) **The day before the test,** make sure you get a good night's sleep.

2) **On the day of the test,** be sure to eat a good hearty breakfast! Also, be sure to arrive at school on time.

3) **During the test:**

- **Read every question carefully.**

  - Do not spend too much time on any one question. Work steadily through all questions in the section.
  - Attempt all of the questions even if you are not sure of some answers.
  - If you run into a difficult question, eliminate as many choices as you can and then pick the best one from the remaining choices. Intelligent guessing will help you increase your score.
  - Also, mark the question so that if you have extra time, you can return to it after you reach the end of the section.
  - Some questions may refer to a graph, chart, or other kind of picture. Carefully review the graphic before answering the question.
  - Be sure to include explanations for your written responses and show all work.

- **While Answering Multiple-Choice (EBSR) questions.**

  - Select the bubble corresponding to your answer choice.
  - Read **all** of the answer choices, even if think you have found the correct answer.

- **While Answering TECR questions.**

  - Read the directions of each question. Some might ask you to drag something, others to select, and still others to highlight. Follow all instructions of the question (or questions if it is in multiple parts)

Chapter 2 - Reading: Literature

The objective of the Reading Literature standards is to ensure that the student is able to read and comprehend literature (which includes stories, drama and poetry) related to Grade 8.

To help students master the necessary skills, information to help the student understand the concepts related to the standard is given. Along with this, we encourage the student to go through the resources available online on EdSearch to gain an in depth understanding of these concepts. The EdSearch page for each lesson can be accessed with the help of the url or the QR code provided.

A small map is provided after each passage or text in which the student can enter the details as understood from the literary text. Doing this will help the student to refer to key points that help in answering the questions with ease.

Chapter 2

Lesson 1: Textual Evidence

Inferences: Conclusions reached or judgments made after reading and thinking about the meaning of a statement or proposal. These conclusions or judgments are not included in the statement or proposal.

Let us understand the concept with an example.

Global Warming

Scientists tell us that changes in our climate are happening. Average temperatures around the world are getting higher. The planet's average surface temperature has risen about 2.0 degrees Fahrenheit since the late 19th century. The warmest year on record was 2016, according to a report compiled by the National Oceanic and Atmospheric Administration's Center for Weather and Climate at the National Centers for Environmental Information. This report is based on contributions from scientists from around the world, and includes data collected by environmental monitoring stations and instruments located on land, water, ice, and in space. This report also noted the following changes attributed to the warming of the earth:

- The amount of carbon dioxide in the atmosphere reached its highest level in the past 60 years
- The temperatures of seawater at the surface were the highest ever recorded
- Global sea levels were the highest ever recorded
- The ice caps in Greenland and Antarctica are melting.

This increase in global temperatures is called global warming. Global warming is caused by the increase in certain gases (such as carbon dioxide) in the atmosphere that occurs when warmth from the sun is trapped in the Earth's atmosphere by a layer of gases and water vapor. They refer to this phenomenon as the "greenhouse effect." And how do these gases enter the atmosphere? From the burning of fossil fuels such as oil, coal and gas which are used in the manufacture of products and as byproducts from the use of gasoline to fuel vehicles. Other forms of pollution also contribute to the greenhouse effect as does deforestation and other actions that decrease the number of plants on earth (plants absorb carbon dioxide during photosynthesis and release oxygen as a byproduct).

Your *assignment*:

Part 1. To analyze the text and summarize its main ideas, and quote from the text-specific statements that support the main ideas.
Part 2. What do you infer (draw a conclusion or opinion from the text that is not stated in the text) from the text?

10

Here is an example of what you might write.

Part 1:

Main idea #1: Our climate is changing. Average temperatures around the world are getting higher. Proof: A report compiled by the National Oceanic and Atmospheric Administration's Center for Weather and Climate at the National Centers for Environmental Information cites several statistics that support the idea that global warming is taking place. The fact that scientists from around the world contributed to this report and the report used data from monitoring stations from several locations on earth provide credibility to the results of the report.

Main idea #2: These changes in climate are having harmful effects on humans, plants and animals. Proof: Carbon dioxide reduces air quality which is not healthy for humans and animals to breathe. Water is essential for living creatures; without enough water they die. Global warming decreases the amount of water on the planet. Some creatures cannot adapt quickly to changes in climates and will die, and those that migrate can be forced to change their migration patterns.

Main idea #3: Most scientists agree that human activities are the most important causes of global warming. Examples: using fossil fuels like oil, gas and coal in the manufacture of products and as byproducts from the use of gasoline to fuel vehicles. Other forms of pollution also contribute to the greenhouse effect as does deforestation.

Part 2:

I am inferring that if we do not reverse the trend in global warming, there will be results that are harmful to humans, plants and animals. The supply of fresh water will become increasingly scarce as higher temperatures increase evaporation and without adequate fresh water, large numbers of humans, plants and animals will die. Also, in the short term, flooding will occur as melting glaciers and ice caps increase the volume of ocean saltwater. Carbon dioxide reduces air quality which is not healthy for humans and animals to breathe, although plants need it for photosynthesis, but deforestation because of logging and commercial and residential development reduces the numbers of plants.

I am also inferring from this data that organizations interested in maintaining a healthy environment on earth need volunteers and funds to advance their programs.

You can scan the QR code given below or use the url to access additional EdSearch resources including videos and mobile apps related to *Textual Evidence* .

ed Search   *Textual Evidence*

URL	QR Code
http://www.lumoslearning.com/a/rl81	

Question 1-5 are based on the poem below.

Sympathy

I lay in sorrow, deep distressed;
My grief a proud man heard;
His looks were cold, he gave me gold,
But not a kindly word.

My sorrow passed-I paid him back
The gold he gave to me;
Then stood erect and spoke my thanks
And blessed his charity.

I lay in want, and grief, and pain;
A poor man passed my way;
He bound my head, He gave me bread,
He watched me day and night.

How shall I pay him back again
For all he did to me ?
Oh, gold is great, but greater far
Is heavenly sympathy.
-        Charles Mackay

1. The reader can tell from the third stanza that the poet is

   Ⓐ caring for a patient with a head injury.
   Ⓑ wanting company.
   ⬤ watched and fed night and day by a poor man.
   Ⓓ greedy.

2. According to the poet, what did he feel was most important?

   Ⓐ giving away food
   Ⓑ blessing charity
   ⬤ sympathy
   Ⓓ gold

3. What does the first stanza tell us about the poet?

   ⬤ The poet experienced an event which made him deeply sorrowful.
   Ⓑ The poet wrote this poem when he was a proud man.
   Ⓒ The poet wrote this poem when he was in need of money.
   Ⓓ The poet was friends with the proud man.

4. Which line in the poem tells you that the poet is grateful to the poor man?

Ⓐ How shall I pay him back again, for all he did to me?
Ⓑ I lay in want, in grief and pain;
Ⓒ His looks were cold, he gave me gold. But not a kindly word.
Ⓓ Then stood erect and spoke my thanks, and blessed his charity.

5. How did the proud man treat the poet when he lay in sorrow and deep distress?

Ⓐ in an affectionate way
Ⓑ in an aloof, unsympathetic manner
Ⓒ with a lot of concern
Ⓓ with respect and kindness

Question 6 and 7 are based on the poem below.

The Mountain and The Squirrel	The Arrow and the Song
The mountain and the squirrel Had a quarrel; And the former called the latter, "Little Prig." Bun replied "You are doubtless very big; But all sorts of things and weather Must be taken in together To make up a year And a sphere. And I think it no disgrace To occupy my place. If I'm not so large as you, Your are not so small as I, And not half so spry; I'll not deny you make A very pretty squirrel track; Talents differ; all is well and wisely put; If I cannot carry forests on my back, Neither can you crack a nut" Ralph Waldo Emerson (1803 - 1882)	I shot an arrow into the air It fell to earth, I knew not where; For, so swiftly it flew, the sight Could not follow it in its flight. I breathed a song into the air It fell to earth, I knew not where For who has sight so keen and strong That it can follow the flight of song? Long, long afterward, in an oak I found the arrow, still unbroke And the song, from beginning to end I found again in the heart of a friend. H. W. Longfellow (1807 - 1882)

6. Which line in "The Mountain and the Squirrel" told the reader that the squirrel recognizes everyone has a different talent?

Ⓐ Talents differ; all is well and wisely put;
Ⓑ You are doubtless very big;
Ⓒ And I think it no disgrace
   To occupy my place.
Ⓓ I'll not deny you make
   A very pretty squirrel track;

7. Which of the following statements about "The Mountain and the Squirrel" and "The Arrow and the Song" is true?

Ⓐ A squirrel is the narrator in both.
Ⓑ Both incorporate nature in the text.
Ⓒ Both are written in first person.
Ⓓ Both are about friendship.

Question 8-10 are based on the poem below.

The Lake Isle of Innisfree

I will arise and go now, and go to Innisfree,
And a small cabin build there, of clay and wattles made:
Nine bean-rows will I have there, a hive for the honey-bee;
And live alone in the bee-loud glade.

And I shall have some peace there, for peace comes dropping slow,
Dropping from the veils of the morning to where the cricket sings;
There midnight's all a glimmer, and noon a purple glow,
And evening full of the linnet's wings.

I will arise and go now, for always night and day
I hear lake water lapping with low sounds by the shore;
While I stand on the roadway, or on the pavements grey,
I hear it in the deep heart's core.

W.B. Yeats

About the poet:
William Butler Yeats was an Irish poet and a dramatist. He was one of the foremost figures of 20th-century literature and was the driving force behind the Irish literary revival. Together with Lady Gregory and Edward Martin, Yeats founded the Abbey Theatre. He served as its chief during its early years and was a pillar of the Irish literary establishment in his later years.

The well-known poem explores the poet's longing for the peace and tranquillity of Innisfree, a place where he spent a lot of time as a boy. This poem is a lyric.

image obtained from freephotosbank.com

8. Which line tells the reader Yeats is day-dreaming of Innisfree?

Ⓐ Nine bean-rows will I have there, a hive for the honey-bee;
Ⓑ And I shall have some peace there, for peace comes dropping slow,
Ⓒ And evening full of the linnet's wings.
Ⓓ While I stand on the roadway, or on the pavements grey

9. What does the description after the poem tell us about Yeats?

Ⓐ He was a key person in the development of Irish economy.
Ⓑ He was a key person in the development of Irish literacy.
Ⓒ He was not a Nobel Prize winner.
Ⓓ all of the above

10. Part A

According to the poem and the description, which of the following statements about the author would be true?

Ⓐ Yeats was very famous and loved literature.
Ⓑ Yeats was a writer and wrote a lot of poems and plays.
Ⓒ Yeats was an Irish man and a key person in the development of Irish literature.
Ⓓ All of the above.

10. Part B

Which line of the poem provides evidence that the author wants to build a cabin in Innisfree?

Ⓐ I will arise and go now, and go to Innisfree,
Ⓑ And a small cabin build there, of clay and wattles made:
Ⓒ Dropping from the veils of the morning to where the cricket sings;
Ⓓ I will arise and go now, for always night and day

Question 11 is based on the passage below.

Patrick couldn't believe it. The most important day of his life so far; the day he had been waiting for had finally arrived! He was so excited to show the coaches how hard he had been working on his pitching. He just knew he would make the team this year. Looking at the clock, Patrick realized he was running late. "Bye, Mom," he yelled as he scrambled out of the house. Backing down the driveway, he saw his mom run out of the house, and it looked like she was trying to get his attention. He didn't have time to wait, so he drove off.

Although the school was only five minutes away, the drive felt like an eternity. Two red lights later, Patrick screeched into the parking lot, slammed the car into park, and ran around to the trunk to get his bat bag. It wasn't there. Every piece of equipment he needed to prove himself to the coaches this year was in that bag.

11. Part A

What was Patrick's mom likely trying to tell him?

Ⓐ "Don't drive too fast!"
Ⓑ "Don't be late for tryouts!"
Ⓒ "Be careful driving!"
Ⓓ He forgot his bat bag!

11. Part B

The reader can tell from the story that Patrick _____.

Ⓐ had tried out for the team before and not made it.
Ⓑ was a fast runner.
Ⓒ was not at all ready for tryouts.
Ⓓ was not excited to tryout for the team.

Question 12 is based on the passage below.

It had been a year since Lauren had seen Bailey. Bailey's family had moved to Qatar leaving Lauren to face the world without her best friend. Anxiously, Lauren waited at the arrival gate hoping to glimpse a peek at her childhood friend. She knew after eleven hours in the air, Bailey would be exhausted, but she could hardly wait to catch up. Moments later, the doors to the gate flung open, and there she was, her best friend, Bailey.

Once home, the hours passed like minutes as the girls laughed and giggled sharing moments from the last year. It felt as if they had never been apart. But Lauren felt like Bailey was holding something back.

12. Part A

What details in the passage supports that Lauren was anxious to meet her friend Bailey?

Ⓐ She knew after eleven hours in the air, Bailey would be exhausted, but she could hardly wait to catch up.

Ⓑ Anxiously, Lauren waited at the arrival gate hoping to glimpse a peek at her childhood friend.

Ⓒ Moments later, the doors to the gate flung open and there she was, her best friend, Bailey.

Ⓓ All of the above

12. Part B

What did Lauren feel about Bailey in the concluding sentence of the passage?

Ⓐ Bailey was moving home.

Ⓑ Bailey had a secret she wasn't sharing.

Ⓒ Bailey loved her new home in Qatar.

Ⓓ None of the above

Chapter 2

Lesson 2: Inferences

You can scan the QR code given below or use the url to access additional EdSearch resources including videos and mobile apps related to *Inferences*.

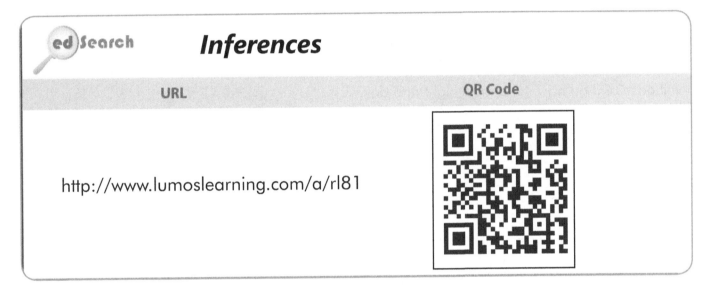

ed Search

Inferences

URL	QR Code
http://www.lumoslearning.com/a/rl81	

Question 1 and 2 are based on the poem below.

The Lake Isle of Innisfree

I will arise and go now, and go to Innisfree,
And a small cabin build there, of clay and wattles made:
Nine bean-rows will I have there, a hive for the honey-bee;
And live alone in the bee-loud glade.

And I shall have some peace there, for peace comes dropping slow,
Dropping from the veils of the morning to where the cricket sings;
There midnight's all a glimmer, and noon a purple glow,
And evening full of the linnet's wings.

I will arise and go now, for always night and day
I hear lake water lapping with low sounds by the shore;
While I stand on the roadway, or on the pavements grey,
I hear it in the deep heart's core.

W.B. Yeats

About the poet:
William Butler Yeats was an Irish poet and a dramatist. He was one of the foremost figures of 20th-century literature and was the driving force behind the Irish literary revival. Together with Lady Gregory and Edward Martin, Yeats founded the Abbey Theatre. He served as its chief during its early years and was a pillar of the Irish literary establishment in his later years.

The above well-known poem explores the poet's longing for the peace and tranquility of Innisfree, a place where he spent a lot of time as a boy. This poem is a lyric.

1. After reading the poem what can you say the poet is yearning for?

Ⓐ the lake water and the sound it makes
Ⓑ the beehive and sound of the bees
Ⓒ the peace and tranquility of Innisfree
Ⓓ none of the above

2. According to the poem, what do you think the age of the author is?

Ⓐ He is old and ready to retire.
Ⓑ He is a very young boy.
Ⓒ He is in his mid thirties.
Ⓓ He is a baby.

Question 3 is based on the paragraph below.

Elizabeth had done it again. She was in such a hurry; she didn't check to make sure she had everything she needed for the drive to work. Just as she slammed the door behind her, she realized, too late, that she wasn't going anywhere fast.

3. What did Elizabeth forget?

- Ⓐ her running shoes
- Ⓑ her keys
- Ⓒ her briefcase
- Ⓓ her workout clothes

Question 4 is based on the paragraph below.

When Samantha saw the new boy in class, her heart started pounding so fast and loudly that she was certain everybody could hear it. She straightened her posture and gently swept her bangs behind her right ear. As the boy sat down next to her, she gave him a quick glance and then a friendly smile. She was sure he noticed her bright red cheeks as she bent over her paper.

4. Which of the following can be inferred about Samantha based on the above passage?

- Ⓐ She thought the boy had a nice backpack.
- Ⓑ She was scared of the boy.
- Ⓒ She thought the boy was cute.
- Ⓓ She thought the boy was mean.

Question 5 is based on the paragraph below.

Maya and her family were headed to the beach one sunny summer afternoon. When they arrived, Maya noticed a family seemed to be having what appeared to be a garage sale, which was a curious sight to see in the beach parking lot. They were selling used personal items that you would normally find in one's house like pots, pans, dishes, a CD player, and various other items. There appeared to be a mother, father, and two children, a boy and a girl about Maya's age. Maya could tell that the family was not there to enjoy the beach as they were not dressed for the beach. Their clothes were far too warm for the beautiful day and were tattered, torn, and quite dingy. Suddenly, Maya remembered that she had a twenty dollar bill in her pocket that she had received for her birthday.

5. Based on the information in the passage, infer what you think will happen next.

- Ⓐ Maya will buy something from the family's garage sale.
- Ⓑ Maya will want to buy something, but she already has all of those items in her house, so she won't buy anything.
- Ⓒ Maya will give the money to her family.
- Ⓓ Maya will use the money for snacks for the family.

Question 6 is based on the story below.

After reading the story, enter the details in the map below. This will help you to answer the questions that follow.

Haley was putting the finishing touches on her famous apple pie when the phone rang. She dashed to answer it. After all, this might be the call that she had been waiting for. Even though her hands were still covered in flour, she grabbed the phone before it could ring a second time.

"Hello. You've reached the Williams residence," she said, trying to make her voice sound calm and collected.

"Is this Haley Williams?" asked the voice on the other end of the line.

"Yes, it is. How may I help you?" Haley replied.

"Ms. Haley Williams, we are proud to announce that you are a finalist in the National Pie Competition. The championship round will be held next weekend in Tampa, Florida. You and your family are invited to join us. Good luck!"

"Why thank you very much," Haley said graciously. "I am looking forward to it." After hanging up, Haley took a deep breath and let out an ear-piercing scream of excitement. She jumped up and down and ran around the kitchen with glee. In the pandemonium, her apple pie was knocked off the counter and landed on the floor, where her two puppies immediately began to gobble it down. Haley just laughed at the mess. As she cleaned the floor she began to think very carefully about her plan for the upcoming week.

With the big competition only one week away, Haley decided that she better make three pies every day. This practice would allow her to experiment with the crust , the filling, and the baking time. She wanted to do everything she possibly could to ensure that her pie was a winner.

Her friend, Max, who was thrilled to find out that Haley was a finalist, offered his kitchen for practice. Haley thanked him. She knew that cooking in an unfamiliar kitchen would be excellent practice for the competition.

Haley worked hard all week, doing nothing but baking pies. Not every pie turned out well. Some had a soggy crust or burned a little on the top. Haley threw out the bad pies and carefully wrapped the successful pies and delivered them to her neighbors and friends. They were all delighted by the surprise and wished Haley good luck at the competition.

The day before the competition, Haley packed up all of the things she would need. She brought her favorite rolling pin for good luck. When she arrived in Tampa, Florida, she went straight to her hotel and got a good night's rest. The competition started early the next morning, and Haley wanted to be ready.

The day of the competition seemed to fly by in one big blur. Haley was one of twelve finalists. Each finalist had their own counter top on which to prepare their pie and their own oven in which to bake it. Once everyone was set up at their station, the master of ceremonies officially started the clock, and everyone got to work. Every contestant had 90 minutes to prepare and bake their pies. Haley mixed and rolled out her pie dough. Then she peeled and sliced her apples, laying them carefully inside the crust. She seasoned the pie with cinnamon and sugar and laid strips of dough on top. She brushed the pie crust with butter and glanced at the clock. She was right on schedule; her pie took 45 minutes to bake and there were just 47 minutes left on the clock.

Haley opened the oven door, but she immediately noticed that something was wrong.

She didn't feel a rush of dry heat in her face, and she realized that she had forgotten to preheat the oven. The oven wasn't hot, and it would take several minutes to reach the correct temperature.

Haley felt her heart sink into her stomach. How could she forget such an important step? In all her practice, she had never forgotten to preheat the oven. Haley figured that she didn't stand a chance of winning, but she refused to give up. She put her pie in the oven and set the oven to the correct temperature.

With 30 seconds left in the competition, Haley removed her pie from the oven. It wasn't golden on the top, but it looked like it was cooked through. Haley sighed, disappointed that she had blown her chances at winning. But she delivered her pie to the judges and hoped for the best.

After tasting each pie and deliberating for hours, the judges handed the results to the master of ceremonies. "In third place….Haley Williams!" the voice boomed over the loud speaker. Haley couldn't believe her ears. She walked to the front of the room to accept her trophy with a smile on her face. She knew that if it hadn't been for her mistake, she might have won the grand prize.

But, she just hugged her trophy, congratulated herself on her accomplishment, and promised herself that she would do better next year.

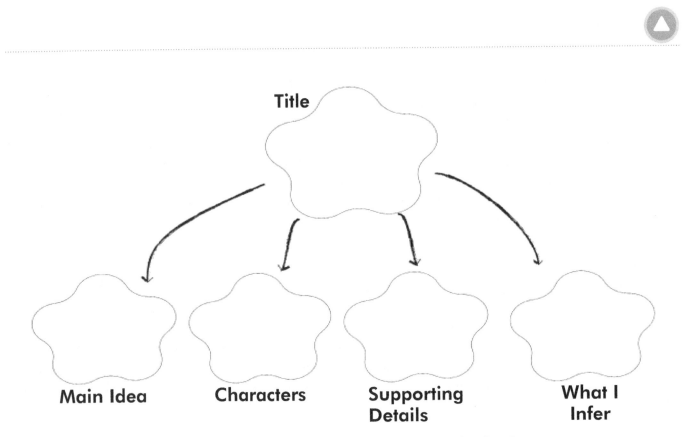

Title

Main Idea   Characters   Supporting   What I
                                       Details   Infer

6. What can be inferred from Haley's reaction to the phone ringing?

Ⓐ   She isn't concerned about the phone call.
Ⓑ   She doesn't think washing her hands is important.
Ⓒ   She is expecting an important phone call.
Ⓓ   She is enjoying talking to her family.

Question 7 is based on the paragraph below.

Henry sat eagerly in the waiting area of the airport. Over the last year, he'd been putting away a little money each month into what he called his "vacation fund." He bought travel books and researched all of the sites he wanted to see. Now all he had to do was wait until his flight was called.

7. What can you infer about Henry's trip?

Ⓐ   It was a spur of the moment idea.
Ⓑ   It is something he has looked forward to for a long time.
Ⓒ   It is to a place he's been before.
Ⓓ   It is to an exotic location.

Question 8 is based on the paragraph below.

She pulled hard at the doorknob. The door was difficult to budge. Finally inside, she brushed aside the cobwebs, leaving footprints in the dust on the floor.

8. What can be inferred from this description?

Ⓐ The place she is entering hasn't been used in a long time.
Ⓑ The house she is entering is a new structure.
Ⓒ The door was locked.
Ⓓ She has just bought the house and is preparing to move in.

Question 9 is based on the paragraph below.

When Melody's mom came home and discovered the vase in pieces on the counter, she said nothing; instead she pursed her lips, put her hand on her left hip and glared at Melody.

9. What can the reader infer about Melody's mom?

Ⓐ Melody's mom is mad at Melody for breaking the vase. She is waiting for an explanation.
Ⓑ Melody's mom had a long day at work and just needs a moment to think.
Ⓒ Melody's mom cannot talk due to some dental work she had done earlier in the day.
Ⓓ Melody's mom is surprised that her kitchen is so clean.

The Mountain and The Squirrel	The Arrow and the Song
The mountain and the squirrel Had a quarrel: And the former called the latter, "Little Prig." Bun replied, "You are doubtless very big: But all sorts of things and weather Must be taken in together To make up a year And a sphere. And I think it no disgrace To occupy my place. If I'm not so large as you You are not so small as I, And not half so spry; I'll not deny you make A very pretty squirrel track; Talents differ; all is well and wisely Put; If I cannot carry forests on my back, Neither can you crack a nut." **RALPH WALDO EMERSON (1803 -1882)**	I shot an arrow into the air It fell to earth, I knew not where: For, so swiftly it flew, the sight Could not follow it in its flight. I breathed a song into the air It fell to earth, I knew not where For who has sight so keen and strong That it can follow the flight of song? Long, long afterward, in an oak I found the arrow, still unbroke And the song, from beginning to end I found again in the heart of a friend. **H.W. LONGFELLOW (1807 -1882)**

10. Part A

What do you think the poet is trying to tell us in the "The Arrow and the Song"?

Ⓐ Actions and words can leave a lasting impact on others.
Ⓑ It is dangerous to shoot arrows into the air.
Ⓒ Arrows shot into the air sound like a beautiful song.
Ⓓ None of the above

10. Part B

What do you think is the poet trying to tell us in both poems?

Ⓐ What goes around comes around.
Ⓑ The actions we perform or the thoughts we express will leave their mark.
Ⓒ We must think before we do our actions.
Ⓓ The arrow and the song both fell to the ground.

11. When the thunder began to roar, Mary leapt under her covers and put her hands over her ears.

   What can be inferred from Mary's reaction to the storm? Circle the correct answer choice.

   Ⓐ She enjoys thunderstorms.
   Ⓑ She cannot hear well.
   Ⓒ She is afraid of thunderstorms.
   Ⓓ She likes to sleep.

Question 12 is based on the paragraph below.

She pulled hard at the doorknob. The door was difficult to budge. Finally inside, she brushed aside the cobwebs, leaving footprints in the dust on the floor.

12. What can be inferred from this description?

The room hasnt been used in a long time due to the door being hard to open, the cobwebs, & the foot prints left in the dust.

Question 13 is based on the paragraph below.

Justin had Mark's deep brown eyes and his button nose. At only three years old, he already showed signs of Mark's sense of humor and optimism. Mark was proud that Justin had inherited some of his traits.

13. Based on the description above, one could infer that Justin _____

   Select the correct answer choice from the 4 options given below and fill in the blank.

   Ⓐ is friends with Mark
   Ⓑ is Mark's brother
   Ⓒ is Mark's son
   Ⓓ is Mark's sister

Chapter 2

Lesson 3: Theme

Before answering questions related to this standard, you need to understand the terms "Main Idea", "Inference", "Plots" and "Characters(relationship to the characters)".

Main Idea: It is the main thought or message being conveyed about the topic. To figure out the main idea, ask yourself: What is being said about the person, thing, or idea (the topic). The main idea is usually the first sentence of the passage. The rest of the passage usually has the supporting ideas and details.

Inference: This is a conclusion reached by a reader after reading the information in a passage. The reader uses the information in the passage to reach this conclusion on his/her own; it has not been stated by the author.

Character(s)

The actions and thoughts and emotions of the main (major) character(s) have the most influence, are the most important, to the plot. There may be other less important characters (known as minor or secondary characters) in the story, but they will have less influence on the plot.

Plots

A plot describes the most important events and relationships in a story. Events may be actions that characters take, or actions that affect characters.

Actions that affect characters may be actions taken by other characters or by natural forces (ex. tornado or fire).

Relationships describe the way characters interact with other characters; the other characters may be other humans, supernatural beings, live plants or animals, or non-living characters. Interactions between or among characters can take place at different levels. What do we mean by different levels? If an author writes about one character talking to another, or about an event that all characters are experiencing together, without any mention of what each character is thinking, that is a single level. It means that each character is completely aware of everything that is said or done. If the author adds what a character is thinking but not saying out loud, that is a second level, because the other character does not know what the first character is thinking. The same reasoning applies if two characters talk about another character and the other character is not aware of what was said. If a story includes the description of a dream, the dream is on a second level; the events in the dream are not taking place in the real world in which the dreamer lives.

Setting

Setting refers to the location where an event or a relationship takes place, or to the time period in which an event or relationship takes place.

You can scan the QR code given below or use the url to access additional EdSearch resources including videos and mobile apps related to *Theme*.

ed)Search **Theme**

URL	QR Code
http://www.lumoslearning.com/a/rl82	

1. What is the difference between a theme and a main idea?

(A) A theme is the message of a story, and the main idea is what the story is about.
(B) A theme is a summary, and the main idea is a paraphrase.
(C) A theme tells what the symbols mean, and the main idea is a symbol.
(D) A theme is what a student writes, and a main idea is what the story is mainly about.

2. What is a universal theme?

(A) a story that takes place in outer space
(B) a theme that is implied
(C) a common theme that could apply to anyone, anywhere, anytime
(D) a theme that includes an adventure across the universe

3. The theme of a story:

(A) is always a statement.
(B) is usually a single word, such as "love."
(C) is a question.
(D) none of the above.

4. What is the best way to find a theme in a story?

(A) look at the first sentence of the story.
(B) look at the names of the characters in a story.
(C) look at the details in the story to find a larger meaning.
(D) look at reviews of the story.

5. What is an implied theme?

(A) a theme that is straightforward and requires no guessing
(B) a theme that is indirectly stated through characters, plot, and setting of a story
(C) a theme that is common throughout many stories that are told across many different cultures
(D) a theme that is clearly stated by the main character in the story

Question 6 is based on the story below.

After reading the story, enter the details in the map below. This will help you to answer the questions that follow.

The Fox and the Cat - An Aesop's Fable

A Fox was boasting to a Cat of its clever devices for escaping its enemies.
"I have a whole bag of tricks," he said, "which contains a hundred ways of escaping my enemies."
"I have only one," said the Cat; "but I can generally manage with that."
Just at that moment they heard the cry of a pack of hounds coming towards them, and the Cat immediately scampered up a tree and hid herself in the boughs.
"This is my plan," said the Cat. "What are you going to do?"

The Fox thought first of one way, then of another, and while he was debating the hounds came nearer and nearer, and at last the Fox in his confusion was caught up by the hounds and soon killed by the huntsmen. The Cat, who had been looking on, said, "Better one safe way than a hundred on which you cannot reckon."

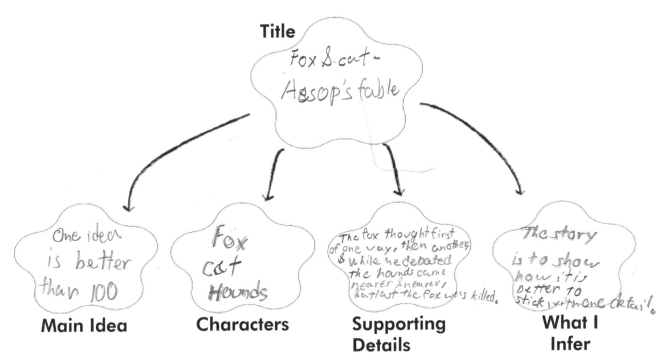

Title
Fox & cat - Aesop's fable

Main Idea
One idea is better than 100

Characters
Fox
cat
Hounds

Supporting Details
The Fox thought first of one way, then another & while he debated the hounds came nearer & nearer, but last the Fox was killed.

What I Infer
The story is to show how it's better to stick with one detail.

6. What is the theme of this story?

   Ⓐ   It is good to make friends with strangers.
   Ⓑ   It is better to be a cat than a fox.
   ●   Having one solid plan is better than having many possible ones.
   Ⓓ   Foxes are not as smart as cats.

Question 7 is based on the story below.

The Ungrateful Son
by Jacob and Wilhelm Grimm

Once, a man was sitting with his wife before their front door. They had a roasted chicken, which they were about to eat together. Then the man saw that his aged father was approaching, and he hastily took the chicken and hid it, for he did not want to share it with him. The old man came, had a drink, and went away. Now the son wanted to put the roasted chicken back onto the table, but when he reached for it, it had turned into a large toad, which jumped into his face and sat there and never went away again. If anyone tried to remove it, it looked venomously at him as though it would jump into his face, so that no one dared to touch it. And the ungrateful son was forced to feed the toad every day, or else it would eat from his face. And thus, he went to and fro in the world without rest.

7. Part A
What is the theme of this story?

Ⓐ The theme of the story is to always share what you have to share.
Ⓑ The theme of the story is to not be afraid of toads because they can keep you from saving someone's life.
Ⓒ The theme of the story is that you should always feed yourself first, and then you will be strong enough to help others.
Ⓓ The theme of the story is that you should always share your chicken with your parents.

7. Part B
The theme of The Ungrateful Son is implied because _____.

Ⓐ It is indirectly stated, and the reader has to determine the theme through the actions of the characters.
Ⓑ It is explicitly stated and the reader does not have to guess at all.
Ⓒ It is obvious and doesn't require much thought.
Ⓓ None of the above

Question 8 is based on the story below.

The Fox and the Crow Aesop's Fable

A Fox once saw a Crow fly off with a piece of cheese in its beak and settle on a branch of a tree. "That's for me, as I am a Fox," said Master Reynard, and he walked up to the foot of the tree. "Good-day, Mistress Crow," he cried. "How well you are looking today: how glossy your feathers; how bright your eye. I feel sure your voice must surpass that of other birds, just as your figure does; let me hear but one song from you that I may greet you as the Queen of Birds." The Crow lifted up her head and began to caw her best, but the moment she opened her mouth, the piece of cheese fell to the ground,

32

only to be snapped up by Master Fox. "That will do," said he. "That was all I wanted. In exchange for your cheese, I will give you a piece of advice for the future."

8. What is the theme of this story?

Ⓐ   Help out your friends.
Ⓑ   Don't trust flatterers.
Ⓒ   Sometimes, a song is necessary.
Ⓓ   You should never have to work for food.

Question 9 is based on the story below.

After reading the story, enter the details in the map below. This will help you to answer the questions that follow.

Walk-A-Thon

It was clear there weren't enough funds for the 8th-grade graduation ceremony at the end of the year. Big deal – why should I care? I was on the student council, but I never cared about graduation ceremonies.
It costs about $5,000.00 for the rent, equipment, the insurance, and all the other incidentals that pile up when planning a large event. Principal Dorsey told us that he didn't have the money this year. He said that if we wanted to keep the graduation tradition going, we would have to raise the money ourselves. "I'm sure we can live without the ceremony, but it would be nice to have," he told us. Then he left the meeting.

Immediately, Katrina Reynolds shot her hand in the air. She's not very popular, and I always feel kind of sorry for her. "We have to do this, you guys," Katrina gushed. "There is no way we are going to be the only class ever not to have a graduation ceremony."

Then, of course, Abbie Morelle, who was President, shot her hand in the air. I'd been on Student Council for two years, and as far as I could remember, Abbie had never let Katrina say anything without disagreeing with it. "It's very late in the year," Abbie said. "And we already have the Band Land Dance scheduled, which we don't have enough money for. We can't raise $7,000 in, like, two months."

Paulie Roman, who was treasurer, said, "According to my records, it would be more like $7,012, although we can't be certain of the precise cost of unspecified expenses related to the ceremony."

I didn't care. To me, 8th-grade is pure misery, no matter what you do. If you have a great graduation ceremony at the end of it, that's like saying, "We had such a great time in all of our boring classes and with all of the bullies every day. Let's have a party to celebrate them!" But I was all for a fundraiser if it would get Abbie Morelle off Katrina's back.

I said, "Let's do a walk-a-thon. We could raise a lot of money that way."

"Walk-a-thons are stupid," Abbie said.

Paulie Roman asked, "How much money could we raise with a walk-a-thon?"

I said, "When we did a walk-a-thon for cancer research in elementary school, we raised $4,000. This school is twice as big, and people can walk farther."

"Yeah," Abbie said, "but that was for cancer. Why would anyone give us money for a graduation ceremony? Plus, someone has to organize it, and it's complicated."

That got me mad enough that I had to say, "It's not that complicated. I'll do it."

What was I thinking? I spent the next month doing almost nothing except organizing that walk-a-thon. I hate walk-a-thons, and I hate talking to people about money. I ended up doing way more than I ever wanted to.

Within the first two weeks, I could see that we weren't going to get enough. It was because we weren't raising money for something important, like cancer. So I started telling people that the money would also go for cancer research. Then, when I saw how many people were ready to give more, I just told them it was all for cancer research. I got hundreds of parents signed up, and I got businesses to do-nate food and decorations.

Abbie was completely jealous.

The walk-a-thon was almost a success, too. But the day before, Principal Dorsey called me into his office. He wanted to know if it was true that I had been telling people that the money would go to can-cer research because he had understood the money was going for our 8th-grade graduation party. I didn't answer. He said that he was going to call some of the people who pledged money to ask them if I had said anything about cancer.

"It was the only way I could raise enough money!" I answered back, knowing the lie had caught up with me.

"Well, it was the wrong thing to do." Principal Dorsey replied. "Now, you are going to have to contact every person who donated and let them know the truth. You also may not have enough money for a graduation party now."

I knew I should never have volunteered to lead this.

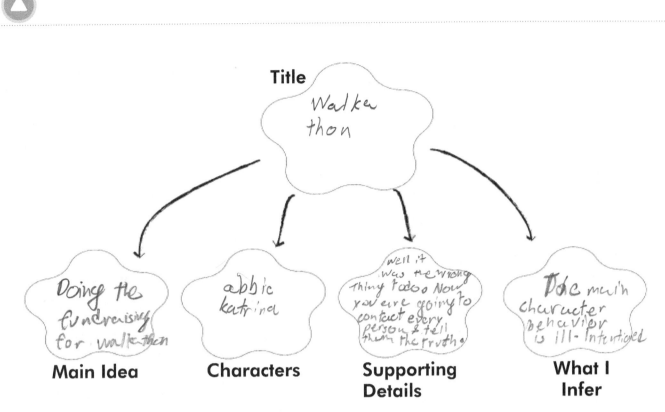

Title
Walka
thon

Main Idea
Doing the
fundraising
for walk-a-thon

Characters
abbie
katrina

**Supporting
Details**
well it
was the wrong
thing to do Now
you are going to
contact every
person & tell
them the truth.

**What I
Infer**
The main
character
behavior
is ill-intentioned

9. What is the theme of this story?

Ⓐ Don't volunteer to do things.
Ⓑ Principals can be very stern.
Ⓒ Make sure your intentions are pure, or the results will be disastrous.
Ⓓ Walk-a-thons are not the best money-makers.

Question 10 is based on the story below.

The Laundry

Charlie's parents always assigned him chores around the house. They would often ask him to trim the lawn, wash the dishes, and feed the dog. However, his chores never included laundry. He relied on his mother to wash his clothes for him. Charlie was an outstanding student and was recently accepted to a top college. The college he planned to attend was in New York City. Charlie was nervous about leaving Texas, where he grew up, and being so far away from his family, but he knew that the college in New York was the perfect fit for him. Before he left, his mother decided that she had better show him how to wash his own clothes because she wouldn't be there to do it for him anymore. She showed Charlie how to sort his clothes into two piles: whites and colors.

Then she showed him how much soap to use and told him when to use hot or warm water and when to use cold water. Next, she explained the different settings on the dryer and told him to be careful not to dry certain items on high heat. Charlie didn't pay much attention. He didn't see what could happen or what was so complicated about washing clothes. He planned on packing mostly t-shirts and jeans and figured that it would be hard to mess up something so simple. When Charlie arrived at school, he was completely overwhelmed with all of the exciting things to do and new people to meet. He was also careful to dedicate plenty of time to his schoolwork because he wanted to impress his professors and earn good grades. One morning Charlie woke up and found that he had no clean clothes to wear. His schedule had been so packed with activities and studying that he had managed to get through the first month of school without doing any laundry. That night, Charlie piled his soiled clothes into a large basket and headed to his dormitory's laundry room. He shoved all of his clothes into a washer, poured in the soap, and pressed the start. Half an hour later, he opened the washer and started moving the clothes into the dryer. It was then that he realized that he had skipped one very significant step. All of his white t-shirts and socks had turned pink. He had forgotten to sort his colors from his whites. Charlie had received a bright red t-shirt with his new school's logo across the front. The red dye had bled in the wash, turning all of his white clothes pink. Charlie was unhappy about his destroyed wardrobe, but he figured that there was absolutely nothing to do except to put the clothes in the dryer and hope for the best. So he transferred the clothes to a dryer and set the heat to high. After all, he was anxious to get back upstairs to his studies. An hour later, Charlie removed his clothes from the dryer and headed straight back to his dorm room. The following morning, he reached for one of his favorite t-shirts. It was slightly pink now, but he didn't have enough money to replace all of his newly pink clothes. He would have to wear them, pink or not. As he pulled the shirt over his head, he noticed that it seemed tight. He looked at himself in the mirror.

The shirt had shrunk in the dryer. It looked like he had tried to squeeze into his little sister's pink t-shirt. All Charlie could do was laugh. He called his mom and asked her to repeat her laundry instructions again.

This time, Charlie took notes.

10. What is the theme of this story?

Circle the correct answer choice.

Ⓐ Pay close attention when you are learning something new.
Ⓑ Always ask for help.
Ⓒ Learn how to do your laundry when you are young.
Ⓓ Always have your parents do your laundry.

Chapter 2

Lesson 4: Objective Summary

You can scan the QR code given below or use the url to access additional EdSearch resources including videos and mobile apps related to *Objective Summary*.

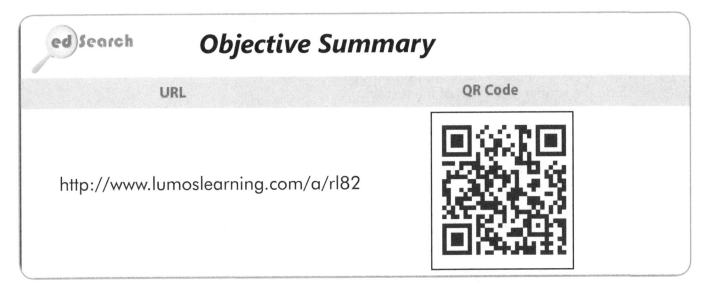

edSearch

Objective Summary

URL	QR Code
http://www.lumoslearning.com/a/rl82	

1. What is an objective summary?

(A) a restatement of the main idea of a text with the addition of the writer's opinion on the idea

(B) a restatement of the main idea of a text without the addition of the writer's opinion of the idea

(C) a paraphrase of the text with a focus on the writer's opinion and how it affects the main idea of the passage

(D) a paraphrase of the text with a focus on the reader's opinion

2. An objective summary should _____ .

(A) include supporting details

(B) be brief, accurate, and objective

(C) include both main points and supporting details

(D) include the reader's opinion of the text

3. An objective summary should always _____ .

(A) clearly show your opinions of the text

(B) clearly communicate a summary of the text

(C) clearly indicate all the characters in the text

(D) include at least four sentences

Question 4 is based on the passage below.

It had been a year since Lauren had seen Bailey. Bailey's family had moved to Qatar leaving Lauren to face the world without her best friend. Anxiously, Lauren waited at the arrival gate hoping to glimpse a peek at her childhood friend. She knew after eleven hours in the air, Bailey would be exhausted; but, she could hardly wait to catch up. Moments later, the doors to the gate flung open, and there was her best friend, Bailey.

Once home, the hours passed like minutes as the girls laughed and giggled sharing moments from the last year. It felt as if they had never been apart. But Lauren felt like Bailey was holding something back.

4. What is the best summary for this passage?

(A) After a year abroad, Lauren was excited about seeing her best friend and catching up.

(B) Lauren was too excited about seeing her best friend Bailey, and even though she knew Bailey was tired from her flight, she probably talked her ear off.

(C) Bailey had been gone a year.

(D) Bailey was Lauren's best friend and though she had been gone a year, she really didn't want to come back.

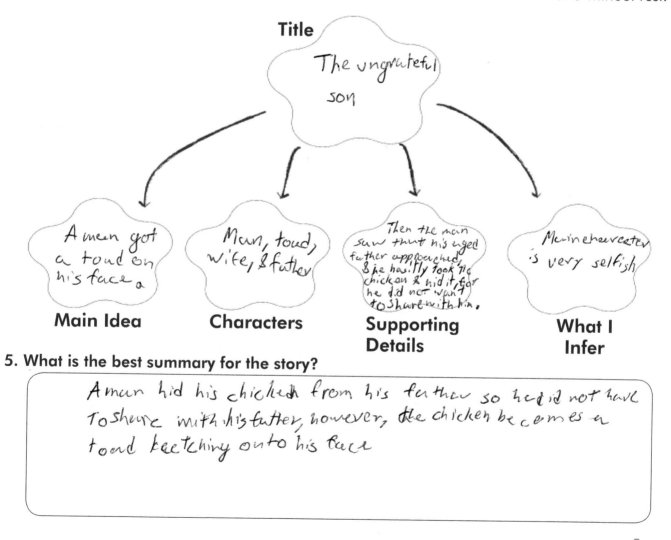

Question 5 is based on the story below.

After reading the story, enter the details in the map below. This will help you to answer the questions that follow.

The Ungrateful Son
by Jacob and Wilhelm Grimm

Once, a man was sitting with his wife before their front door. They had a roasted chicken which they were about to eat together. Then the man saw that his aged father was approaching, and he hastily took the chicken and hid it, for he did not want to share it with him. The old man came, had a drink, and went away. Now the son wanted to put the roasted chicken back onto the table, but when he reached for it, it had turned into a large toad, which jumped into his face and sat there and never went away again. If anyone tried to remove it, it looked venomously at him as though it would jump into his face, so that no one dared to touch it. And the ungrateful son was forced to feed the toad every day, or else it would eat from his face. And thus he went to and fro in the world without rest.

Title

The ungrateful son

Main Idea

A man got a toad on his face a

Characters

Man, toad, wife, & father

Supporting Details

Then the man saw that his aged father approached, & he hastily took the chicken & hid it, for he did not want to share with him.

What I Infer

Main character is very selfish

5. **What is the best summary for the story?**

A man hid his chicken from his father so he did not have to share with his father, however, the chicken becomes a toad keetching onto his face

Question 6 is based on the passage below.

When I was finished with my doctor's appointment, I made my way to the lobby. My mom was going to pick me up, but knowing how she was always late, I realized I had some time to spare. I took a seat in the lobby and smiled politely at the three elderly people sitting near me. There were two women and an old man. Then I dug into my backpack for my library book.

Soon, one of the women and the man left. It was just me and the beautiful gray-haired woman in the lobby.

6. What is the best summary for this passage?

Ⓐ A boy went to the lobby and waits for his mother.

Ⓑ After a doctor's appointment, the narrator waits in the lobby for his mother to pick him up. At the end, only he and a woman remain in the lobby.

Ⓒ The narrator, who must be impatient, waits for his mother in the lobby.

Ⓓ The narrator reads a library book in the lobby while waiting for his mother.

Question 7 is based on the passage below.

The Laundry

Charlie's parents always assigned him chores around the house. They would often ask him to trim the lawn, wash the dishes, and feed the dog. However, his chores never included laundry. He relied on his mother to wash his clothes for him. Charlie was an outstanding student and was recently accepted to a top college. The college he planned to attend was in New York City. Charlie was nervous about leaving Texas, where he grew up, and being so far away from his family, but he knew that the college in New York was the perfect fit for him. Before he left, his mother decided that she had better show him how to wash his own clothes because she wouldn't be there to do it for him anymore. She showed Charlie how to sort his clothes into two piles: whites and colors.

7. What is the best summary for this story?

Ⓐ Charlie is going away to college and is nervous about not being in Texas anymore.

Ⓑ Charlie is going to New York City for college. He has done many chores in the past but not laundry.

Ⓒ Charlie is going to college in New York City and needs to learn how to do his laundry before he leaves. His mother teaches him how to sort his clothes.

Ⓓ Charlie has done many chores in the past. He is nervous about leaving Texas but knows the college he is going to will be a good fit.

Question 8 is based on the passage below.

From **Chapter 5 of Peter Pan** by J.M. Barrie

"He lay at his ease in a rough chariot drawn and propelled by his men, and instead of a right hand, he had the iron hook with which ever and anon he encouraged them to increase their pace. As dogs, this terrible man treated and addressed them, and as dogs, they obeyed him. In-person he was ca-daverous [dead looking] and [dark faced], and his hair was dressed in long curls, which at a little distance looked like black candles, and gave a singularly threatening expression to his handsome countenance. His eyes were of the blue of the forget-me-not, and of a profound melancholy, save when he was plunging his hook into you, at which time two red spots appeared in them and lit them up horribly. A man of indomitable courage, it was said that the only thing he shied at was the sight of his own blood, which was thick and of an unusual color. But undoubtedly the grimmest part of him was his iron claw."

8. Which choice best summarizes the personality of the character in the following excerpt?

Ⓐ James Hook was a scary man because he had the face of a dead person and had dark curly hair and a hook for his right hand. He treated his men like dogs, and they obeyed him as such. When he was angry, his eyes turned from blue to red.

Ⓑ James Hook used his appearance to assert his authority in ways that forced others into doing what he wanted. He spoke to and treated his men like dogs, and they were forced to listen. Only the sight of his own blood could waver his courage.

Ⓒ James Hook was a scary man.

Ⓓ James Hook was a scary man. James Hook used his appearance to assert his authority in ways that forced others into doing what he wanted. He spoke to and treated his men like dogs, and they were forced to listen. Only the sight of his own blood could waver his courage.

Question 9 is based on the passage below.

The Emperor Penguin is the only penguin species that breeds during the Antarctic winter. It treks 31–75 miles over the ice to breeding colonies, which may include thousands of penguins. The female lays a single egg, which is then incubated by the male while the female returns to the sea to feed; parents subsequently take turns foraging at sea and caring for their chick in the colony. The average lifespan of the Emperor Penguin is 20 years, although observations suggest that some Emperor Penguins may live to 50 years of age.

9. Read the summary below. Select the answer below that best explains why the summary provided cannot be considered a proper objective summary.

Breeding during the winter in Antarctica is specific to the Emperor Penguin. The Emperor Penguin travels far; they will travel anywhere from 31 – 75 miles in the freezing cold to meet many other penguins for breeding. This is known as a breeding colony and a colony can have thousands of penguins. The father penguins sit on the eggs while the mothers go and hunt for food at sea. After the chick is born, the mother and father take turns taking care of the baby and going off to feed. Emperor Penguins, on average, live to be about 20 years old, but some have been known to live up to 50 years.

Ⓐ   The summary is incorrect because it includes the writer's opinion.
Ⓑ   The summary is perfect and should be considered proper.
Ⓒ   The summary is incorrect because it is not a summary; it is a paraphrase of the passage.
Ⓓ   The summary is incorrect because it is not accurate.

Question 10 is based on the story below.

After reading the story, enter the details in the map below. This will help you to answer the questions that follow.

Walk-A-Thon

It was clear there weren't enough funds for the 8th-grade graduation ceremony at the end of the year. Big deal – why should I care? I was on the Student Council, but I never cared about graduation ceremonies.

It costs about $5,000.00 for the rent, equipment, the insurance, and all the other incidentals that pile up when planning a large event. Principal Dorsey told us that he didn't have the money this year. He said that if we wanted to keep the graduation tradition going, we would have to raise the money ourselves. "I'm sure we can live without the ceremony, but it would be nice to have," he told us. Then he left the meeting.

Immediately, Katrina Reynolds shot her hand in the air. She's not very popular and I always feel kind of sorry for her. "We have to do this, you guys," Katrina gushed. "There is no way we are going to be the only class ever not to have a graduation ceremony."

Then, of course, Abbie Morelle, who was President, shot her hand in the air. I'd been on Student Council for two years and as far as I could remember, Abbie had never let Katrina say anything without disagreeing with it. "It's very late in the year," Abbie said. "And we already have the Band Land Dance scheduled, which we don't have enough money for. We can't raise $7,000 in, like, two months."

Paulie Roman, who was treasurer, said, "According to my records, it would be more like $7,012, although we can't be certain of the precise cost of unspecified expenses related to the ceremony."

I didn't care. To me, 8th-grade is pure misery, no matter what you do. If you have a great graduation ceremony at the end of it, that's like saying, "We had such a great time in all of our boring classes, and with all of the bullies every day. Let's have a party to celebrate them!" But I was all for a fundraiser if it would get Abbie Morelle off Katrina's back.

I said, "Let's do a walk-a-thon. We could raise a lot of money that way."

"Walk-a-thons are stupid," Abbie said.

Paulie Roman asked, "How much money could we raise with a walk-a-thon?"

I said, "When we did a walk-a-thon for cancer research in elementary school, we raised $4,000. This school is twice as big and people can walk farther."

"Yeah," Abbie said, "but that was for cancer. Why would anyone give us money for a graduation ceremony? Plus, someone has to organize it, and it's complicated."

That got me mad enough that I had to say, "It's not that complicated. I'll do it."

What was I thinking? I spent the next month doing almost nothing except organizing that walk-a-thon. I hate walk-a-thons, and I hate talking to people about money. I ended up doing way more than I ever wanted to.

Within the first two weeks I could see that we weren't going to get enough. It was because we weren't raising money for something important, like cancer. So I started telling people that the money would also go for cancer research. Then, when I saw how many people were ready to give more, I just told them it was all for cancer research. I got hundreds of parents signed up, and I got businesses to donate food and decorations.

Abbie was completely jealous.

The walk-a-thon was almost a success, too. But the day before, Principal Dorsey called me into his office. He wanted to know if it was true that I had been telling people that the money would go to cancer research, because he had understood the money was going to our 8th-grade graduation party. I didn't answer. He said that he was going to call some of the people who pledged money to ask them if I had said anything about cancer.

"It was the only way I could raise enough money!" I answered back, knowing the lie had caught up with me.

"Well, it was the wrong thing to do." Principal Dorsey replied. "Now, you are going to have to contact every person who donated and let them know the truth. You also may not have enough money for a graduation party now."

I knew I should never have volunteered to lead this.

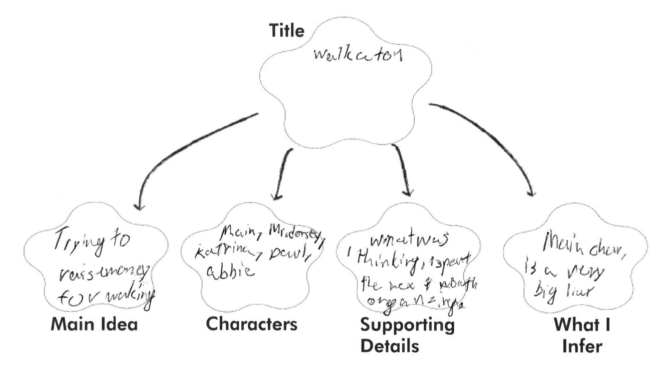

Title
walkaton

Main Idea
Trying to reis emoney for working

Characters
Main, Mr. dorsey, katrina, pawl, abbie

Supporting Details
what was I thinking, spent the nex month organizing

What I Infer
Main char, is a very big liar

10. Which is the best summary of the story?

Ⓐ Student Council members learn that they do not have enough money for an 8th-grade graduation ceremony. They decide to raise money through a walk-a-thon which the narrator volunteers to lead.

Ⓑ Student Council members learn that they do not have enough money for an 8th-grade graduation ceremony. They decide to raise money through a walk-a-thon which the narrator volunteers to lead. Fund raising doesn't go as well as anticipated and the 8th-grade graduation party is in jeopardy. The Student Council members were probably really mad after all their hard work.

Ⓒ The 8th-grade class did not have enough money for a graduation party. They tried to raise money, but failed.

Ⓓ Student Council members learn that they do not have enough money for an 8th-grade graduation ceremony. They decide to raise money through a walk-a-thon which the narrator volunteers to lead. Fund raising doesn't go as well as anticipated and the 8th-grade graduation party is in jeopardy.

Question 11 is based on the story below.

The Ant and the Grasshopper Aesop's Fable

In a field, one summer's day, a grasshopper was hopping about, chirping and singing to its heart's content. A group of ants walked by, grunting as they struggled to carry plump kernels of corn. "Where are you going with those heavy things?" asked the grasshopper. Without stopping, the first ant replied, "To our anthill. This is the third kernel I've delivered today."

"Why not come and sing with me," teased the grasshopper, "instead of working so hard?"

"We are helping to store food for the winter," said the ant, "and think you should do the same."

"Winter is far away, and it is a glorious day to play," sang the grasshopper. But the ants went on their way and continued their hard work.

The weather soon turned cold. All the food lying in the field was covered with a thick white blanket of snow that even the grasshopper could not dig through.

Soon the grasshopper found itself dying of hunger. He staggered to the ants' hill and saw them handing out corn from the stores they had collected in the summer. He begged them for something to eat.

"What!" cried the ants in surprise, "haven't you stored anything away for the winter? What in the world were you doing all last summer?"

"I didn't have time to store any food," complained the grasshopper; "I was so busy playing music that before I knew, it the summer was gone."

The ants shook their heads in disgust, turned their backs on the grasshopper, and went on with their work.

11. What is the best summary for the story?

> Ants sturing their food during summer to use in the winter, while the grasshopper was playing & dying.

Question 12 is based on the story below.

When I was finished with my doctor's appointment, I made my way to the lobby. My mom was going to pick me up, but knowing how she was always late, I realized I had some time to spare. I took a seat in the lobby and smiled politely at the three elderly people sitting near me. There were two women and an old man. Then I dug into my backpack for my library book.

Soon, one of the women and the man left. It was just me and the beautiful gray- haired woman in the lobby.

12. What is the best summary for the story?

> After a doctors appointment the character is waiting for his mom.

Chapter 2

Lesson 5: Plot

You can scan the QR code given below or use the url to access additional EdSearch resources including videos and mobile apps related to *Plot*.

ed Search   *Plot*

URL	QR Code
http://www.lumoslearning.com/a/rl82	

1. What are the elements of plot?

- Ⓐ prelude, beginning, interlude, middle, end
- Ⓑ introduction, setting, action, conflict, falling action
- Ⓒ introduction, rising action, climax, falling action, resolution
- Ⓓ beginning, middle, end

2. What are the two main types of conflict?

- Ⓐ internal and external
- Ⓑ interior and exterior
- Ⓒ good and bad
- Ⓓ big and little

3. What is the plot of a story?

- Ⓐ the message that the author is trying to convey
- Ⓑ the series of events that make up the story
- Ⓒ the use of characters in a story
- Ⓓ the part of a story where the characters decide what they are going to do

Question 4-7 are based on the story below.

Walk-A-Thon

It was clear there weren't enough funds for the 8th-grade graduation ceremony at the end of the year. Big deal – why should I care? I was on the student council, but I never cared about graduation ceremonies.

It costs about $5,000.00 for the rent, equipment, the insurance, and all the other incidentals that pile up when planning a large event. Principal Dorsey told us that he didn't have the money this year. He said that if we wanted to keep the graduation tradition going, we would have to raise the money ourselves. "I'm sure we can live without the ceremony, but it would be nice to have," he told us. Then he left the meeting.

Immediately, Katrina Reynolds shot her hand in the air. She's not very popular, and I always feel kind of sorry for her. "We have to do this, you guys," Katrina gushed. "There is no way we are going to be the only class ever not to have a graduation ceremony."

Then, of course, Abbie Morelle, who was President, shot her hand in the air. I'd been on Student Council for two years, and as far as I could remember, Abbie had never let Katrina say anything without disagreeing with it. "It's very late in the year," Abbie said. "And we already have the Band Land Dance scheduled, which we don't have enough money for. We can't raise $7,000 in, like, two months."

Paulie Roman, who was treasurer, said, "According to my records, it would be more like $7,012, although we can't be certain of the precise cost of unspecified expenses related to the ceremony."

I didn't care. To me, 8th-grade is pure misery, no matter what you do. If you have a great graduation ceremony at the end of it, that's like saying, "We had such a great time in all of our boring classes and with all of the bullies every day. Let's have a party to celebrate them!" But I was all for a fundraiser if it would get Abbie Morelle off Katrina's back.

I said, "Let's do a walk-a-thon. We could raise a lot of money that way."

"Walk-a-thons are stupid," Abbie said.

Paulie Roman asked, "How much money could we raise with a walk-a-thon?"

I said, "When we did a walk-a-thon for cancer research in elementary school, we raised $4,000. This school is twice as big, and people can walk farther."

"Yeah," Abbie said, "but that was for cancer. Why would anyone give us money for a graduation ceremony? Plus, someone has to organize it, and it's complicated."

That got me mad enough that I had to say, "It's not that complicated. I'll do it."

What was I thinking? I spent the next month doing almost nothing except organizing that walk-a-thon. I hate walk-a-thons, and I hate talking to people about money. I ended up doing way more than I ever wanted to.

Within the first two weeks, I could see that we weren't going to get enough. It was because we weren't raising money for something important, like cancer. So I started telling people that the money would also go for cancer research. Then, when I saw how many people were ready to give more, I just told them it was all for cancer research. I got hundreds of parents signed up, and I got businesses to donate food and decorations.

Abbie was completely jealous.

The walk-a-thon was almost a success, too. But the day before, Principal Dorsey called me into his office. He wanted to know if it was true that I had been telling people that the money would go to cancer research because he had understood the money was going for our 8th-grade graduation party. I didn't answer. He said that he was going to call some of the people who pledged money to ask them if I had said anything about cancer.

"It was the only way I could raise enough money!" I answered back, knowing the lie had caught up with me.

"Well, it was the wrong thing to do." Principal Dorsey replied. "Now, you are going to have to contact every person who donated and let them know the truth. You also may not have enough money for a graduation party now."

I knew I should never have volunteered to lead this.

4. Part A
What is the major type of conflict in this story?

Ⓐ external: man vs fate
Ⓑ external: man vs man
Ⓒ internal: man vs himself
Ⓓ external: man vs nature

Part B
What is the conflict in this story?

Ⓐ there is not enough money for an 8th-grade graduation party
Ⓑ who is most popular
Ⓒ who will organize the walk-a-thon
Ⓓ whether or not to have graduation

5. Part A
What is the exposition in this story?

Ⓐ I didn't care. To me, 8th-grade is pure misery, no matter what you do. If you have a great graduation ceremony at the end of it, that's like saying, "We had such a great time in all of our boring classes, and with all of the bullies every day. Let's have a party to celebrate them!" But I was all for a fundraiser if it would get Abbie Morelle off Katrina's back.

Ⓑ He wanted to know if it was true that I had been telling people that the money would go to cancer research, because he had understood the money was going for our 8th-grade graduation party.

Ⓒ Principal Dorsey told us that he didn't have the money this year. He said that if we wanted to keep the graduation tradition going, we would have to raise the money ourselves.

Ⓓ It was clear there weren't enough funds for the 8th-grade graduation ceremony at the end of the year. Big deal – why should I care? I was on the Student Council, but I never cared about graduation ceremonies.

Part B
What is the most important event in the rising action of this story?

Ⓐ when the narrator volunteers to take charge of the walk-a-thon
Ⓑ when the narrator lies about why she is collecting the money
Ⓒ when the narrator gets called into the principal's office
Ⓓ when the principal says there will be no graduation

6. **Part A**
What is the climax of this story?

Ⓐ when the narrator volunteers to be in charge of the walk-a-thon
Ⓑ when the narrator lies about why she is collecting the money
Ⓒ when the principal calls the narrator to the office and the narrator confesses to lying about the cause
Ⓓ when the narrator makes Abbie jealous

Part B
What is the most important event in the falling action of this story?

Ⓐ when the narrator learns she must contact all the donors
Ⓑ when the narrator learns there will be no graduation party
Ⓒ when the narrator makes Abbie jealous
Ⓓ when the narrator organizes the walk-a-thon

7. **What is the resolution of this story?**

Ⓐ when the narrator volunteers to be in charge of the walk-a-thon
Ⓑ when the narrator is called to the principal's office
Ⓒ when the narrator learns there will be no graduation party
Ⓓ when Abbie gets jealous

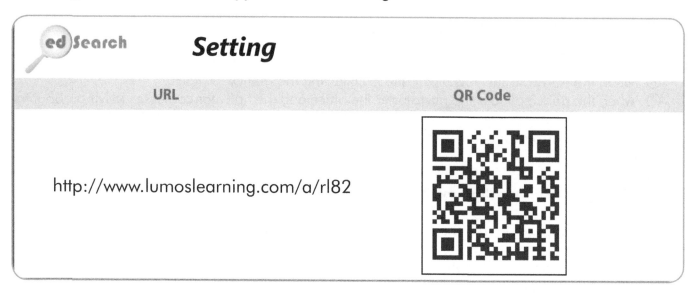

Chapter 2

Lesson 6: Setting

You can scan the QR code given below or use the url to access additional EdSearch resources including videos and mobile apps related to *Setting*.

ed Search

Setting

URL	QR Code
http://www.lumoslearning.com/a/rl82	

1. During which part of a story is the setting usually introduced?

- Ⓐ introduction
- Ⓑ rising action
- Ⓒ climax
- Ⓓ resolution

2. Can there be more than one setting in a story?

- Ⓐ yes
- Ⓑ no
- Ⓒ only if the story is really long
- Ⓓ only if the story is really short

3. Which of the following can convey setting?

- Ⓐ the name of the characters
- Ⓑ the age of the characters
- Ⓒ the culture of the characters
- Ⓓ the thoughts of a character

4. What does the setting tell us about a story?

- Ⓐ the names of the characters
- Ⓑ the time and place of action in the story
- Ⓒ the mood of the story
- Ⓓ one of the above

Question 5 is based on the story below.

Megan couldn't believe her luck. She had been standing in line with her best friend Jessica for thirty minutes. Their excitement was mounting as they neared the front of the line for the famed Greased Lightning roller coaster. Just as they took their seats, the clouds opened up. Soaking wet and disappointed, the girls followed the directions of the ride employees and took shelter under the nearby canopies.

5. Which of the following does not help the reader to gain a sense of the setting?

- Ⓐ the time of day
- Ⓑ the weather
- Ⓒ the time of year
- Ⓓ the mood of the main character

Question 5 is based on the passage below.

It had been a year since Lauren had seen Bailey. Bailey's family had moved to Qatar leaving Lauren to face the world without her best friend. Anxiously, Lauren waited at the arrival gate hoping to glimpse a peek at her childhood friend. She knew after eleven hours in the air, Bailey would be exhausted; but, she could hardly wait to catch up. Moments later, the doors to the gate flung open, and there was her best friend, Bailey.

Once home, the hours passed like minutes as the girls laughed and giggled sharing moments from the last year. It felt as if they had never been apart. But Lauren felt like Bailey was holding something back.

6. What is the primary setting for this passage?

- Ⓐ an airport
- Ⓑ Lauren's house
- Ⓒ Bailey's house
- Ⓓ There is not enough information to determine the setting.

Question 6 is based on the paragraph below.

From **Chapter 5 of Peter Pan** by J.M. Barrie

"He lay at his ease in a rough chariot drawn and propelled by his men, and instead of a right hand, he had the iron hook with which ever and anon he encouraged them to increase their pace. As dogs, this terrible man treated and addressed them, and as dogs, they obeyed him. In-person he was cadaverous [dead looking] and [dark faced], and his hair was dressed in long curls, which at a little distance looked like black candles, and gave a singularly threatening expression to his handsome countenance. His eyes were of the blue of the forget-me-not, and of a profound melancholy, save when he was plunging his hook into you, at which time two red spots appeared in them and lit them up horribly. A man of indomitable courage, it was said that the only thing he shied at was the sight of his own blood, which was thick and of an unusual color. But undoubtedly the grimmest part of him was his iron claw."

7. What is the setting of the above paragraph from the excerpt?

Question 8 is based on the story below.

The Laundry

Charlie's parents always assigned him chores around the house. They would often ask him to trim the lawn, wash the dishes, and feed the dog. However, his chores never included laundry. He relied on his mother to wash his clothes for him. Charlie was an outstanding student and was recently accepted to a top college. The college he planned to attend was in New York City. Charlie was nervous about leaving Texas, where he grew up, and being so far away from his family; but, he knew that the college in New York was the perfect fit for him. Before he left, his mother decided that she had better show him how to wash his own clothes because she wouldn't be there to do it for him anymore. She showed Charlie how to sort his clothes into two piles: whites and colors.

Then she showed him how much soap to use and told him when to use hot or warm water and when to use cold water. Next, she explained the different settings on the dryer and told him to be careful not to dry certain items on high heat. Charlie didn't pay much attention. He didn't see what could happen or what was so complicated about washing clothes. He planned on packing mostly t-shirts and jeans and figured that it would be hard to mess up something so simple.

When Charlie arrived at school, he was completely overwhelmed with all of the exciting things to do and new people to meet. He was also careful to dedicate plenty of time to his schoolwork because he wanted to impress his professors and earn good grades. One morning Charlie woke up and found that he had no clean clothes to wear. His schedule had been so packed with activities and studying that he had managed to get through the first month of school without doing any laundry. That night, Charlie piled his soiled clothes into a large basket and headed to his dormitory's laundry room. He shoved all of his clothes into a washer, poured in the soap, and pressed the start. Half an hour later, he opened the washer and started moving the clothes into the dryer. It was then that he realized that he had skipped one very significant step. All of his white t-shirts and socks had turned pink. He had forgotten to sort his colors from his whites. Charlie had received a bright red t-shirt with his new school's logo across the front. The red dye had bled in the wash, turning all of his white clothes pink. Charlie was unhappy about his destroyed wardrobe, but he figured that there was absolutely nothing to do except to put the clothes in the dryer and hope for the best. So he transferred the clothes to a dryer and set the heat to high. After all, he was anxious to get back upstairs to his studies. An hour later, Charlie removed his clothes from the dryer and headed straight back to his dorm room. The following morning, he reached for one of his favorite t-shirts. It was slightly pink now, but he didn't have enough money to replace all of his newly pink clothes. He would have to wear them, pink or not. As he pulled the shirt over his head, he noticed that it seemed tight. He looked at himself in the mirror. The shirt had shrunk in the dryer. It looked like he had tried to squeeze into his little sister's pink t-shirt. All Charlie could do was laugh. He called his mom and asked her to repeat her laundry instructions again.

This time, Charlie took notes.

8. What is the first setting of this excerpt?

Ⓐ Texas
Ⓑ New York
Ⓒ a laundromat
Ⓓ There is not enough information to determine the setting.

Question 9 is based on the story below.

I sat with my mother, a friendly and courageous woman, on the back porch of our country home. The thermometer read 100 degrees, and even the plants seemed to sweat in the heat.

9. Which of the following does not help the reader to better understand the setting of the story?

Ⓐ "the back porch"
Ⓑ "thermometer read 100 degrees"
Ⓒ "a friendly and courageous woman"
Ⓓ "our country home"

Question 10 is based on the paragraph below.

University of California Berkeley scientists confirmed that a cluster of fossilized bones found in Silicon Valley are likely the remains of a mammoth. The giant beast would have roamed the area between 10,000 and 40,000 years ago. A pair of elephant-like tusks, a huge pelvic bone, and the animal's rib cage were found by an amateur naturalist who was walking a dog along a canal near San Jose's Guadalupe River. It could be the remains of a Columbian mammoth, according to paleontologists who expect to study the site.

10. What is the setting of this article?

Ⓐ Columbia
Ⓑ University of California Berkeley
Ⓒ a canal near the Guadalupe River in the Silicon Valley
Ⓓ Berkeley

Question 11 is based on the paragraph below.

From Chapter 1 of Bullets and Billets by Bruce Bainsfather

Gliding up the Seine, on a transport crammed to the lid with troops, in the still, cold hours of a November morning, was my debut into the war. It was about 6 a.m. when our boat silently slipped along past the great wooden sheds, posts and complications of Havre Harbour. I had spent most of the twelve-hour trip down somewhere in the depths of the ship, dealing out rations to the hundred men that I had brought with me from Plymouth. This sounds a comparatively simple process, but not a bit of it. To begin with, the ship was filled with troops to bursting point, and the mere matter of proceeding from one deck to another was about as difficult as trying to get round to see a friend at the other side of the ground at a Crystal Palace Cup final.

11. What is the setting of this excerpt?

Lesson 7: Character

You can scan the QR code given below or use the url to access additional EdSearch resources including videos and mobile apps related to *Character*.

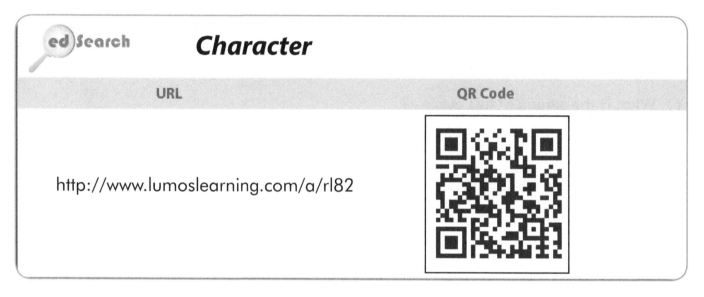

ed Search	**Character**	
URL		**QR Code**
http://www.lumoslearning.com/a/rl82		

1. What is a round character?

  Ⓐ a character who has many personality traits
  Ⓑ a character who has very few personality traits
  Ⓒ a character who changes throughout the story
  Ⓓ a character who does not change throughout the story

2. Who or what is the protagonist of a story?

  Ⓐ the main character with the problem
  Ⓑ the character that is the least interesting
  Ⓒ the character that is the most interesting
  Ⓓ main character's opposing force

3. Who or what is the antagonist in a story?

  Ⓐ the main character of a story
  Ⓑ the main character's opposing force
  Ⓒ the character that is the least interesting
  Ⓓ the character that is the most interesting

4. What is a static character?

  Ⓐ a character that changes during the course of the story
  Ⓑ a character that does not change during the course of the story
  Ⓒ a character with a smaller role that is not important to the development of the story
  Ⓓ a character with a large role that is not vital to the development of the story

5. What is a dynamic character?

  Ⓐ a character that changes during the course of the story
  Ⓑ a character that does not change during the course of the story
  Ⓒ a character with a smaller role that is not important to the development of the story
  Ⓓ a character with a large role that is not vital to the development of the story

Question 6 and 7 are based on the story below.

Walk-A-Thon

It was clear there weren't enough funds for the 8th-grade graduation ceremony at the end of the year. Big deal – why should I care? I was on the student council, but I never cared about graduation ceremonies.

It costs about $5,000.00 for the rent, equipment, the insurance, and all the other incidentals that pile up when planning a large event. Principal Dorsey told us that he didn't have the money this year. He said that if we wanted to keep the graduation tradition going, we would have to raise the money ourselves. "I'm sure we can live without the ceremony, but it would be nice to have," he told us. Then he left the meeting.

Immediately, Katrina Reynolds shot her hand in the air. She's not very popular, and I always feel kind of sorry for her. "We have to do this, you guys," Katrina gushed. "There is no way we are going to be the only class ever not to have a graduation ceremony."

Then, of course, Abbie Morelle, who was President, shot her hand in the air. I'd been on Student Council for two years, and as far as I could remember, Abbie had never let Katrina say anything without disagreeing with it. "It's very late in the year," Abbie said. "And we already have the Band Land Dance scheduled, which we don't have enough money for. We can't raise $7,000 in, like, two months."

Paulie Roman, who was treasurer, said, "According to my records, it would be more like $7,012, although we can't be certain of the precise cost of unspecified expenses related to the ceremony."

I didn't care. To me, 8th-grade is pure misery, no matter what you do. If you have a great graduation ceremony at the end of it, that's like saying, "We had such a great time in all of our boring classes and with all of the bullies every day. Let's have a party to celebrate them!" But I was all for a fundraiser if it would get Abbie Morelle off Katrina's back.

I said, "Let's do a walk-a-thon. We could raise a lot of money that way."

"Walk-a-thons are stupid," Abbie said.
Paulie Roman asked, "How much money could we raise with a walk-a-thon?"

I said, "When we did a walk-a-thon for cancer research in elementary school, we raised $4,000. This school is twice as big, and people can walk farther."

"Yeah," Abbie said, "but that was for cancer. Why would anyone give us money for a graduation ceremony? Plus, someone has to organize it, and it's complicated."

That got me mad enough that I had to say, "It's not that complicated. I'll do it."

What was I thinking? I spent the next month doing almost nothing except organizing that walk-a-thon. I hate walk-a-thons, and I hate talking to people about money. I ended up doing way more than I ever wanted to.

Within the first two weeks, I could see that we weren't going to get enough. It was because we weren't raising money for something important, like cancer. So I started telling people that the money would also go for cancer research. Then, when I saw how many people were ready to give more, I just told

them it was all for cancer research. I got hundreds of parents signed up, and I got businesses to donate food and decorations.

Abbie was completely jealous.

The walk-a-thon was almost a success, too. But the day before, Principal Dorsey called me into his office. He wanted to know if it was true that I had been telling people that the money would go to cancer research because he had understood the money was going for our 8th-grade graduation party. I didn't answer. He said that he was going to call some of the people who pledged money to ask them if I had said anything about cancer.

"It was the only way I could raise enough money!" I answered back, knowing the lie had caught up with me.

"Well, it was the wrong thing to do." Principal Dorsey replied. "Now, you are going to have to contact every person who donated and let them know the truth. You also may not have enough money for a graduation party now."

I knew I should never have volunteered to lead this.

6. Part A
What sort of character is the narrator?

Ⓐ major
Ⓑ minor
Ⓒ middle
Ⓓ weak

Part B
Who or what is the main antagonist in this story?

Ⓐ unnamed narrator
Ⓑ Abbie Morelle
Ⓒ Paulie Roman
Ⓓ none of the above

7. Part A
What sort of character is Principal Dorsey?

Ⓐ major
Ⓑ minor
Ⓒ middle
Ⓓ weak

7. Part B
What type of character is Abbie Morelle?

Ⓐ round
Ⓑ flat
Ⓒ bumpy
Ⓓ none of the above

Question 8 and 9 are based on the story below.

Excerpt from **Stave One of A Christmas Carol** by Charles Dickens

(1) "What else can I be," returned the uncle [Scrooge], "when I live in such a world of fools as this? Merry Christmas! Out upon Merry Christmas! What's Christmas time to you but a time for paying bills without money; a time for finding yourself a year older, but not an hour richer; a time for balancing your books and having every item in 'em through a round dozen of months presented dead against you? If I could work my will," said Scrooge indignantly, "every idiot who goes about with 'Merry Christmas' on his lips should be boiled with his own pudding, and buried with a stake of holly through his heart. He should!"

Excerpt from **Stave Five of A Christmas Carol** by Charles Dickens

(2) "A merry Christmas, Bob!" said Scrooge [the uncle], with an earnestness that could not be mistaken, as he clapped him on the back. "A merrier Christmas, Bob, my good fellow, than I have given you, for many a year! I'll raise your salary, and endeavor to assist your struggling family, and we will discuss your affairs this very afternoon, over a Christmas bowl of smoking bishop, Bob! Make up the fires, and buy another coal-scuttle before you dot another, Bob Cratchit!"

8. What type of characterization does Dickens use to describe Scrooge (the uncle)?

Ⓐ indirect characterization
Ⓑ direct characterization
Ⓒ false characterization
Ⓓ none of the above

9. What type of character is Scrooge (the uncle)?

Ⓐ flat
Ⓑ static
Ⓒ round
Ⓓ dynamic

Question 10 and 11 are based on the story below.

Excerpt from the **Foreword of A Princess of Mars** by Edgar Rice Burroughs

My first recollection of Captain Carter is of the few months he spent at my father's home in Virginia, just prior to the opening of the Civil War. I was then a child of but five years, yet I well remember the tall, dark, smooth-faced, athletic man whom I called Uncle Jack.

He seemed always to be laughing; and he entered into the sports of the children with the same hearty good fellowship he displayed toward those pastimes in which the men and women of his own age indulged; or he would sit for an hour at a time entertaining my old grandmother with stories of his strange, wild life in all parts of the world. We all loved him, and our slaves fairly worshipped the ground he trod.

He was a splendid specimen of manhood, standing a good two inches over six feet, broad of shoulder and narrow of hip, with the carriage of the trained fighting man. His features were regular and clear cut, his hair black and closely cropped, while his eyes were of a steel gray, reflecting a strong and loyal character, filled with fire and initiative. His manners were perfect, and his courtliness was that of a typical southern gentleman of the highest type.

His horsemanship, especially after hounds, was a marvel and delight even in that country of magnificent horsemen. I have often heard my father caution him against his wild recklessness, but he would only laugh, and say that the tumble that killed him would be from the back of a horse yet unfoaled. When the war broke out he left us, nor did I see him again for some fifteen or sixteen years. When he returned it was without warning, and I was much surprised to note that he had not aged apparently a moment, nor had he changed in any other outward way. He was, when others were with him, the same genial, happy fellow we had known of old, but when he thought himself alone I have seen him sit for hours gazing off into space, his face set in a look of wistful longing and hopeless misery; and at night he would sit thus looking up into the heavens, at what I did not know until I read his manuscript years afterward.

10. What sort of characterization is used in this excerpt?

- Ⓐ direct characterization
- Ⓑ indirect characterization
- Ⓒ false characterization
- Ⓓ none of the above

11. What type of character is Captain Carter?

- Ⓐ flat
- Ⓑ static
- Ⓒ round
- Ⓓ dynamic

Lesson 8: Analyzing Literature

Definition: Analyze means to examine carefully, critically and in detail so as to bring out the essential elements of whatever you are analyzing.

The text below presents two accounts of what happened at an event. The event was a town meeting arranged by a candidate for mayor to present his program, if elected and to answer questions from voters who attended.

The president of the local voter organization's point of view, as expressed in a letter to the members of her organization.

Dear members: I attended the recent town meeting organized by a local candidate for Mayor Brian Jones. As you know, he is a newcomer to local politics but is considered a threat by the current mayor and his administration because he has been criticizing them for excessive spending and a lack of cost controls. This administration has been in office for many years and is well connected in this city.

When Mr. Jones scheduled a town hall meeting here, he publicized it with posters; we also publicized it but the local paper would not. The meeting was well attended and Mr. Jones explained the plans and programs he would present to the town council for approval. That part went according to plan. But during the question and answer period, several of those in attendance, who I recognized as friends and supporters of the mayor, asked loaded questions designed to make Mr. Jones look bad; some of the questions implied actions or views on his part that I recognized were false. When anyone tried to criticize their questions, and especially tried to defend him, they were shouted down by the mayor's friends. Emotions on both sides flared to the point that a couple of fist fights started but were quickly broken up by police officers serving as security at the meeting. They disbursed the crowd but arrested a couple of Mr. Jones's friends for disturbing the peace, even though it was the mayor's friends who provoked them and started the fights.

I am appalled by the biased article by the reporter who covered this meeting for the local newspaper. I wrote a letter criticizing the article and sent it to the newspaper, but of course it was not published.

The newspaper reporter's point of view, as expressed in the newspaper article he wrote.
Headline: **Riot erupts at Jones's town hall meeting**

Mayoral candidate Brian Jones held a town hall meeting last night that ended when police were called to quell a riot. After Jones made a speech about his political platform, a question and answer period followed. Jones either refused to answer some questions or provided answers that antagonized members of the audience, especially answers which criticized the mayor and his administration. Rather than try to maintain calm, Jones continued on with inflammatory comments that caused heated arguments between his supporters and detractors which led to several fist fights and the arrival of police. This is in contrast to a town hall held by the mayor two weeks ago that was conducted in a professional manner.

Your assignment: Use actual examples of dialogue or incidents from the text to show how they cause actions to take place and/or reveal details about a character and/or force a decision to be made.

Here is what you might write:

The newspaper article allowed me to make some judgments about the character of the newspaper reporter. It revealed that the reporter had a strong negative bias toward Mr. Jones's candidacy for mayor even before he attended the town hall meeting. I inferred (concluded or judged) this because he worked for a newspaper that refused to publicize the meeting, and after the meeting, refused to publish the letter from the president of the local voter organization. A truly professional reporter of honest character would have reported on the programs Mr. Jones proposed to accomplish. He would also have reported on the discussions during the question and answer period. But this reporter did not, which I inferred was because of his negative bias.

After reading the letter from the president of the voter organization, I made some judgements about the friends of the mayor who attended the meeting. They were arrogant and rude to the candidate, there to antagonize him and try to dissuade others from voting for him, by raising falsehoods, interrupting anyone who spoke in favor of him, and asking trick questions designed to elicit answers that could be used against him. These actions caused the president of the voter's organization to decide to take action by writing the letter shown above to her members, which I infer would most likely convince them to vote for Mr. Jones.

You can scan the QR code given below or use the url to access additional EdSearch resources including videos and mobile apps related to *Analyzing Literature*.

ed)Search

Analyzing Literature

URL	QR Code
http://www.lumoslearning.com/a/rl83	

Question 1 and 2 are based on the story below.

The Laundry

Charlie's parents always assigned him chores around the house. They would often ask him to trim the lawn, wash the dishes, and feed the dog. However, his chores never included laundry. He relied on his mother to wash his clothes for him. Charlie was an outstanding student and was recently accepted to a top college. The college he planned to attend was in New York City. Charlie was nervous about leaving Texas, where he grew up, and being so far away from his family; but, he knew that the college in New York was the perfect fit for him. Before he left, his mother decided that she had better show him how to wash his own clothes because she wouldn't be there to do it for him anymore. She showed Charlie how to sort his clothes into two piles: whites and colors.

Then she showed him how much soap to use and told him when to use hot or warm water and when to use cold water. Next, she explained the different settings on the dryer and told him to be careful not to dry certain items on high heat. Charlie didn't pay much attention. He didn't see what could happen or what was so complicated about washing clothes. He planned on packing mostly t-shirts and jeans and figured that it would be hard to mess up something so simple.

When Charlie arrived at school, he was completely overwhelmed with all of the exciting things to do and new people to meet. He was also careful to dedicate plenty of time to his schoolwork because he wanted to impress his professors and earn good grades. One morning Charlie woke up and found that he had no clean clothes to wear. His schedule had been so packed with activities and studying that he had managed to get through the first month of school without doing any laundry. That night, Charlie piled his soiled clothes into a large basket and headed to his dormitory's laundry room. He shoved all of his clothes into a washer, poured in the soap, and pressed the start. Half an hour later, he opened the washer and started moving the clothes into the dryer. It was then that he realized that he had skipped one very significant step. All of his white t-shirts and socks had turned pink. He had forgotten to sort his colors from his whites. Charlie had received a bright red t-shirt with his new school's logo across the front. The red dye had bled in the wash, turning all of his white clothes pink. Charlie was unhappy about his destroyed wardrobe, but he figured that there was absolutely nothing to do except to put the clothes in the dryer and hope for the best. So he transferred the clothes to a dryer and set the heat to high. After all, he was anxious to get back upstairs to his studies. An hour later, Charlie removed his clothes from the dryer and headed straight back to his dorm room. The following morning, he reached for one of his favorite t-shirts. It was slightly pink now, but he didn't have enough money to replace all of his newly pink clothes. He would have to wear them, pink or not. As he pulled the shirt over his head, he noticed that it seemed tight. He looked at himself in the mirror.

The shirt had shrunk in the dryer. It looked like he had tried to squeeze into his little sister's pink t-shirt. All Charlie could do was laugh. He called his mom and asked her to repeat her laundry instructions again.

This time, Charlie took notes.

1. Which statement best describes Charlie's parents' expectations of him?

Ⓐ They let Charlie do whatever he wants since he's smart and will probably make good decisions.
Ⓑ They expect Charlie to help around the house and earn good grades in school.
Ⓒ They don't expect much from Charlie since he probably won't fulfill their expectations.
Ⓓ They expect Charlie to do all the work around the house while earning straight A's.

2. Part A
What does this excerpt reveal about Charlie?

Ⓐ Charlie did not ask his mother for help with his clothes.
Ⓑ Charlie did not listen carefully to his mother's instructions on how to wash his clothes.
Ⓒ Charlie tried to enjoy doing his laundry.
Ⓓ Charlie is so eager to get his homework completed on time that he forgets the laundry instructions.

2. Part B
After Charlie had a mishap with his laundry, he laughed. What does this reveal about Charlie's character?

Ⓐ Charlie is the kind of person who realizes what's done is done; all he can do is try again.
Ⓑ Charlie is the kind of person who laughs wildly when he isn't sure how to react to stressful situations.
Ⓒ Charlie is the kind of person who laughs at the misfortune of others.
Ⓓ Charlie is the kind of person who laughs when he isn't sure what to do.

Question 3-5 are based on the story below.

Excerpt from **Stave Five of A Christmas Carol** by Charles Dickens

(1) "What else can I be," returned the uncle [Scrooge], "when I live in such a world of fools as this? Merry Christmas! Out upon Merry Christmas! What's Christmas time to you but a time for paying bills without money; a time for finding yourself a year older, but not an hour richer; a time for balancing your books and having every item in 'em through a round dozen of months presented dead against you? If I could work my will," said Scrooge indignantly, "every idiot who goes about with 'Merry Christmas' on his lips should be boiled with his own pudding, and buried with a stake of holly through his heart. He should!"

Excerpt from **Stave Five of A Christmas Carol** by Charles Dickens

(2) "A merry Christmas, Bob!" said Scrooge [the uncle], with an earnestness that could not be mistaken, as he clapped him on the back. "A merrier Christmas, Bob, my good fellow, than I have given

you, for many a year! I'll raise your salary, and endeavor to assist your struggling family, and we will discuss your affairs this very afternoon, over a Christmas bowl of smoking bishop, Bob! Make up the fires, and buy another coal-scuttle before you dot another, Bob Cratchit!"

3. What is the significance of this dialogue from both excerpts?

Ⓐ This dialogue is significant because it shows that Scrooge wants to wish the person he's addressing a Merry Christmas.

Ⓑ This dialogue is significant because it is important for the reader to know Scrooge's feelings about Christmas.

Ⓒ This dialogue is significant because Scrooge wants to make sure everyone knows he dislikes Christmas.

Ⓓ This dialogue is significant because it shows Scrooge cannot wait for Christmas morning to come, so he can rip open his presents.

4. What is the most important purpose of this dialogue?

Ⓐ It allows the reader to really understand the change that Scrooge underwent in the story.

Ⓑ It allows the reader to see that Scrooge liked Christmas all along.

Ⓒ It allows the reader to see that nothing could change Scrooge's opinion of Christmas.

Ⓓ None of the above

5. Why is it important to understand what characters can reveal to readers?

Ⓐ It allows readers to see and understand how characters interact with the setting.

Ⓑ It allows readers to see and understand how characters interact with other characters.

Ⓒ It allows readers to see and understand how the actions of a character can drive the plot.

Ⓓ All of the above

Question 6 and 7 are based on the passage below.

Casey Jones-A Tennessee Legend
-retold by S.E. Schlosser

Casey Jones, that heroic railroad engineer of the Cannonball, was known as the man who always brought the train in on time. He would blow the whistle, so it started off soft but would increase to a wail louder than a banshee before dying off so that people would recognize that whistle and know when Casey was driving past.

April 29, 1900, Casey brought the Cannonball into Memphis dead on time. As he was leaving, he found out one of the other engineers was sick and unable to make his run. So Casey volunteered to help out his friend. He pulled the train out of the station about eleven p.m., an hour and thirty-five minutes late. Casey was determined to make up the time. As soon as he could, he highballed out of

Memphis (highballing means to go very fast and take a lot of risks to get where you are headed) and started making up for the lost time.

About four a.m., when he had nearly made up all the time on the run, Casey rounded a corner near Vaughn, Mississippi, and saw a stalled freight train on the track. He shouted for his fireman to jump. The fireman made it out alive, but Casey Jones died in the wreck, one hand on the brake and one on the whistle chord.

6. Which of the statements below best describes Casey Jones?

Ⓐ He was a large, friendly man known to most as the Cannonball.
Ⓑ He was a courageous, and punctual man.
Ⓒ He was so concerned about being punctual, he was not careful when driving.
Ⓓ None of the above

7. What do Casey's actions in the last paragraph reveal about him?

Ⓐ He wasn't very smart because he didn't jump off the train in time.
Ⓑ He did not care for his firemen.
Ⓒ Up to his very last act, he was courageous.
Ⓓ None of the above

Question 8 is based on the passage below.

The Grasshopper and the Ants-Aesop's Fable

In a field, one summer's day, a grasshopper was hopping about, chirping and singing to its heart's content. A group of ants walked by, grunting as they struggled to carry plump kernels of corn. "Where are you going with those heavy things?" asked the grasshopper. Without stopping, the first ant replied, "To our anthill. This is the third kernel I've delivered today."

"Why not come and sing with me," teased the grasshopper, "instead of working so hard?"

"We are helping to store food for the winter," said the ant, "and think you should do the same."

"Winter is far away, and it is a glorious day to play," sang the grasshopper. But the ants went on their way and continued their hard work.

The weather soon turned cold. All the food lying in the field was covered with a thick white blanket of snow that even the grasshopper could not dig through.

Soon the grasshopper found itself dying of hunger. He staggered to the ants' hill and saw them handing out corn from the stores they had collected in the summer. He begged them for something to eat.

"What!" cried the ants in surprise, "haven't you stored anything away for the winter? What in the world were you doing all last summer?"

"I didn't have time to store any food," complained the grasshopper; "I was so busy playing music that before I knew, it the summer was gone."

The ants shook their heads in disgust, turned their backs on the grasshopper, and went on with their work.

8. Part A
What does the response of the first ant to the grasshopper reveal for readers?

- Ⓐ He is taking his work seriously.
- Ⓑ He doesn't like grasshoppers.
- Ⓒ He likes to work alone.
- Ⓓ He has just started working and doesn't want to be bothered.

Part B
What does the grasshopper's response to the ant reveal about the grasshopper?

- Ⓐ He is trying to be responsible.
- Ⓑ He is afraid of the ant.
- Ⓒ He is not very responsible.
- Ⓓ He is very similar to the ant.

Part C
What do the ants' response to the grasshopper reveal about the ants' opinion of the grasshopper's attitude?

- Ⓐ They are proud of what the grasshopper has done.
- Ⓑ They want to become friendlier with the grasshopper.
- Ⓒ They are unsure of what to say to the grasshopper.
- Ⓓ They can't believe the grasshopper would be so careless.

Chapter 2

Lesson 9: Meaning and Tone

Definitions:

1. Figurative: Figurative language is a language where the meaning of a word or phrase is different from the literal (primary or strict or dictionary) meaning. Another way of defining figurative is: using language that has another meaning besides its normal definition.

2. Connotative: Connotative meanings suggest that there is an associated or secondary meaning of a word or expression, in addition to its primary meaning, that the reader or listener will have to identify himself/herself, since it is not stated in the text.

Let us understand the concept with an example.

Sympathy
By Charles McKay

I lay in sorrow, deep distressed;
My grief a proud man heard;
His looks were cold, he gave me gold
But not a kindly word.
My sorrow passed, I paid him back
The gold he gave to me;
Then stood erect and spoke my thanks,
And blessed his charity.

I lay in want, in grief and pain;
A poor man passed my way;
He bound my head, he gave me bread,
He watched me night and day.
How shall I pay him back again,
For all he did to me?
Oh, gold is great, but greater far
Is heavenly sympathy!

Your assignment: Determine the meanings of keywords or phrases in the poem, especially where figurative language is used or where there are connotative meanings and analyze the impact of specific words and phrases on meaning and tone.

What you might write:

The poet makes a moral judgement in the statement "Oh, gold is great, but greater far Is heavenly sympathy!" which connotes that having feelings of compassionate is more important than having material things without compassion. He reinforces that thought in the verses "His looks were cold, he gave me gold But not a kindly word." which implies that the kindly word was needed more than the gold to help the grieving person. You can infer that although the proud man was generous enough to give the sufferer gold, it was a material gift given without compassion, which shows that he was not a very compassionate person. Furthermore, it was easier for the grieving man to pay back the gold and consider the transaction complete than to repay the poor man who gave emotional and physical caring to the sufferer.

"But not a kindly word" has a negative tone, a tone disparaging of the proud man's character. And perhaps you could connote sarcasm in the line "And blessed his charity." and regard it as an insincere compliment. The verses "How shall I pay him back again, For all he did to me?" has a tone of appreciation, gratefulness.

This poem can be thought of as an allusion to another story: the parable of the good Samaritan in the Christian bible.

You can scan the QR code given below or use the url to access additional EdSearch resources including videos and mobile apps related to *Meaning and Tone*.

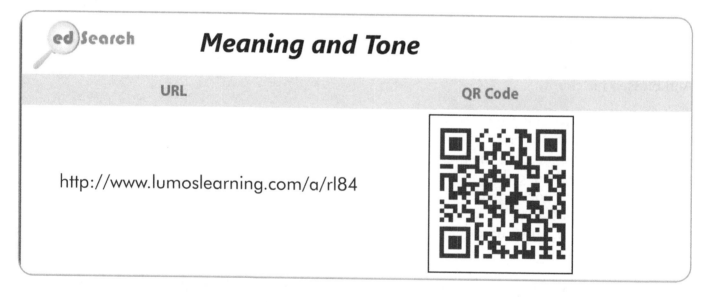

URL	QR Code
http://www.lumoslearning.com/a/rl84	

ed)Search

Meaning and Tone

1. What is the tone of a piece of literature?

    Ⓐ   the rhythm of the words when read out loud
    Ⓑ   the level of sound with which it should be read
    Ⓒ   the author's attitude about the subject and/or the readers
    Ⓓ   none of the above

2. What is the tone of this sentence?

Tonight's homework is to read thirty pages in the textbook.

    Ⓐ   neutral
    Ⓑ   dramatic
    Ⓒ   angry
    Ⓓ   friendly

3. What is the tone of the below sentence?

Oh great! My thoughtful teacher gave us homework again tonight! Sure, I have nothing better to do than read thirty pages out of an outdated textbook. I don't have a life.

    Ⓐ   expectant
    Ⓑ   sad
    Ⓒ   sarcastic
    Ⓓ   adoring

4. What is the tone of the below sentence?

I simply cannot believe that after all the reading we have done this week, we have to read thirty pages tonight. This is an outrage!

    Ⓐ   angry
    Ⓑ   gleeful
    Ⓒ   skeptical
    Ⓓ   questioning

Question 5 is based on the passage below.

Excerpt from Because of Winn-Dixie
by Kate DiCamillo

The Open Arms had mice. They were there from when it was a Pick-It-Quick and there were lots of good things to eat in the building, and when the Pick-It-Quick became the Open Arms Baptist Church of Naomi, the mice stayed around to eat all the leftover crumbs from the potluck suppers. The preacher kept on saying he was going to have to do something about them, but he never did. Because the truth is, he couldn't stand the thought of hurting anything, even a mouse.

Well, Winn-Dixie saw that mouse, and he was up and after him. One minute, everything was quiet and serious and the preacher was going on and on and on; and the next minute, Winn-Dixie looked like a furry bullet, shooting across the building, chasing that mouse. He was barking and his feet were skidding all over the polished Pick-It-Quick floor, and people were clapping and hollering and pointing. They really went wild when Winn-Dixie actually caught the mouse.

5. What is the tone in this excerpt?

- Ⓐ romantic
- Ⓑ unemotional
- Ⓒ enthusiastic
- Ⓓ morose

Question 6 is based on the passage below.

From **Narrative of the Life of Frederick Douglass, an American Slave**

This battle with Mr. Covey was the turning point in my career as a slave. It rekindled the few expiring embers of freedom, and revived within me a sense of my own manhood.

6. What is the tone of the statement above?

- Ⓐ encouraging
- Ⓑ sarcastic
- Ⓒ unemotional
- Ⓓ sorrowful

Question 7-9 are based on the excerpt below.

Excerpt from **"The Story of the Wild Huntsman"** by Heinrich Hoffmann

This is the Wild Huntsman that shoots the hares
With the grass-green coat he always wears:
With game-bag, powder-horn and gun,
He's going out to have some fun.
He finds it hard, without a pair
Of spectacles, to shoot the hare:
He put his spectacles upon his nose, and said,
"Now I will shoot the hares, and kill them dead."
The hare sits snug in leaves and grass
And laughs to see the green man pass

7. What is the tone of this excerpt?

- Ⓐ   joyous
- Ⓑ   formal
- Ⓒ   serious
- Ⓓ   comical

8. In this sentence, what does "snug" most likely mean?

- Ⓐ   seaworthiness
- Ⓑ   fitting closely
- Ⓒ   privacy
- Ⓓ   humorous

9. In this excerpt, what does "spectacles" most likely means?

- Ⓐ   something unusual
- Ⓑ   something one would be curious about
- Ⓒ   dramatic display
- Ⓓ   glasses

Question 10 is based on the passage below.

The Ungrateful Son
By Jacob and Wilhelm Grimm

Once a man was sitting with his wife before their front door. They had a roasted chicken which they were about to eat together. Then the man saw that his aged father was approaching, and he hastily took the chicken and hid it, for he did not want to share it with him. The old man came, had a drink, and went away. Now the son wanted to put the roasted chicken back onto the table, but when he reached for it, it had turned into a large toad, which jumped into his face and sat there and never went away again. If anyone tried to remove it, it looked venomously at him as though it would jump into his face, so that no one dared to touch it. And the ungrateful son was forced to feed the toad every day, or else it would eat from his face. And thus he went to and fro in the world without rest.

10. Part A
In this story, what does "hastily" most likely means?

Ⓐ hurriedly
Ⓑ slowly
Ⓒ carefully
Ⓓ quietly

Part B
In this story, "venomously" most closely means

Ⓐ poisonous
Ⓑ acting like a snake
Ⓒ showing strong anger
Ⓓ striking

Question 11 and 12 are based on the passage below.

Once upon a midnight dreary, while I pondered, weak and weary,
Over many a quaint and curious volume of forgotten lore,
While I nodded, nearly napping, suddenly there came a tapping,
As of some one gently rapping, rapping at my chamber door.
''Tis some visitor,' I muttered, 'tapping at my chamber door-
Only this, and nothing more.'

Ah, distinctly I remember it was in the bleak December,
And each separate dying ember wrought its ghost upon the floor.
Eagerly I wished the morrow;- vainly I had sought to borrow

From my books surcease of sorrow- sorrow for the lost Lenore-
For the rare and radiant maiden whom the angels name Lenore-
Nameless here for evermore.

And the silken sad uncertain rustling of each purple curtain
Thrilled me- filled me with fantastic terrors never felt before;
So that now, to still the beating of my heart, I stood repeating,
''Tis some visitor entreating entrance at my chamber door-
Some late visitor entreating entrance at my chamber door;-
This it is, and nothing more.'

Presently my soul grew stronger; hesitating then no longer,
'Sir,' said I, 'or Madam, truly your forgiveness I implore;
But the fact is I was napping, and so gently you came rapping,
And so faintly you came tapping, tapping at my chamber door,
That I scarce was sure I heard you'- here I opened wide the door;-
Darkness there, and nothing more.

Deep into that darkness peering, long I stood there wondering, fearing,
Doubting, dreaming dreams no mortals ever dared to dream before;
But the silence was unbroken, and the stillness gave no token,
And the only word there spoken was the whispered word, 'Lenore!'
This I whispered, and an echo murmured back the word, 'Lenore!'-
Merely this, and nothing more.

Back into the chamber turning, all my soul within me burning,
Soon again I heard a tapping somewhat louder than before.
'Surely,' said I, 'surely that is something at my window lattice:
Let me see, then, what thereat is, and this mystery explore-
Let my heart be still a moment and this mystery explore;-
'Tis the wind and nothing more.'

Open here I flung the shutter, when, with many a flirt and flutter,
In there stepped a stately raven of the saintly days of yore;
Not the least obeisance made he; not a minute stopped or stayed he;
But, with mien of lord or lady, perched above my chamber door-
Perched upon a bust of Pallas just above my chamber door-
Perched, and sat, and nothing more.

Then this ebony bird beguiling my sad fancy into smiling,
By the grave and stern decorum of the countenance it wore.
'Though thy crest be shorn and shaven, thou,' I said, 'art sure no craven,
Ghastly grim and ancient raven wandering from the Nightly shore-
Tell me what thy lordly name is on the Night's Plutonian shore!'
Quoth the Raven, 'Nevermore.'

Much I marvelled this ungainly fowl to hear discourse so plainly,
Though its answer little meaning- little relevancy bore;
For we cannot help agreeing that no living human being
Ever yet was blest with seeing bird above his chamber door-
Bird or beast upon the sculptured bust above his chamber door,
With such name as 'Nevermore.'

But the raven, sitting lonely on the placid bust, spoke only
That one word, as if his soul in that one word he did outpour.
Nothing further then he uttered- not a feather then he fluttered-
Till I scarcely more than muttered, 'other friends have flown before-
On the morrow he will leave me, as my hopes have flown before.'
Then the bird said, 'Nevermore.'

Startled at the stillness broken by reply so aptly spoken,
'Doubtless,' said I, 'what it utters is its only stock and store,
Caught from some unhappy master whom unmerciful Disaster
Followed fast and followed faster till his songs one burden bore-
Till the dirges of his Hope that melancholy burden bore
Of 'Never- nevermore'.'

But the Raven still beguiling all my fancy into smiling,
Straight I wheeled a cushioned seat in front of bird, and bust and door;
Then upon the velvet sinking, I betook myself to linking
Fancy unto fancy, thinking what this ominous bird of yore-
What this grim, ungainly, ghastly, gaunt and ominous bird of yore
Meant in croaking 'Nevermore.'

This I sat engaged in guessing, but no syllable expressing
To the fowl whose fiery eyes now burned into my bosom's core;
This and more I sat divining, with my head at ease reclining
On the cushion's velvet lining that the lamplight gloated o'er,
But whose velvet violet lining with the lamplight gloating o'er,

She shall press, ah, nevermore!

Then methought the air grew denser, perfumed from an unseen censer
Swung by Seraphim whose footfalls tinkled on the tufted floor.
'Wretch,' I cried, 'thy God hath lent thee- by these angels he
hath sent thee
Respite- respite and nepenthe, from thy memories of Lenore!
Quaff, oh quaff this kind nepenthe and forget this lost Lenore!'
Quoth the Raven, 'Nevermore.'

'Prophet!' said I, 'thing of evil!- prophet still, if bird or
devil!-
Whether Tempter sent, or whether tempest tossed thee here ashore,
Desolate yet all undaunted, on this desert land enchanted-
On this home by horror haunted- tell me truly, I implore-
Is there- is there balm in Gilead?- tell me- tell me, I implore!'
Quoth the Raven, 'Nevermore.'

'Prophet!' said I, 'thing of evil- prophet still, if bird or
devil!
By that Heaven that bends above us- by that God we both adore-
Tell this soul with sorrow laden if, within the distant Aidenn,
It shall clasp a sainted maiden whom the angels name Lenore-
Clasp a rare and radiant maiden whom the angels name Lenore.'
Quoth the Raven, 'Nevermore.'

'Be that word our sign in parting, bird or fiend,' I shrieked,
upstarting-
'Get thee back into the tempest and the Night's Plutonian shore!
Leave no black plume as a token of that lie thy soul hath spoken!
Leave my loneliness unbroken!- quit the bust above my door!
Take thy beak from out my heart, and take thy form from off my
door!'
Quoth the Raven, 'Nevermore.'

And the Raven, never flitting, still is sitting, still is sitting
On the pallid bust of Pallas just above my chamber door;
And his eyes have all the seeming of a demon's that is dreaming,
And the lamplight o'er him streaming throws his shadow on the
floor;
And my soul from out that shadow that lies floating on the floor
Shall be lifted- nevermore!

Synopsis of THE RAVEN

The poem is set on a dreary night while the narrator is reading by a dying fire in attempts to forget his love, Lenore's death. He hears a tapping at his door and finds nothing. The tap then gets louder. The narrator realizes it is coming from a window. When he opens the window, a raven flies in and sits above the door.

He is then sort of interested and amused by the bird. He asks the bird what his name is, but the raven only says, "Nevermore". This surprises the narrator that the bird can talk. He says the bird will fly out of his life like others have. The bird again says, "Nevermore" leading the narrator to think he has had a cruel master. He thinks that is the only word the bird knows.

The narrator is curious to see what the raven will do and pulls up a chair directly in front of him. He wants to learn more about the bird. He lets his mind wander to his lost love Lenore. He feels the presence of angels and now believes this could be a sign from God. When he asks the bird, the raven replies the negative comment again. Now the narrator becomes angry and feels the raven is a devil or evil bird. The word, "Nevermore" is again repeated. The man is outraged and tells the bird to leave. It does not. The narrator falls into a deep state of depression.

11. Why do you think the raven was chosen to be used in this poem? Write your answer in the box below.

12. The narrator in the poem thinks that the raven could have been sent by two different forces. What are they? Write your answer in the box below.

Lesson 10: Compare and Contrast

CAUSE AND EFFECT STRUCTURE: This structure presents a relationship between the cause of an event, idea, or concept and the effects of carrying out that event, idea, or concept.

Let us understand the concept with an example.

The Obesity Epidemic

Publisher's Note: The first paragraph states the main idea of the article.

In the United States population, 30% of adults and 17% of children are obese, according to the American Heart Association. And by 2020, 83% of men and 72% of women are expected to be overweight or obese, according to research presented at the Heart Association's scientific meeting in 2011.

Publisher's Note: The next paragraph states the cause associated with the main idea.

What is causing so many people to be obese? More sedentary lifestyles are one factor. Sitting and watching television, driving instead of walking, not exercising enough. Nutrition is another. So much of our food is processed, which means fat and sugar are added. Also, we frequently eat portions larger than our bodies need, and we often snack between meals.

Publisher's Note: The next paragraph states the effects from the cause associated with the main idea.

Being obese has negative health and health expense disadvantages. According to the Centers for Disease Control and Prevention:

- Obesity-related conditions include heart disease, stroke, type 2 diabetes, high blood pressure, arthritis and certain types of cancer, some of the leading causes of preventable death.
- The estimated annual medical cost of obesity in the U.S. was $147 billion in 2008 U.S. dollars; the medical costs for people who are obese were $1,429 higher than those of normal weight.

Publisher's Note: Sometimes there will be a paragraph following the effects paragraph that explains a solution to the problem described in the main idea.

What can people do about reducing their obesity?

- Exercise: The Centers for Disease Control (CDC) recommends 2.5 hours of moderate aerobic exercise per week, along with 2 days of strength training.

- Nutrition: Controlling the intake of carbohydrates is one important action. Also, eating less processed food, less refined grains and bread and more vegetables are also important. You need to add lean protein to every meal and every snack, along with moderate amounts of healthy fats.

COMPARE-CONTRAST STRUCTURE: This type of text examines the similarities and differences between two or more people, events, concepts, ideas, etc.

Global Warming

For many years, scientists have been studying the effects of temperature on living organisms on planet Earth. In the last few years, there has been an increase in the earth's atmospheric and oceanic temperatures, which has been called global warming. Global warming has been recognized as a very important environmental phenomenon that can have dramatic and devastating effects on the environment of planet Earth.

Scientists in one group, we'll call it Group A, believe the theory that global warming is caused by the increase in certain gases (such as carbon dioxide) in the atmosphere that occurs when warmth from the sun is trapped in the Earth's atmosphere by a layer of gases (such as carbon dioxide) and water vapor. They refer to this as the "greenhouse effect." This group believes that human activities, such as manufacturing, deforestation and pollution are the primary contributors to the greenhouse effect. Scientists in another group, we'll call it Group B, believe the theory that global warming is not just a recent phenomenon, but is a natural phenomenon that has been occurring for thousands of years as part of a cycle of warming and cooling of the Earth's atmosphere, and that human activity is only a minor contributor

Also, they mention that some experts point out that natural cycles in the Earth's orbit can alter the planet's exposure to sunlight, which may explain the current trend. Earth has indeed experienced warming and cooling cycles roughly every hundred thousand years due to these orbital shifts, but such changes have occurred over the span of several centuries.

What you might write:

The cause and effect structure is very logical and easy for a reader to understand the text. It is very logical to explain the cause of an event or action first, then explain the effects of that action. This structure gives the reader enough information to intelligently evaluate a concluding paragraph asking the reader to take some action (donation of money or time) to resolve the problem caused by the effects. The compare-contrast structure is also a logical way to communicate information to a reader. In its most effective format, it will start by presenting a description of the main idea or issue to be dealt with, which was done in the example above. Then it will present the opinions of one group, then the opinions of the other group, clearly spelled out so the reader can tell how the groups differ or agree in their positions on the issue. This is what was done in the example above.

Sometimes, when the main topic has several subtopics, the writer might list each subtopic separately with the position of each group included. Otherwise, the entire position of a group can be described followed by the entire position of the other group.

There may also be a concluding paragraph recommending how the issue should be resolved.

You can scan the QR code given below or use the url to access additional EdSearch resources including videos and mobile apps related to *Compare and Contrast*.

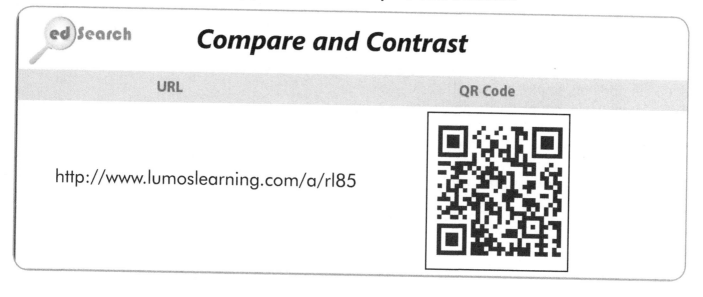

URL	QR Code
http://www.lumoslearning.com/a/rl85	

1. When you are comparing two things, what are you looking for?

   (A) similarities
   (B) differences
   (C) similarities and differences
   (D) none of the above

2. Which of the following group of signal words would you most likely find in a paper comparing two things?

   (A) in addition, finally, above all
   (B) meanwhile, coupled with, for instance
   (C) likewise, as well, the same as
   (D) although, however, contrary to

3. Which of the following graphic organizers is most effectively used to compare and contrast?

   (A) Venn diagram
   (B) Brace map
   (C) Fish bone map
   (D) Tree map

4. When you are contrasting two things, what are you looking for?

   (A) similarities
   (B) differences
   (C) similarities and differences
   (D) none of the above

5. In a Venn diagram, where does the "common" information belong?

   (A) in the middle
   (B) on the right
   (C) on the left
   (D) no where

6. Which of the following group of signal words would you most likely find in a paper contrasting two things?

   (A) in addition, finally, above all
   (B) meanwhile, coupled with, for instance
   (C) likewise, as well, the same as
   (D) although, however, contrary to

Question 7 and 8 are based on the poems below.

The Mountain and The Squirrel	The Arrow and the Song
The mountain and the squirrel Had a quarrel; And the former called the latter, "Little Prig." Bun replied "You are doubtless very big; But all sorts of things and weather Must be taken in together To make up a year And a sphere. And I think it no disgrace To occupy my place. If I'm not so large as you, You are not so small as I, And not half so spry; I'll not deny you make A very pretty squirrel track; Talents differ; all is well and wisely put; If I cannot carry forests on my back, Neither can you crack a nut" **Ralph Waldo Emerson** (1803 - 1882)	I shot an arrow into the air It fell to earth, I knew not where; For, so swiftly it flew, the sight Could not follow it in its flight. I breathed a song into the air It fell to earth, I knew not where For who has sight so keen and strong That it can follow the flight of song? Long, long afterward, in an oak I found the arrow, still unbroke And the song, from beginning to end I found again in the heart of a friend. **H. W. Longfellow** (1807 - 1882)

7. Both poems share a similar setting which is _____.

- Ⓐ nature
- Ⓑ the mountains
- Ⓒ a lake
- Ⓓ a tree

8. Part A
   What is one comparison the reader can make about both poems?

- Ⓐ Both the poems were written during the 19th century.
- Ⓑ One of the poems was written in the 20th century.
- Ⓒ Both the poems were written in the 20th century.
- Ⓓ One of the poems was written in the 19th century.

8. Part B
A difference between the poems is _____.

Ⓐ dialogue
Ⓑ point of view
Ⓒ both A & B
Ⓓ none of the above

Question 9 and 10 are based on the passage below.

Henry Wordsworth Longfellow was an American poet who lived from 1807 to 1882. Longfellow was born and raised in the region of Portland, Maine. Longfellow was enrolled in dame school at the age of only three. By age six, when he entered Portland Academy, he was able to read and write quite well. He graduated from Bowdoin College in Brunswick, Maine, in 1822. At Bowdoin, he met Nathaniel Hawthorne, who became his lifelong friend. After several journeys overseas, Longfellow settled for the last forty-five years of his life in Cambridge, Massachusetts. Longfellow was one of the five members of the group known as the Fireside Poets. During his years at the college, he wrote textbooks in French, Italian, and Spanish and a travel book, Outre-mer: A Pilgrimage Beyond the Sea Longfellow was such an admired figure in the United States during his life that his 70th birthday in 1877 took on the air of a national holiday, with parades, speeches, and the reading of his poetry. He had become one of the first American celebrities. His work was immensely popular during his time and is still today, although some modern critics consider him too sentimental. His poetry is based on familiar and easily understood themes with simple, clear, and flowing language. His poetry created an audience in America and contributed to creating American mythology.

Ralph Waldo Emerson was an American essayist, poet, and leader of the trancendentalist movement in the early 19th century. He was born and brought up in Boston, Massachusetts. Emerson lost his father at the age of 8 and was subsequently sent to Boston Latin School at the age of 9. He went to Harvard College at the age of 14 and graduated in 1821. Emerson made his living as a schoolmaster and then went to Harvard Divinity School and emerged as a Unitarian Minister in 1829. A dispute with church officials over the administration of the Communion service and misgivings about public prayer led to his resignation in 1832. In the 1840's Emerson was hospitable to Nathanial Hawthorne and his family, influencing Hawthorne during his three joyous years with Emerson. Emerson was noted as being a very abstract and difficult writer who nevertheless drew large crowds for his speeches. The heart of Emerson's writing were his direct observations in his hournals, which he started keeping as a teenager at Harvard. Emerson has written a lot of essays on, History, Self-reliance, love, friendship, heroism etc... He died in 1882 and is buried in the sleepy hollow Cemetery, Concord, Massachusetts. His house, which he bought in 1835 in Concord, Massachusetts, is now open to the public as the Ralph Waldo Emerson house.

9. According to the above passages, what is common between the above writers?

   Ⓐ   Both the writers were born in America.
   Ⓑ   Both the writers lived at the same time (19th Century).
   Ⓒ   Both the writers were associated with Nathaniel Hawthorne.
   Ⓓ   All of the above.

10. Did the synopsis help you to understand the poem better? Explain your answer. Write your answer in the box below.

Chapter 2

Lesson 11: Producing Suspense and Humor

You can scan the QR code given below or use the url to access additional EdSearch resources including videos and mobile apps related to *Producing Suspense and Humor*.

edSearch	**Producing Suspense and Humor**	
URL		**QR Code**
http://www.lumoslearning.com/a/rl86		

1. **Which of the following is an example of a pun?**

   Ⓐ A boiled egg every morning is hard to beat.
   Ⓑ Nicholas went to buy some camouflage pants the other day, but he couldn't find any.
   Ⓒ Our social studies teacher says her globe means the world to her.
   Ⓓ all of the above

2. **What literary elements can add humor to a story?**

   Ⓐ pun
   Ⓑ setting or situation
   Ⓒ irony
   Ⓓ all of the above

3. **What is the best definition of irony?**

   Ⓐ interesting dialogue between characters
   Ⓑ a scene in which something is complex and difficult to understand
   Ⓒ surprising, funny, or interesting contradictions
   Ⓓ a line that is straight to the point

Question 4 is based on the poem below.

Excerpt from **The Story of the Wild Huntsman** by Heinrich Hoffmann

This is the Wild Huntsman that shoots the hares
With the grass-green coat he always wears:
With game-bag, powder-horn and gun,
He's going out to have some fun.
He finds it hard, without a pair
Of spectacles, to shoot the hare:
He put his spectacles upon his nose, and said,
"Now I will shoot the hares, and kill them dead."
The hare sits snug in leaves and grass
And laughs to see the green man pass

4. **The author creates humor through his description of** _____.

   Ⓐ the laughing rabbit
   Ⓑ the hunter who is excited to kill a rabbit
   Ⓒ the hunter who is over-prepared to hunt
   Ⓓ the description of the spectacle

Question 5 is based on the paragraph below.

It was a cold and windy evening. The clouds had a haunting presence in the sky. Cindy walked briskly down the street, conscious of the quiet around her. As she approached her front door, she noticed something wasn't right. There was a light on inside, and she thought she could hear someone running down the stairs. Her husband, however, wasn't due home for a couple of hours.

5. This description builds a sense of _____.

- Ⓐ irony
- Ⓑ suspense
- Ⓒ humor
- Ⓓ confusion

Question 6 is based on the paragraph below.

In the story Romeo and Juliet by William Shakespeare, Romeo commits suicide because he thinks that Juliet is dead. However, the reader knows that she is just in a deep sleep because she took a potion that made her appear dead.

6. What type of irony does Shakespeare use?

- Ⓐ dramatic irony
- Ⓑ verbal irony
- Ⓒ situational irony
- Ⓓ none of the above

Question 7 is based on the paragraph below.

A man wakes up early to wash his car before a trip to the park to watch a baseball game. After the game, he realizes that he parked under a tree filled with birds and now his car is covered in white splattered patches. The man said with a loud sigh, "Gee, I sure am glad I woke up early to wash my car."

7. What type of irony does the author use?

- Ⓐ dramatic irony
- Ⓑ verbal irony
- Ⓒ situational irony
- Ⓓ none of the above

Question 8 is based on the paragraph below.

During a ceremony to release two rehabilitated seals into the ocean, the seals are attacked and killed by whales.

8. What type of irony does the author use?

Ⓐ dramatic irony
Ⓑ verbal irony
Ⓒ situational irony
Ⓓ none of the above

Question 9 is based on the paragraph below.

Caitlin saved for years to be able to afford her dream vacation to Tahiti. The morning of her flight she received a phone call from a talk show. If she answered the question correctly she would win a vacation. To her surprise, she answered the question correctly, and the host announced she had won an all-expense paid vacation to Tahiti.

9. What type of irony does the author use?

Ⓐ situational irony
Ⓑ verbal irony
Ⓒ dramatic irony
Ⓓ all of the above

Question 10 is based on the paragraph below.

Kyle knew he needed to study for his biology test, but he was so close to beating the next level of his video game that he just couldn't tear himself away from the screen. An hour later, his mom came into his room and said, "Kyle, when you are finished the very important task of beating this level, why don't you consider opening up your binder and studying for your biology test?"

10. What type of irony does the author use?

Ⓐ situational irony
Ⓑ verbal irony
Ⓒ dramatic irony
Ⓓ building suspense

Question 11 and 12 are based on the details below.

The Tempest, Act III, Scene II [Be not afeard]

William Shakespeare, 1564 - 1616

Caliban speaks to Stephano and Trinculo.

Be not afeard; the isle is full of noises,
Sounds and sweet airs, that give delight, and hurt not.
Sometimes a thousand twangling instruments
Will hum about mine ears; and sometime voices,
That, if I then had waked after long sleep,
Will make me sleep again: and then, in dreaming,
The clouds methought would open, and show riches
Ready to drop upon me; that, when I waked,
I cried to dream again.

11. Describe what not to be afraid of? Write your answer in the box below.

12. Why did he want to dream again? Write your answer in the box below.

Chapter 2

Lesson 12: Media and Literature

Presented below are two reviews of the film Cinderella. Following that is an example of what you might write in comparing the film and the book, assuming you read the storybook version of Cinderella by Ruth Sanderson.

Two Reviews of Walt Disney Pictures Cinderella
By Alex Reif, Alex's Movie blog, January 29, 2015 and by Spencer Higham, Cinderella Plot Summary, on the IMDb website, 2015

Walt Disney Pictures' latest live action fairytale is a retelling of the evergreen classic Cinderella. The story starts with young Ella, who lives with her wealthy parents in a beautiful estate in a peaceful kingdom. From a young age, she is taught by her mother to believe in the existence and presence of magic, allowing her to befriend the many animals on the estate, particularly the mice.

Everything is perfect until her mother contracts a fatal illness. On her deathbed, she makes Ella promise that she'll always have courage and show kindness to others. Years later, her father decides to remarry to bring some happiness back to the house, but soon after he passes away, Ella's stepmother reveals her true cold, wicked nature. Desperate for money, she dismisses the servants and forces Ella to do all the work. Even worse, she gives Ella's room to the stepsisters, forces her to sleep in the attic, and won't even let her eat with the family. One morning, after Ella, not wanting to sleep in the cold attic, sleeps by the fireplace; her soot-covered face leads her stepsisters to mock and dub her as Cinderella. Crushed by their cruelty, Ella goes for a ride in the woods, where she encounters a hunting party and meets one of the hunters who claims to be an apprentice named Kit who lives in the palace. Unknown to her, he's actually the only son of the land's dying king. Despite never learning her name, Kit (a nickname given to him by his father) is enchanted by Ella's charm, kindness, and a unique outlook on life and becomes obsessed with her.

Kit is being forced by his dying father to choose a bride. Desperately hoping to see the mystery girl again, he convinces his father to throw a ball and invite everyone in the kingdom, regardless of status. When she hears about the ball, Ella dreams of attending to find Kit. However, her stepmother Lady Tremaine has other plans for Cinderella.

Ella's chances of attending the ball are destroyed by her stepmother and stepsisters, but she soon discovers that she has a Fairy Godmother who transforms her into a beautiful princess with a horse-drawn coach which whisks her away to the ball. There she discovers that Kit is really the prince and that he is just as much a prisoner as she is, just in different ways. She runs away at midnight just before the spell breaks without giving him her name. Now the prince must have the courage to follow his heart to find Ella so they can both live happily ever after.

Here is what you might write, after seeing this film and reading the storybook version of Cinderella by Ruth Sanderson.

The film gives more details about Ella's life with her parents before her mother dies, including her mother's advice: ""Have courage and be kind." The book devotes just one sentence to this: "Once upon a time there was a gentleman who, after his beloved first wife died, married a widow with two daughters." In the film, her father passes away, leaving her to try and "Have courage and be kind." in spite of the cruel treatment by her stepmother and her two stepdaughters. In the book, her father remains alive, although too weak in temperament to defend her and stand up to her step-relatives until the very end, when he calls the prince's attention to Ella when the prince is seeking the woman for whom the glass slipper will fit. The book never mentions Ella's name; she is referred to as "the girl" until given the name "Cinderella," a derogatory name given by the stepdaughters in the book and film when they see her with her clothes covered with cinder ash from the fireplace.

In the book, Cinderella never meets Kit until she attends the ball. Both the film and the book show actions the stepmother takes to prevent Ella from attending the ball, although the actions are different between the two media. Both media introduce a Fairy Godmother whose magic creates a carriage, horses, a coachman, two footmen, and a beautiful gown and glass slippers with which Cinderella attends the ball. Both include the Godmother's warning that the magic wears off at midnight.

The similarities in both versions continue: they portray her as having exceptional beauty that attracts the prince's attention; at the stroke of midnight she makes a hurried exit from the ball, dropping a glass shoe which the prince finds; and in seeking the shoe's owner the prince eventually visits Ella's house. The film adds another plot in which the stepmother identifies Ella as the object of the prince's search and makes an effort to win royalty for her and her daughters while dissuading Kit to search for "the mystery girl." She fails and when the prince finally reaches Ella's house, both media create different circumstances by which the prince discovers Ella, in spite of the efforts by the stepmother to hide her, and since the shoe fits, both media describe a happy ending of marriage and lives lived happily ever after for Ella and the prince. The book ends with the birds, with whom Ella has always loved, attacking the step-relatives when they are outside the house, as Ella and the prince leave, forcing them back into the house never to venture outside again. The film merely has them forced to leave the kingdom forever.

While the film has live action, the book has beautifully drawn illustrations. Both have worthwhile elements to them, and both are worth seeing or reading.

You can scan the QR code given below or use the url to access additional EdSearch resources including videos and mobile apps related to *Media and Literature.*

URL	QR Code
http://www.lumoslearning.com/a/rl87	

Media and Literature

ed Search

Question 1-3 are based on the paragraph below.

Casey Jones-A Tennessee Legend
-retold by S.E. Schlosser

Casey Jones, that heroic railroad engineer of the Cannonball, was known as the man who always brought the train in on time. He would blow the whistle, so it started off soft but would increase to a wail louder than a banshee before dying off so that people would recognize that whistle and know when Casey was driving past.

April 29, 1900, Casey brought the Cannonball into Memphis dead on time. As he was leaving, he found out one of the other engineers was sick and unable to make his run. So Casey volunteered to help out his friend. He pulled the train out of the station about eleven p.m., an hour and thirty-five minutes late. Casey was determined to make up the time. As soon as he could, he highballed out of Memphis (highballing means to go very fast and take a lot of risks to get where you are headed) and started making up for the lost time.

About four a.m., when he had nearly made up all the time on the run, Casey rounded a corner near Vaughn, Mississippi, and saw a stalled freight train on the track. He shouted for his fireman to jump. The fireman made it out alive, but Casey Jones died in the wreck, one hand on the brake and one on the whistle chord.

1. **What medium of publication would be best to use if you wanted to make it possible for people to see Casey Jones operating the train?**

   Ⓐ a video
   Ⓑ digital text
   Ⓒ a traditional book
   Ⓓ none of the above

2. **What are the advantages of using media to present a particular topic or idea?**

   Ⓐ It can create a picture for viewers to see
   Ⓑ It provides a clear voice for viewers to hear
   Ⓒ Both A and B
   Ⓓ None of the above

3. **If you want to see one person's visual interpretation of a character's appearance, what medium of publication would be best to use?**

   Ⓐ movie version of a text
   Ⓑ print text
   Ⓒ digital text
   Ⓓ none of the above

4. What is multimedia?

Ⓐ A medium used to present information

Ⓑ Using more than one medium of expression or communication.

Ⓒ Multiple books

Ⓓ None of the above

5. What medium of publication would be best to quickly publish your opinion about a current topic?

Ⓐ Research paper

Ⓑ Newspaper article

Ⓒ Blog

Ⓓ None of the above

6. What is the difference between an article written in a newspaper and a blog post?

Ⓐ Newspapers are available only in printed format whereas blogs are published online.

Ⓑ Newspaper articles are reliable resources while blogs are opinions.

Ⓒ Blogs have to be proven true, and newspapers do not.

Ⓓ None of the above

Question 7 and 8 are based on the poem below.

The Lake Isle of Innisfree

I will arise and go now, and go to Innisfree,
And a small cabin build there, of clay and wattles made:
Nine bean-rows will I have there, a hive for the honey-bee;
And live alone in the bee-loud glade.
And I shall have some peace there, for peace comes dropping slow,
Dropping from the veils of the morning to where the cricket sings;
There midnight's all a glimmer, and noon a purple glow,
And evening full of the linnet's wings.
I will arise and go now, for always night and day
I hear lake water lapping with low sounds by the shore;
While I stand on the roadway, or on the pavements grey,
I hear it in the deep heart's core.
W. B. Yeats

About the poet:
William Butler Yeats was an Irish poet and a dramatist. He was one of the foremost figures of 20th-century literature and was the driving force behind the Irish literary revival. Together with Lady

Gregory and Edward Martin, Yeats founded the Abbey Theater. He served as its chief during its early years and was a pillar of the Irish literary establishment in his later years.

The above well-known poem explores the poet's longing for the peace and tranquility of Innisfree, a place where he spent a lot of time as a boy. This poem is a lyric.

7. **Part A**

Which medium of publication, the poem or the picture, gives you a better visualization of the lake?

   Ⓐ the picture
   Ⓑ the poem
   Ⓒ neither
   Ⓓ both

7. **Part B**

Which medium of publication, the poem or the picture, appeals to more than one of the five senses?

   Ⓐ the picture
   Ⓑ the poem
   Ⓒ neither
   Ⓓ both

8. **Part A**

Which medium of publication, the poem or the picture, is the best to visualize the lake and its surroundings?

   Ⓐ the picture
   Ⓑ the poem
   Ⓒ neither
   Ⓓ both

8. **Part B**
   Which medium of publication, the poem or the picture, would be best to use on a travel brochure to attract people to the lake?

   Ⓐ the picture
   Ⓑ the poem
   Ⓒ neither
   Ⓓ both

Chapter 2

Lesson 13: Modern Fictions and Traditional Stories

Let us understand the concept with an example.

The Gregory Maguire novel Wicked: The Life and Times of the Wicked Witch of the West[1], published in 1995, is presented here as the modern work of fiction that the standard calls for. We'll refer to it in this essay as Wicked. The traditional story called for by the standard is The Wonderful Wizard of Oz[2] by Frank Baum, published in 1900. We'll refer to it as Oz. The two stories are compared for their similarities and differences. Here is what you might write, after reading both stories.

1. Both stories are told by a narrator, a third person who is not a character in the stories.

2. Both include the characters of Elphaba, the Wicked Witch of the West, Dorothy and her dog Toto, the Wizard of Oz, Glinda the Good Witch, the tinman, the lion and the scarecrow.

3. Wicked focuses mostly on Elphaba, devoting four of five sections describing her parents, how her green skin and sharp teeth came about, her violent personality, and her childhood in their home country of Munchkinland, where animals talk and strive to be treated like first-class citizens; her attendance at college and transformation into a supporter of animal rights by a self-aware professor who is a Goat, who is one of several talking animals with civil rights equal to humans, who is her mentor, and who also opposes the treatment of other talking animals by the Wizard of Oz; her conflict with Madame Morrible, a puppet of the Wizard of Oz, who arranged the murder of the professor; her meeting with the Wizard of Oz, who rebuffs her when she pleads for animal rights; and her moving to Emerald City to continue to work on animal rights and plans to kill Madame Morrible, a plot that fails. There are other events such as killings and disappointments that negatively affect Elphaba. There is so much detail and so many other characters and events that the plot can be hard to follow; it is hard to keep all the characters straight in your mind. It is not until the fifth section that Dorothy and Toto arrive in Oz and interact with Elphaba.

Oz, on the other hand, is more straightforward in its description of events, and there are fewer characters and fewer details about interrelationships; it is easier reading than Wicked.

4. Oz uses vocabulary suitable for children, and does not include scary, violent descriptions. The language in Wicked is written for adults, children, and describes violent imagery and sexual situations.

5. Oz focuses mostly on Dorothy and her companions the Tinman, the Lion and the Scarecrow, giving details of how she connected with them and convinced them to join her on her trip to see the Wizard of Oz with requests for his help. In Oz the Wizard promises to grant their wishes if they kill Elphaba.

6. In both stories, Elphaba, the Wicked Witch of the West has a grudge against Dorothy, because the farmhouse that Dorothy and Toto were hiding in was picked up by a cyclone in Kansas and deposited in the kingdom of Oz, killing Elphaba's sister when it landed. In both stories, Elphaba sends out animals (wolves in Wicked, dogs, crows and bees in Oz) to kill Dorothy, Tinman, Lion and Scarecrow, and they are killed instead, but Elphaba uses the magic in the Golden Cap to capture them. In a confrontation, in Wicked, Elphaba's broom catches fire and Dorothy throws water on her to put out the fire, and the wicked witch melts. In Oz, it just says that Dorothy throws water on Elphaba in anger after a confrontation and the wicked witch melts. Dorothy, with some help from Glinda, uses the Golden Cap to return her and Toto to Kansas, and the Tinman, Lion and Scarecrow to new kingdoms they will rule. In both stories, the Wizard, exposed as just an ordinary human, leaves Emerald City.

7. In Oz, Winged Monkey characters play a role in getting Dorothy and her companions home.

Footnotes:

[1] **Wicked: The Life and Times of the Wicked Witch of the West** is a novel written by Gregory Maguire and illustrated by Douglas Smith and published 9/1/1995 by Willian Morrow & Company, New York, New York. The sources of much of the information in this article are reviews published in Wikipedia and in Publisher's Weekly fiction book review published 10/30/1995.

[2] **The Wonderful Wizard of Oz** is a book written by author L. Frank Baum and illustrated by W. W. Denslow, published by the George M. Hill Company, Chicago, Illinois, May 17, 1900. The source of much of the information in this article is a Wikipedia entry.

You can scan the QR code given below or use the url to access additional EdSearch resources including videos and mobile apps related to *Modern Fictions and Traditional Stories*.

ed)Search — **Modern Fictions and Traditional Stories**

URL	QR Code
http://www.lumoslearning.com/a/rl89	

1. What is a motif?

(A) the major characters in the story
(B) how the story ends
(C) the plot
(D) a recurring element or idea in a story

2. Which of the following is/are a popular motif(s) in traditional stories?

(A) good vs. evil
(B) a test of courage
(C) children who are heroes
(D) all of the above

Question 3-5 are based on the story below.

The Ant and the Grasshopper Aesop's Fable

In a field, one summer's day, a grasshopper was hopping about, chirping and singing to its heart's content. A group of ants walked by, grunting as they struggled to carry plump kernels of corn. "Where are you going with those heavy things?" asked the grasshopper.

Without stopping, the first ant replied, "To our anthill. This is the third kernel I've delivered today." "Why not come and sing with me," teased the grasshopper, "instead of working so hard?" "We are helping to store food for the winter," said the ant, "and think you should do the same." "Winter is far away, and it is a glorious day to play," sang the grasshopper. But the ants went on their way and continued their hard work.

The weather soon turned cold. All the food lying in the field was covered with a thick white blanket of snow that even the grasshopper could not dig through.

Soon the grasshopper found itself dying of hunger. He staggered to the ants' hill and saw them handing out corn from the stores they had collected in the summer. He begged them for something to eat. "What!" cried the ants in surprise, "haven't you stored anything away for the winter? What in the world were you doing all last summer?"

"I didn't have time to store any food," complained the grasshopper; "I was so busy playing music that before I knew it, the summer was gone."

The ants shook their heads in disgust, turned their backs on the grasshopper, and went on with their work.

3. What is the lesson of this fable?

Ⓐ It's okay to have fun.
Ⓑ Do not help those around you.
Ⓒ Work hard to prepare for the future.
Ⓓ Listen to what you are told.

4. What type of story is "The Ant and the Grasshopper"?

Ⓐ a fairy tale
Ⓑ a fable
Ⓒ a myth
Ⓓ folktale

5. How does the reader know "The Ant and the Grasshopper" is a fable?

Ⓐ Animal characters play the role of humans.
Ⓑ There is a moral or lesson.
Ⓒ The story is short.
Ⓓ all of the above

Question 6 is based on the paragraph below.

There is a boy who has three brothers. His bike is broken so he goes to borrow one of his brother's. His oldest brother's bike is way too big. His younger brother's bike still has training wheels on it and is too small. His second oldest brother's bike works perfectly though, and that is the one he borrowed.

6. What traditional story does this remind you of?

Ⓐ "Little Red Riding Hood"
Ⓑ The Story of "Goldilocks and the Three Bears"
Ⓒ "Rumpelstiltskin"
Ⓓ "Snow White and the Seven Dwarfs"

LumosLearning.com

Question 7-9 are based on the story below.

You read a story about a young girl who battles against all odds to overcome the hardships of homelessness and discrimination to go to Harvard and become extremely successful.

7. What is a popular motif in this story?

Ⓐ good vs. evil
Ⓑ a test of courage
Ⓒ children who are heroes
Ⓓ true love

8. In the classic fairy tale "Cinderella," what do the characters of Cinderella and the stepmother stand for?

Ⓐ fun vs. boring
Ⓑ good vs. evil
Ⓒ young vs. old
Ⓓ traditional vs. non-traditional

9. "When someone declares an event to be a ""modern day Cinderella story"" they mean _____.

Fill in the blank after selecting the correct answer choice from the 4 options given below."

Ⓐ someone poor or common becomes successful
Ⓑ someone has evil step-sisters
Ⓒ someone rides a carriage
Ⓓ someone is the most beautiful in her family

Question 10 is based on the story below.

Casey Jones-A Tennessee Legend
-retold by S.E. Schlosser

Casey Jones, that heroic railroad engineer of the Cannonball, was known as the man who always brought the train in on time. He would blow the whistle, so it started off soft but would increase to a wail louder than a banshee before dying off so that people would recognize that whistle and know when Casey was driving past.

April 29, 1900, Casey brought the Cannonball into Memphis dead on time. As he was leaving, he found out one of the other engineers was sick and unable to make his run. So Casey volunteered to help out his friend. He pulled the train out of the station about eleven p.m., an hour and thirty-five minutes late. Casey was determined to make up the time. As soon as he could, he highballed out of Memphis (highballing means to go very fast and take a lot of risks to get where you are headed) and started making up for the lost time.

About four a.m., when he had nearly made up all the time on the run, Casey rounded a corner near Vaughn, Mississippi, and saw a stalled freight train on the track. He shouted for his fireman to jump. The fireman made it out alive, but Casey Jones died in the wreck, one hand on the brake and one on the whistle chord.

10. What type of story is Casey Jones?

- Ⓐ fairy tale
- Ⓑ fable
- Ⓒ myth
- Ⓓ folktale

End of Reading: Literature

Answer Key and
Detailed Explanations

Chapter 2: Reading: Literature

Lesson 1: Textual Evidence

Question No.	Answer	Detailed Explanations
1.	C	Answer choice C is correct. Lines 3 and 4 in the third stanza provide the text evidence. There is no text evidence supporting answer choices A, B or D.
2.	C	Answer choice C is correct and directly stated in the last two lines of the poem. Answer choice D is incorrect. While the poet does recognize gold is good, he states sympathy is greater. Answer choices A and B do not provide evidence to support the question.
3.	A	Answer choice A is correct because the first line of the poem indicates the poet's sorrow. The other answer choices are incorrect as there is no evidence in the first stanza to support them.
4.	A	Answer choice A is correct because the poet understands that sympathy is invaluable. Answer choice D is incorrect because it refers to the rich man who gave the poet gold. Answer choices B and C do not provide text evidence to support the gratefulness of the poet.
5.	B	Answer choice B is correct. Text evidence supporting this answer can be found in the first stanza, lines 3 and 4. There is no evidence to support answer choices A, C or D.
6.	A	Answer choice A is correct because the squirrel is telling the mountain that it's okay for everyone to have their own talent. Answer choice B is incorrect because the squirrel is describing the mountain, not its talent. Answer choice C is incorrect because the squirrel is simply commenting on its own size. Answer choice D is incorrect because the squirrel is commenting on an attribute of the mountain.
7.	B	Answer choice B is correct because both poems incorporate the use of nature in the narrative. Answer choice A is incorrect because a squirrel only narrates a portion of "The Mountain and the Squirrel." Answer choice C is incorrect because only "The Arrow and the Song" is written in first person. "The Mountain and the Squirrel" is written in third person. Answer choice D is incorrect because only "The Arrow and the Song" is about friendship.

Question No.	Answer	Detailed Explanations
8.	D	Answer choice D is correct because this describes Yeats standing on a road or a sidewalk is likely on his way to or from work. Answer choices A, B and C are incorrect because they are simply describing Innisfree.
9.	B	Answer choice B is correct. Text evidence can be found in the second sentence of the biographical information. Answer choice A is incorrect because neither the poem nor the passage refers to the Irish economy. Answer choice C is incorrect because there is no information regarding the Nobel Prize.
10. Part A	D	Answer choice D is correct because all of the answers are supported by evidence from the text.
10. Part B	B	Answer choice B is correct as it states and describes the cabin in Innisfree. Answer choices A, C and D are incorrect as they do not provide evidence of a cabin in Innisfree.
11. Part A	D	Answer choice D is correct. Patrick was in such a hurry he did not check to see if his bag was in the trunk of his car. His mom realized he had left it and ran out to remind him. There is no evidence to support answer choices A, B, or C.
11. Part B	A	Answer choice A is correct. The word this in the sentence, "he just knew he would make the team this year" indicates that Patrick has tried out before and not made the team. There is no evidence to support answer choices B, C, or D.
12. Part A	D	Answer choice D is correct. The first line of the passage states that it had been an year since Lauren had seen Bailey. All the answer choices hint that Lauren was missing Bailey and hence was really anxious to meet her.
12. Part B	B	Answer choice B is correct. In the last line of the passage, the narrator tells the reader that Lauren felt like Bailey was holding something back. This means Bailey had a secret she wasn't willing to share. Answer choices A and C are not supported by any evidence in the text.

LumosLearning.com

Lesson 2: Inferences

Question No.	Answer	Detailed Explanations
1.	C	Answer choice C is correct. The poet, Yeats, is describing Innisfree as very peaceful and tranquil. All the descriptions that he uses indicate peace and tranquility. Answer choices A and B are incorrect because they are too specific. Each of them contributes to the overall peace and tranquility.
2.	A	Answer choice A is correct. The poet is thinking about where he will retire and fondly thinks about Innisfree as he walks to or from work. Answer choices B, C and D cannot be supported by the text.
3.	B	Answer choice B is correct. Elizabeth was going to drive to work but could not because she did not have her keys. She locked them in the house. Answer choices A and C are not supported in the text.
4.	C	Answer choice C is correct. Samantha's heart pounding loudly, her friendly smile and blushing all indicate she thought the boy was cute. Answer choices A, B and D are not supported by the text. Nothing in the text referring to the boy's backpack, and the boy's actions were not discussed, so the reader cannot draw an inference based on his behavior.
5.	A	Answer choice B is incorrect because Maya realizes the family is needy based on both their actions and the state of their clothes. Hence, answer choice A is correct.
6.	C	Answer choice C is correct. Haley is so eager to answer the phone, she doesn't even take a moment to wash the flour off her hands. Answer choice A is incorrect because it is not supported in the text. Answer choice B is incorrect because it is likely Haley doesn't wash her hands because of her eagerness to answer the phone call.
7.	B	Answer choice B is correct because Henry has been saving his money for a year and did research on his destination. Answer choice A is incorrect because Henry has been saving his money, so the trip was planned. Answer choice C is incorrect because Henry did research on his destination. Answer choice D cannot be inferred from the text.
8.	A	Answer choice A is correct. The door was hard to open because it hadn't been opened in quite some time. Additionally, there were cobwebs in the room and dust on the floor meaning no one had entered the room in a long time. Answer choice B is incorrect because it is unlikely a new building would have cobwebs and a layer of dust in it. Answer choice C is incorrect because she was able to get in. The door was not locked, just stuck. Answer choice D is incorrect because there is no evidence to support the inference.

Question No.	Answer	Detailed Explanations
9.	A	Answer choice A is correct. Melody's mom's body language leads the reader to believe she is angry, and her silence and body language indicate she is angry. Answer choice B is incorrect because her body language indicates she is angry, not tired. Answer choice C is incorrect because there is nothing in the passage to lead the reader to believe any dental work was done. Answer choice D is incorrect because there is nothing in the passage to indicate that the kitchen was clean.
10. Part A	A	Answer choice A is correct. The arrow represents words or actions said, and those words or actions are sometimes said or done without regard to how they impact others. We don't know where they will land just as the poet did not know where his arrow would land and did not give much thought to his actions. Answer choices B and C are not supported by the text.
10. Part B	B	Answer choice B is correct. Both poems include characters who either say or do something; they did not think anyone would notice or care about. Answer choice A is incorrect because neither poem supports this statement. Answer choices C and D are not supported by any evidence to support this inference.
11	C	Answer choice C is correct. When Mary covers her head and ears, this shows the reader she is frightened and trying to hide from the storm. Answer choices A, B, and D cannot be supported by the text.
12	-	The door was hard to open because it hadn't been opened in quite some time. Additionally, there were cobwebs in the room and dust on the floor meaning no one had entered the room in a long time.
13	C	Answer choice C is correct. Mark has inherited some of the traits and characteristics of his father. Answer choices A, B and D cannot be inferred from the text.

Lesson 3: Theme

Question No.	Answer	Detailed Explanations
1.	A	Answer choice A is correct. The theme of a piece is the underlying message of a piece of literature, and the main idea is a statement that tells what the piece is about. Answer choices B, C and D are incorrect and unreasonable.
2.	C	Answer choice C is correct. A universal theme is one that can be found in many stories and pieces of literature and can be applied to any situation, any person or any era. It does not include character names. Answer choices A and D are incorrect. Neither answer is reasonable. Answer choice B is incorrect as the universal theme is not always implicit (not clearly stated). It is sometimes explicit (clearly stated).
3.	A	Answer choice A is correct. The theme is always a statement as opposed to a one word description. Answer choices B, C, and D are incorrect.
4.	C	Answer choice C is correct. Readers should look for details in the story to help determine the theme of the story. It also helps to think about what the main character learns. Answer choices A, B, and D are incorrect as they are not ways to help a reader determine the theme of a story.
5.	B	Answer choice B is correct. The reader determines an implied theme of a story through clues in the story. Answer choices A, C, and D are not definitions of an implied theme.
6.	C	Answer choice C is correct. The Fox bragged to the Cat that he had several ways of escaping his enemy. The Cat only knew one way to escape and used it. The Fox wasted too much time trying to decide which method of escape he should choose and ended up getting caught. Answer choices A, B, and D are not themes of this story.
7. Part A	A	Answer choice A is correct. Had the man offered to share his chicken, it would not have turned into a toad forever requiring attention. Answer choices B, C and D are incorrect because none of them are themes of this story.
7. Part B	A	Answer choice A is correct. The theme is implicitly stated. That is, the reader must use the actions of the man, hiding the roasted chicken so he doesn't have to share, to determine the theme of the text. Answer choices B, C and D are incorrect because they are not reasonable.

Question No.	Answer	Detailed Explanations
8.	B	Answer choice B is correct. The Crow learns that she should not be so trusting of someone who lavishes her with compliments. Considered universally, the theme then becomes don't be trusting of flatterers. Answer choices A, C and D are not themes of this story.
9.	C	Answer choice C is correct. The narrator volunteered to lead the walk-a-thon primarily to get Abbie off Katrina's back. Her intentions were not pure - she did not volunteer in order to help the class earn money for their graduation party. Answer choices A, B, and D are incorrect because they are not themes of the passage. They are not lessons the main character learned that can be applied universally.
10	A	Answer choice A is correct. Charlie learned that he should have listened to his mom when she was giving him instructions on doing the laundry. In this example, the reader thinks about what Charlie learned and then restates the lesson so that it applies universally - pay close attention when you are learning something new. This applies to both Charlie and the world (universal). Answer choices B, C, and D are not themes of this story.

Lesson 4: Objective Summary

Question No.	Answer	Detailed Explanations
1.	B	Answer choice B is correct. An objective summary is one that does not include an opinion. Answer choices A, C, and D are not definitions of an objective summary.
2.	B	Answer choice B is correct. Objective summaries should always be brief, accurate, and objective. Additionally, they should not include details from the text. Answer choices A, C, and D do not describe the attributes of a good objective summary.
3.	B	Answer choice B is correct. An objective summary should adequately summarize the text. Answer choice A is incorrect because an objective summary should not include opinions. Answer choice C is incorrect because a summary should not include information about all the characters in a text. Answer choice D is incorrect because a summary does not have a specific length.
4.	A	Answer choice A is correct. It is brief, accurate and objective. Answer choice B is incorrect as it is not objective or accurate. Answer choice C is incorrect as it does not contain enough information. Answer choice D is incorrect because it is not accurate or objective.
5.	-	A man hid his dinner from his father so he didn't have to share it. Because the man was greedy, the chicken turned into a toad and he was forced to care for it for the rest of his life.
6.	B	Answer choice B is correct. The passage is accurately, objectively, and concisely summarized. Answer choice A is incorrect because it does not give enough information. Answer choice C is incorrect because it does not give enough information nor is it objective. Answer choice D is incorrect because it is not accurate.
7.	C	Answer choice C is correct. The passage is accurate, objective and concise. Answer choice A is incorrect because it is not objective and does not contain enough information. Answer choice B is incorrect because it does not contain enough information. Answer choice D is incorrect because it is not objective nor does it contain enough information.
8	B	Answer choice B is correct. It does not include any opinion and summarize Hook's personality, not his appearance. Answer choice A is incorrect because it summarizes Hook's appearance, not his personality. Answer choice C is incorrect because it is an opinion and does not include a summary of the text. Answer choice D is incorrect because it includes an opinion, "James Hook was a scary man."

Question No.	Answer	Detailed Explanations
9	C	Answer choice C is correct. The summary provided simply paraphrases, or mixes up the words, the passage. Summaries must be original and not paraphrased. Answer choice A is incorrect because the summary is objective. Answer choice B is incorrect because the summary is not perfect. Answer choice D is incorrect because the information contained within the summary is correct. Remember, though, a summary should not be paraphrased.
10	D	Answer choice D is correct. The summary is brief, accurate, and objective. Answer choice A is incorrect because it does not include enough information. Answer choice B is incorrect because it is not objective. Answer choice C is incorrect because it is not accurate.
11.	-	During the summer, the ants stowed food so they would not go hungry during the winter. The grasshopper spent his summer playing music, so when winter came, he had nothing to eat.
12.	-	After a doctor's appointment, the narrator waits in the lobby for his mother to pick him up. In the end, only he and a woman remain in the lobby.

Lesson 5: Plot

Question No.	Answer	Detailed Explanations
1.	C	Answer choice C is correct. There are five elements of a plot. They are the introduction (sometimes identified as the exposition), rising action, climax, falling action, and resolution. Answer choices A, B, and D are incorrect.
2.	A	Answer choice A is correct. The two types of conflict are internal and external. Internal conflict is when the struggle is between the character and himself. External conflict is when an outside force causes the conflict. Answer choices B, C, and D are incorrect.
3.	B	Answer choice B is correct. The plot of the story is the series of events in the story. Answer choices A, C, and D are incorrect.
4. Part A	A	Answer choice A is correct. The conflict is that there is not enough money for a graduation party. This conflict is man vs fate because the students had no direct control. There are other conflicts in the story, but the major conflict is the lack of money. Answer choices B, C, and D are incorrect.
4. Part B	A	Answer choice A is correct. The conflict in the story is that there is not enough money for 8th-grade graduation party. It is worth noting that the reader learns of the conflict in the introduction of the story. Answer choices B, C, and D are incorrect.
5. Part A	D	Answer choice D is correct. The introduction or exposition is where the reader is introduced to the character, setting, and conflict. The exposition occurs at the beginning of the story. Answer choices A, B, and C are incorrect as they are not part of the introduction or exposition of the story.
5. Part B	A	Answer choice A is correct. There are other events that occur in the rising action of the story, but the narrator volunteering to take charge of the walk-a-thon is the most important event as everything that comes next in the story is related to that action. Answer choices B, C, and D are not important events in the rising action of the story.
6. Part A	C	Answer choice C is correct. The climax is the turning point, and the narrator's confession is the turning point. The reader doesn't know if the principal will let the students keep the money or make them return it. Answer choices A, B, and D are not the climax of the story.

Question No.	Answer	Detailed Explanations
6. Part B	A	Answer choice A is correct. The most important event in the falling action is when the narrator learns she must contact all the donors and tell them the truth about what their donations were funding. Answer choices B, C, and D are not part of the falling action of this story.
7.	C	Answer choice C is correct. The resolution of the story occurs when the narrator learns the principal will not allow the money earned to be used for a graduation party. Remember the resolution is the part of the story where the conflict is resolved. In this case, the conflict is that there is not enough money for a graduation party. The resolution to the conflict is that there will be no graduation party. Not all conflicts have a happy resolution. Answer choices A, B, and D are not resolutions to the story.

Lesson 6: Setting

Question No.	Answer	Detailed Explanations
1.	A	Answer choice A is correct. The setting is usually introduced in the introduction or exposition. Note: the setting may change throughout the course of the story. Answer choices B, C, and D are incorrect as the setting is usually introduced in the introduction or exposition of the story.
2.	A	Answer choice A is correct. Stories can have more than one setting as the characters move through the story. Answer choice B, C, and D are incorrect.
3.	C	Answer choice C is correct. The setting of a story can be relayed through the culture of the characters. Answer choices A, B, and D are incorrect.
4.	B	Answer choice B is correct. The setting of the story tells the reader the time and place of action in the story. Answer choices A, C, and D are not part of the setting in the story.
5.	D	Answer choice D is correct. The mood of the main character, also known as the protagonist, cannot help the reader to determine the setting. However, the time of day, weather, and time of year all help to contribute to the setting.
6.	A	Answer choice A is correct. Clues to help the reader understand the setting is in an airport include Lauren waiting at the arrival gate and the reference to eleven hours in the air. Answer choices B, C and D are incorrect.
7.	-	There is not enough information to determine the setting of this excerpt as it is a description of a character.
8.	A	Answer choice A is correct. Charlie is still at his home in Texas. A clue to help the reader understand the setting is in Texas is in the last sentence of the first paragraph, "Before he left..." This information leads the reader to understand that Charlie is still at home in Texas, and his mother is going to show him how to do the laundry before he leaves for school in New York. Answer choices B and C are incorrect because there are no clues to lead the reader to conclude either location is the first setting. Answer choice D is incorrect because there is information that helps determine the setting.

Question No.	Answer	Detailed Explanations
9.	C	Answer choice C is correct. The description of the narrator's mother does not help the reader determine the setting. Answer choices A, B, and D are correct as they all help the reader determine the setting.
10.	C	Answer choice C is correct. The setting is where the fossils were found which is by a canal near the Guadalupe River in the Silicon Valley. Answer choice A is incorrect as the setting is not in Columbia. Answer choice B is incorrect. The scientists working with the fossils are from The University of California Berkeley. Answer choice D is incorrect because the reader is able to determine the setting.
11	-	in a transport boat on the Seine The first sentence of the excerpt describes the setting.

Lesson 7: Character

Question No.	Answer	Detailed Explanations
1.	A	Answer choice A is correct. A round character is one who has many personality traits and is rather complex. Round characters tend to be more involved in the story. Answer choices B, C, and D are incorrect.
2.	A	Answer choice A is correct. The protagonist of a story is the main character. This character is who propels the story forward. Answer choices B, C, and D are incorrect.
3.	B	Answer choice B is correct. The antagonist of a story is opposing force to the main character or protagonist. The antagonist is not always a character. It may be fate or something in nature. Answer choices A, C, and D are incorrect.
4.	B	Answer choice B is correct. A static character does not experience any sort of change during the course of a story. Answer choices A, C, and D are incorrect.
5.	A	Answer choice A is correct. A dynamic character is one who changes during the course of the story due to the events that occur in the story. Answer choices B, C, and D are incorrect.
6. Part A	A	Answer choice A is the correct answer. The narrator is the major character in the story because she is the most important character and propels the story forward. The narrator is also the protagonist. Answer choices B, C and D are incorrect.
6. Part B	D	Answer choice D is correct. The antagonist in this story is the lack of money for the graduation ceremony. The protagonist works to earn money for the ceremony only to find it more difficult than anticipated. In this case, the antagonist is not a who, but a what. Remember the antagonist can be a force which is in direct conflict with the protagonist.
7. Part A	B	Answer choice B is correct. Principal Dorsey is a minor character; however his character is important to the development of the story. Answer choices A, C, and D are incorrect.
7. Part B	B	Answer choice B is correct. The character of Abbie Morelle is flat because the reader does not learn much about her. The author did not provide much information about Abbie, so the reader only gets to see one side of her. Answer choice A is incorrect because the reader does not learn much about the character. Answer choice C is incorrect.

Question No.	Answer	Detailed Explanations
8	A	Answer choice A is correct. Dickens uses indirect characterization to describe the character of Scrooge. Through Scrooge's comments, the reader learns of Scrooge's personality traits. In the first excerpt, the reader learns through Scrooge's commentary that he is penny-pinching and crochety. In the second excerpt, the reader learns through Scrooge's commentary that he is happy and generous. Answer choice B is incorrect because the author does not describe the character of Scrooge to the reader. Answer choices C and D are also incorrect.
9.	D	Answer choice D is correct. The character of Scrooge (the uncle) is dynamic. He undergoes a change from the beginning to the end of the book. At the beginning of the book, Stave One, he is a selfish, penny-pincher not willing to even wish a Merry Christmas to his nephew. At the end of the book, Stave Five, Scrooge undergoes a dramatic change and is now not only willing to wish even a stranger on the street a Merry Christmas, but he's also willing to part with his hard earned money. Answer choices A, B, are incorrect. Answer choice C is incorrect because we do not have enough of the story to determine if Scrooge's character is round. It is worth noting, however, that dynamic characters are usually round.
10.	A	Answer choice A is correct. The author tells the reader about Captain Carter. The reader does not have to make any inferences or guesses about his personality based on what he says or does or what others say about him. Answer choice B is incorrect because indirect characterization means the reader must make inferences about the character based on his actions, comments, or others statements about him. Answer choice C and D are not valid choices.
11.	C	Answer choice C is correct. Captain Carter is a round character. His personality traits are complex, and he seems to be a realistic character. Answer choice A is incorrect because a flat character would not have many personality traits. Answer choice B is incorrect because a static character is one who doesn't change during the course of a story. Flat characters are generally considered static. Answer choices D is incorrect simply because we do not have enough of the story to see a change in Captain Carter. Generally, dynamic characters are considered round.

Lesson 8: Analyzing Literature

Question No.	Answer	Detailed Explanations
1.	B	The story states that Charlie's parents assigned him chores around the house. Because that is not letting Charlie do whatever he wants, answer choice A is incorrect. Also, because he has been earning good grades, it is logical that his parents expect him to continue to earn good grades. Answer choices C and D are incorrect.
2. Part A	B	Answer choice B is correct. Charlie shoves all his laundry into the machine at once which was not part of the laundry instructions his mom gave him. Answer choice A, C, and D could be true, but the reader must consider only the excerpt provided.
2. Part B	A	Answer choice A is correct. Because of Charlie's reaction to his shrunken, miscolored clothes, it is evident he doesn't overreact when faced with obstacles but works to find solutions. Answer choices B, C, and D are incorrect.
3.	B	Answer choice B is correct. Dickens (the author) includes this dialogue so the reader completely understands Scrooge's change in attitude toward Christmas during the story. Answer choices A, C, and D are incorrect.
4.	A	Answer choice A is correct. This dialogue is important because it allows the reader to see the change Scrooge underwent throughout the course of the story. Readers can learn much about characters through their dialogue. Answer choices B, C, and D are incorrect.
5.	D	Answer choice D is correct. When readers are asked what characters' actions reveal, they are essentially being asked to analyze how a character's actions and interactions with the plot, setting, and other characters will move the story forward.
6.	B	Answer choice B is correct. Casey Jones was a courageous man who was concerned about getting his train to its destination on time. Casey did not expect to see another train stalled on the tracks; therefore, he was not prepared to stop. As his last act of courage, Casey warned anyone nearby of impending doom by blowing the whistle and trying to stop the train. Answer choices A, C, and D are incorrect.
7.	C	Answer choice C is correct. As the train rounded the corner, Casey could see disaster ahead and warned the firemen. This is the act of a courageous man. Answer choices A, B, and D are incorrect.

Question No.	Answer	Detailed Explanations
8. Part A	A	Answer choice A is correct. The ant is too busy to stop working and instead carries the kernel while explaining what he is doing to the grasshopper. The ant knows that he must continue with the work in order to be prepared for the upcoming winter. Answer choices B, C, and D are incorrect.
8. Part B	C	Answer choice C is correct. The grasshopper is irresponsible as he is more interested in singing than planning for the future. Answer choices A, B, and D are incorrect.
8. Part C	D	Answer choice D is correct. The ants were working so hard to prepare for the winter; they found it hard to believe that not everyone did the same. Answer choices A, B, and C are incorrect.

Lesson 9: Meaning and Tone

Question No.	Answer	Detailed Explanations
1.	C	Answer choice C is correct. Tone tells the reader the way the author feels about the topic. Tone can be sad, excited, angry, and humorous - really, just about any emotion. Tone is expressed through word choice or phrasing and sometimes uses figurative language. One way to determine the tone of a piece of writing is to ask yourself how the author feels about the topic he or she has written. Answer choices A, B and D are incorrect.
2.	A	Answer choice A is correct. The statement about tone is neutral or indifferent, meaning the writer did not include any language that relays his or her attitude toward the homework assignment. It is just a statement of fact. Answer choice B, C and D are incorrect because the correct tone is neutral.
3.	C	Answer choice C is correct. The author's tone is sarcastic which inspires a slightly humorous atmosphere although he is clearly unhappy about the assignment. Answer choices A, B, and D are incorrect.
4.	A	Answer choice A is correct. The author is angry about the homework assignment. When determining tone, ask yourself how the author feels and what words he or she uses to convey his feelings. Answer choices B, C, and D are incorrect.
5.	C	Answer choice C is correct. The tone of the excerpt is enthusiastic. DiCamillo wants the reader to feel excited while reading this passage. Answer choices A, B, and D are incorrect.
6.	A	Answer choice A is correct. The tone is hopeful and encouraging. Pay close attention to the word choice: turning point, rekindled, revived. These are all words that convey a sense of encouragement. Answer choices B, C and D are incorrect.
7.	D	Answer choice D is correct. The tone is comical as Hoffmann describes the bumbling huntsman and hiding hare. Answer choices A, B, and C are incorrect.
8.	B	Answer choice B is correct. The hare is hiding from the huntsman in the leaves and grass. He is not noticed as the huntsman walks past because he is snug or fitting closely in the leaves and grass. Answer choices A, C, and D are incorrect.

Question No.	Answer	Detailed Explanations
9.	D	Answer choice D is correct. In this excerpt, "spectacles" most closely means glasses. The huntsman realizes he cannot see to hunt without his spectacles or glasses. Humorously, even with his spectacles, or glasses, perched upon his nose, he still does not see the hare hiding. Answer choices A, B, and C are incorrect.
10. Part A	A	Answer choice A is correct. The ungrateful son does not want to share the chicken with his father so he hastily, or quickly, hides it. Decisions made in haste can often end up being poor decisions. Hasty decisions are quick and done without much thought. Answer choices B, C, and D are incorrect.
10. Part B	C	Answer choice C is correct. The frog looked venomously or angrily if someone tried to remove it. Answer choices A, B, and D are incorrect.
11	-	The raven is generally thought to be a bird associated with death, or evil, or something dreaded and bad. Answers need to include points related to this.
12	-	Answer must include God, angels or Heaven- good force or Devil, evil - evil force. In either order, one good, one evil.

Lesson 10: Compare and Contrast

Question No.	Answer	Detailed Explanations
1.	A	The correct answer is A. When you are comparing, you are looking for similarities. When looking at two pieces of text, if you are asked to compare them, you are being asked to look for what is similar within the two pieces of text. Answer choices B, C, and D are incorrect.
2.	C	Answer choice C is correct. A paper or article that is comparing two things will likely use signal words such as likewise, as well, the same as, both, similarly, or too. These are not the only signal words, but they are quite common. Answer choices A, B, and D are incorrect.
3.	A	Answer choice A is correct. A Venn diagram provides space for both comparing (the center where the circle meet) and contrasting (the outer circles). Answer choices B, C, and D are incorrect.
4.	B	The correct answer is B. When you are contrasting, you are looking for differences. When you are looking at two pieces of text, if you are asked about contrasts, you are being asked to tell the difference between the two pieces of text. Answer choices A, C, and D are incorrect.
5.	A	The correct answer is A. Common information in a Venn diagram goes in the middle where the two circles intersect. Contrasting information goes in the outer portions of the circle. Answer choices B, C, and D are incorrect.
6.	D	Answer choice D is correct. A paper or article that is contrasting two things will likely use signal words such as although, however, contrary to, unlike, and unless. These are not the only signal words, but they are quite common. Answer choices A, B, and C are incorrect.
7.	A	Answer choice A is correct. Both poems are set in nature. The reader must make a comparison, remembering to determine what is alike about the setting. Answer choices B, C, and D are incorrect.
8. Part A	A	Answer choice A is correct. When reading text, it is important to read everything on the page, including the dates. Answer choices B, C, and D are incorrect.
8. Part B	C	Answer C is correct. When considering both poems, only "The Mountain and the Squirrel" include dialogue. Additionally, the point of view in each point is different. "The Mountain and the Squirrel" is written in third person point of view. "The Song and the Arrow is written in first person point of view.
9.	D	Answer choice D is correct. According to the passages, Longfellow and Emerson were born in America, lived in the 19th century, and were familiar with Nathaniel Hawthorne.

Question No.	Answer	Detailed Explanations
10.	-	The synopsis usually helps a person to better understand the poem because it gives summaries of each section. The student's answer should reflect this.

Lesson 11: Producing Suspense and Humor

Question No.	Answer	Detailed Explanations
1.	D	Answer choice D is correct. All of the choices are puns.
2.	D	Answer choice D is correct. Irony, puns, setting and situation can all add humor to a story.
3.	C	Answer choice C is correct. Irony is a surprisingly funny, or interesting contradiction. It is a situation that occurs which is the opposite of what is expected to occur. Answer choices A, B, and D are incorrect.
4.	A	Answer choice A is correct. The author creates humor by creating a rabbit that is amused by the bumbling hunter who passes right by him. Answer choices B, C, and D are incorrect.
5.	B	Answer choice B is correct. The author builds suspense by setting up a mood of apprehension and including foreshadowing. Answer choices A, C, and D are incorrect.
6.	A	Answer choice A is correct. Dramatic irony is used because the reader knows something that the character of Romeo does not know. Believing his beloved is dead, he kills himself. Answer choices B, C, and D are incorrect.
7.	B	Answer choice B is correct. Verbal irony is used because the man says he is happy he woke up early to wash his car, but in reality his efforts were futile since his car is now dirty. He did not sincerely mean what he said. Answer choices A, C, and D are incorrect.
8.	C	Answer choice C is correct. Situational irony is used because the reader expects the rehabilitated seals will swim off into the ocean and live happily ever after. Answer choices A, B, and D are incorrect.
9.	A	Answer choice A is correct. Situational irony is used by the author. After saving for years for a dream vacation, one suddenly appears in Caitlin's life. Answer choices B, C, and D are incorrect.
10.	B	Answer choice B is correct. The author uses verbal irony as Kyle's mother doesn't really believe that beating the next level in the video game is important. She is making a point that studying is more important than playing games. Answer choices A, C, and D are incorrect.
11	Noise	This scene describes the type of noises not to be afraid of.
12	his dream was enjoyable	He wanted to redream or continue his dream because it was a good dream.

Lesson 12: Media and Literature

Question No.	Answer	Detailed Explanations
1.	A	Answer choice A is correct because a video allows people to see a visualization.
2.	C	Answer choice C is correct. Media can aide an audience seeing and hearing.
3.	A	Answer choice A is correct. Since the question is asking for a visual interpretation, a movie will show viewers the interpretation of the director.
4.	B	Answer choice B is correct. The definition of multimedia is using more than one medium of expression or communication.
5.	C	Answer choice C is correct because it can be done quickly. While options A and B allow publication, a blog can be posted quickly.
6.	B	Answer choice B is correct because newspapers articles report the facts, while anyone can publish a blog.
7. Part A	A	Answer choice A is correct because the image is only of the lake. The poem speaks of the lake, but it speaks more of the boy's memories associated with the lake.
7. Part B	B	Answer choice B is correct because the poem talks about both sounds and sights.
8. Part A	B	Answer choice B is correct because the question asks about both the lake and its surroundings. The image only shows the lake.
8. Part B	A	Answer choice A is correct because the poem is about the author's personal cabin at the lake; therefore, it's not a travel destination while the image is of the entire lake and therefore open to the public.

LumosLearning.com

Lesson 13: Modern Fictions and Traditional Stories

Question No.	Answer	Detailed Explanations
1.	D	Answer choice D is correct. A motif is an element or idea in a story that recurs in traditional stories. Motifs can be characters, places, objects, actions or even style.
2.	D	Answer choice D is correct. While these are not all the motifs found in traditional stories, they encompass the majority of those stories. Consider the books and stories you read now. Can you find motifs in those that are similar to the motifs in traditional stories? If so, chances are what you are reading is a modern day retelling of a traditional story.
3.	C	Answer choice C is correct. The lesson, or moral, of the story is to work hard and prepare for the future. The grasshopper chose to play while the ants worked hard to gather food for the upcoming winter. Once the cold arrived, the grasshopper had nothing to eat, while the ants had plenty because they prepared.
4.	B	Answer choice B is correct. "The Ant and the Grasshopper" is a fable. It is thought to have originated from Aesop who lived over 2000 years ago. He was a storyteller and many fables are attributed to him.
5.	D	Answer choice D is correct. "The Ant and the Grasshopper" is a fable. Readers can recognize fables by their length, animal characters and lesson.
6.	B	Answer choice B is correct. This story is a loose retelling of the fairy tale, "Goldilocks and the Three Bears" by Robert Southey. Traditional stories are often times retold into modern versions, thus the story lives on and is more applicable to modern times.
7.	B	Answer choice B is correct. The popular motif in this short story is a test of courage (character's actions). This is a loose adaptation of the classic fairy tale "Cinderella".
8.	B	Answer choice B is correct. Remember that fairy tales always include a good character and an evil character. In "Cinderella," Cinderella is the good character and her step-mother is evil, thus their characters represent good vs. evil.
9.	A	Answer choice A is correct. Modern day Cinderellas are people who overcome odds and become successful.
10.	D	Answer choice D is correct. Casey Jones is a folktale that originated in Tennessee. Remember folktales were passed on by word of mouth. This entertaining version may differ from other versions you have heard or read.

Chapter 3 - Reading: Informational Text

The objective of the Reading Informational Text standards is to ensure that the student is able to read and comprehend informational texts (history/social studies, science, and technical texts) related to Grade 8.

To help students master the necessary skills, information to help the student understand the concepts related to the standard is given. Along with this, we encourage the student to go through the resources available online on EdSearch to gain an in depth understanding of these concepts. The EdSearch page for each lesson can be accessed with the help of the url or the QR code provided.

A small map is provided after each passage or text in which the student can enter the details as understood from the literary text. Doing this will help the student to refer to key points that help in answering the questions with ease.

Chapter 3

Lesson 1: Making Inferences Based on Textual Evidence

Let us understand the concept with an example.

Stopping by Woods on a Snowy Evening[1]
By Robert Frost

Whose woods these are I think I know.
His house is in the village though;
He will not see me stopping here
To watch his woods fill up with snow.
My little horse must think it queer
To stop without a farmhouse near
Between the woods and frozen lake
The darkest evening of the year.
He gives his harness bells a shake
To ask if there is some mistake.
The only other sound's the sweep
Of easy wind and downy flake.
The woods are lovely, dark and deep.
But I have promises to keep,
And miles to go before I sleep,
And miles to go before I sleep.

This is what you might write.

"He will not see me stopping here To watch his woods fill up with snow."
I infer that the poet assumes the owner of the woods would be annoyed and suspicious if he saw someone stopping by his woods, just sitting there staring, even though that someone is not doing anything harmful. This assumption is probably based on the poet's own life experience of how people think. How unfortunate if his assumption is true – that we cannot realize and accept the fact that there are those who stop to admire the beauty of nature.

"My little horse must think it queer To stop without a farmhouse near"
The horse is a creature of habit, and apparently the habit of the carriage driver has been to only stop at a place where there are people, and since he cannot speak, the horse communicates his question "Why are we stopping here?" by a shake of his harness.

"The only other sound's the sweep Of easy wind and downy flake. The woods are lovely, dark and deep."

These lines explain what the poet sees and hears, and express his appreciation for the beauty of the woods on this snowy evening and the pleasing sound of snow and wind.

"But I have promises to keep, And miles to go before I sleep, And miles to go before I sleep."

I see an analogy (similarity) here to the lives of many of us. If we do manage to take the time to appreciate beauty, in this case, of nature, we cannot tarry too long – we have promises (or obligations) to keep and many things that we must do before we can stop and rest (either literally sleep or eventually die). But by relating a personal experience, the poet implies in this poem that his life, and because he has shared the experience, our lives, will be more enjoyable if we take the time to pause and appreciate nature, and I choose to imply, to appreciate anything that is beautiful.

[1] *The Poetry of Robert Frost*, edited by Edward Connery Lathem, ©1923, ©1969 by Henry Holt and Company, Inc., renewed 1951, by Robert Frost. Reprinted with permission of Henry Holt and Company, LLC.

You can scan the QR code given below or use the url to access additional EdSearch resources including videos and mobile apps related to *Making Inferences Based on Textual Evidence*.

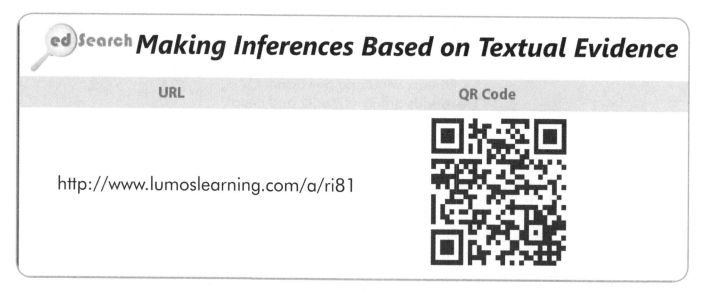

URL	QR Code
http://www.lumoslearning.com/a/ri81	

1. What is an inference?

Ⓐ an answer that is clearly stated in the text
Ⓑ a logical conclusion drawn from evidence in a text
Ⓒ an opinion made from reading a text
Ⓓ a direct quotation found in the text

2. What is the proper way to make a direct citation from a text?

Ⓐ put the citation in italics
Ⓑ underline the citation
Ⓒ put the citation in quotes
Ⓓ make the citation bold

3. What is/are the best way to cite evidence from a text?

Ⓐ summarize
Ⓑ paraphrase
Ⓒ in quotes
Ⓓ all of the above

Question 4-7 are based on the passage below.

Stephen and Joseph Montgolfier were papermakers, but they had been interested in flying for many years. One night, in 1782, Joseph noticed something that gave him an idea. He was sitting in front of the fire when he saw some small pieces of scorched paper being carried up the chimney.

Soon afterwards, the brothers conducted an experiment. They lit a fire under a small silk bag, which was open at the bottom; at once, the bag rose to the ceiling. After this, Stephen and Joseph conducted many more experiments, both indoors and in the open air. Eventually, they built a huge balloon of linen and paper. On June 5th, 1783, they launched their balloon in the village of Annonay.

4. What evidence in the passage shows that the Montgolfier brothers discovered how to make a hot air balloon?

Ⓐ "He was sitting in front of the fire when he saw some small pieces of scorched paper being carried up the chimney."
Ⓑ "Eventually, they built a huge balloon of linen and paper. On June 5th, 1783, they launched their balloon in the village of Annonay."
Ⓒ "After this, Stephen and Joseph conducted many more experiments, both indoors and in the open air."
Ⓓ None of the above

5. What evidence in the text shows that the Montgolfier brothers launched the first successful hot air balloon?

Ⓐ "He was sitting in front of the fire when he saw some small pieces of scorched paper being carried up the chimney."

Ⓑ "Eventually, they built a huge balloon of linen and paper. On June 5th, 1783, they launched their balloon in the village of Annonay."

Ⓒ "After this, Stephen and Joseph conducted many more experiments, both indoors and in the open air."

Ⓓ None of the above

6. What evidence in the text could lead you to infer that the Montgolfier brothers' experienced some trial and error before successfully launching a hot air balloon?

Ⓐ "He was sitting in front of the fire when he saw some small pieces of scorched paper being carried up the chimney."

Ⓑ "Eventually, they built a huge balloon of linen and paper. On June 5th, 1783, they launched their balloon in the village of Annonay."

Ⓒ "After this, Stephen and Joseph conducted many more experiments, both indoors and in the open air."

Ⓓ None of the above

7. Part A
Which specific detail in the above passage describes the first experiment the brothers did?

Ⓐ Stephen and Joseph Montgolfier were papermakers, but they had been interested in flying for many years.

Ⓑ He was sitting in front of the fire when he saw some small pieces of scorched paper being carried up the chimney.

Ⓒ After this, Stephen and Joseph conducted many more experiments, both indoors and in the open air.

Ⓓ They lit a fire under a small silk bag, which was open at the bottom; at once, the bag rose to the ceiling.

7. Part B
The reader can tell from the article that Joseph Montgolfier was very observant because

Ⓐ He created a balloon from paper and linen.

Ⓑ He noticed the small pieces of burnt paper being carried up the chimney.

Ⓒ He found the best location to launch the balloon.

Ⓓ He was interested in flying.

Question 8 is based on the passage below.

TERRORISM— A CHALLENGE

Terrorism is one of the most serious threats and challenges that the world faces today. It is a war against democracy and a crime against humanity. It has crossed national boundaries and has international ramifications. Terrorism, in a way, is a new challenge to humanity in the 21st century.

Terrorism is violence used by a few unlawful, ruthless, heartless, and senseless criminals against fellow human beings. Terrorists have total disregard for human lives including their own. They commit crimes and cause bloodshed without any sense of guilt. To them, their cause is everything, and others are either for it or against it.

Violence is an essential part of terrorism. Terrorism is a systematic use of violence or the threat of violence to achieve specific goals. It attempts to use violence to cause widespread panic, fear, or terror to achieve its ultimate aim.

8. Part A
According to the above passage what is the most important aspect of terrorism?

- Ⓐ violence
- Ⓑ democracy
- Ⓒ national unity
- Ⓓ humanity

8. Part B
Which sentence explains who is targeted by terrorism?

- Ⓐ Terrorism is one of the most serious threats and challenges that the world faces today.
- Ⓑ It is a war against democracy and a crime against humanity.
- Ⓒ Terrorism is violence used by a few unlawful, ruthless, heartless, and senseless criminals against fellow human beings.
- Ⓓ both B and C

Question 9 and 10 are based on the passage below.

The Emperor Penguin is the only penguin species that breeds during the Antarctic winter. It treks 31–75 miles over the ice to breeding colonies, which may include thousands of penguins. The female lays a single egg, which is then incubated by the male while the female returns to the sea to feed; parents subsequently take turns foraging at sea and caring for their chick in the colony. The average lifespan of the Emperor Penguin is 20 years, although observations suggest that some Emperor Penguins may live to 50 years of age.

9. What evidence in the text could lead you to infer both the male and female penguin share equally in the responsibility of raising the chick?

Ⓐ "The average lifespan of the Emperor Penguin is 20 years,"
Ⓑ "The Emperor Penguin is the only penguin species that breeds during the Antarctic winter."
Ⓒ "…parents subsequently take turns foraging at sea and caring for their chick in the colony."
Ⓓ "…some Emperor Penguins may live to 50 years of age."

10. What evidence in the text tells you what the penguins do to survive in the colony after the chick is born?

Ⓐ "The average lifespan of the Emperor Penguin is 20 years,"
Ⓑ "The Emperor Penguin is the only penguin species that breeds during the Antarctic winter."
Ⓒ None of the above

Question 11 and 12 are based on the passage below.

Excerpt from the Foreword of **A Princess of Mars** by Edgar Rice Burroughs

My first recollection of Captain Carter is of the few months he spent at my father's home in Virginia, just prior to the opening of the Civil War. I was then a child of but five years, yet I well remember the tall, dark, smooth-faced, athletic man whom I called Uncle Jack.

He seemed always to be laughing; and he entered into the sports of the children with the same hearty good fellowship he displayed toward those pastimes in which the men and women of his own age indulged; or he would sit for an hour at a time entertaining my old grandmother with stories of his strange wild life in all parts of the world. We all loved him, and our slaves fairly worshipped the ground he trod.

He was a splendid specimen of manhood, standing a good two inches over six feet, broad of shoulder and narrow of hip, with the carriage of the trained fighting man. His features were regular and clear cut, his hair black and closely cropped, while his eyes were of a steel gray, reflecting a strong and loyal character, filled with fire and initiative. His manners were perfect, and his courtliness was that of a typical southern gentleman of the highest type.

11. **Based on the evidence in the text, what can you determine about Captain Carter's personality?**

   Ⓐ He was a happy man.
   Ⓑ He was a hard worker.
   Ⓒ He was ready to go to war.
   Ⓓ He was a friendly man.

12. **Based on the evidence in the text what historical event is about to happen?**

   Ⓐ World War II
   Ⓑ World War I
   Ⓒ Civil War
   Ⓓ The Revolutionary war

Chapter 3

Lesson 2: Central Idea

Let us understand the concept with an example.

Over the course of history in the United States, necessity and economics have combined to change the way we transport cargo, consisting of either living creatures (people, animals and plants) and nonliving items. When the colonies were first settled, walking or riding horses or using horses, oxen or mules with carriages, stagecoaches and wagons were the common forms of transportation on land. But these were relatively slow, limited in the number of passengers or cargo they could carry, and cumbersome when having to deal with natural forces like streams, mountains, forests, heavy snow, heavy rain and the resulting mud. And horses required a lot of care – food, water, shelter, horseshoes, harnesses and saddles.

But then someone invented the steam engine. Steam-driven locomotives, which used plentiful coal and water, could transport many more people and cargo than animals pulling wagons, and at a greater speed over a long-distance. All that was needed were rails (instead of roads), both of which required a lot of initial effort, but once built, required much less effort to maintain. And later on, the hauling power of trains was increased with the introduction of the diesel engine, which had the further advantage of not needing a fireman to keep shoveling coal into the boiler of the steam train. Yes, maintenance was required, but it was worth it because of the long lifespan of the engine and the rails. Steam engines also drove factory machines and fire engines, an improvement over bucket brigades. In 1903, the demonstration of the first heavier than air flight by the Wright brothers ushered in the age of flight. While early aircraft were severely limited in the number of people or amount of cargo they could carry, the development of more powerful gasoline engines increased the cargo carrying capacity, speed and distance an aircraft could fly. And the introduction of the jet engine increased these capabilities even more. Also, the gasoline engine was an important factor in making automobiles more useful than a horse, oxen or mules for transporting cargo. An advantage of aircraft was the speed with which cargo could be transported, for purposes of conducting business meetings, peaceful trade or warfare, and rescue missions.

Your assignment: Apply the requirements of this standard to the text.

Here is what you might write.

The central ideas are necessity drives invention and economics drives invention. The text infers that from the early days of the colonies until today, there were people with ambition and motivation. These ingredients led people to invent things to meet their needs, such as for food, medical treatments or convenience and to influence the economy by creating rewards such as income or property.

Examples of necessities were improvements in fire fighting equipment using steam and gasoline engines, and the use of these and jet engines to rapidly deliver rescuers and their equipment to locations where needed, including remote locations unreachable by road. Vehicles such as ambulances became more efficient, able to transport patients and medical personnel more quickly. Economics drove the inventions of equipment that was faster, more powerful, more versatile and more efficient and cheaper to operate than its predecessors. These inventions made manufacturing more efficient, which meant increased output of products at lower and lower costs. Same with the transportation of goods and services.

You can scan the QR code given below or use the url to access additional EdSearch resources including videos and mobile apps related to *Central Idea*.

ed Search	*Central Idea*
URL	QR Code
http://www.lumoslearning.com/a/ri82	

1. What is a central idea?

Ⓐ the idea stated in the topic sentence
Ⓑ the theme of a piece of literature
Ⓒ a piece of informational text is mainly about someone
Ⓓ the main idea of a piece of informational text

2. What statement(s) is/are true about a central idea?

Ⓐ It can sometimes be found in the title of the text.
Ⓑ It is supported by the details in the text.
Ⓒ It covers the whole text.
Ⓓ All of the above

3. When determining the central idea of a text, it is important not to confuse it with:

Ⓐ the topic
Ⓑ the details
Ⓒ none of the above
Ⓓ both A & B

Question 4 is based on the passage below.

Stephen and Joseph Montgolfier were papermakers, but they had been interested in flying for many years. One night, in 1782, Joseph noticed something that gave him an idea. He was sitting in front of the fire when he saw some small pieces of scorched paper being carried up the chimney.

Soon afterwards, the brothers conducted an experiment. They lit a fire under a small silk bag, which was open at the bottom; at once, the bag rose to the ceiling. After this, Stephen and Joseph conducted many more experiments, both indoors and in the open air. Eventually, they built a huge balloon of linen and paper. On June 5th, 1783, they launched their balloon in the village of Annonay.

4. What is the central idea of this passage?

Ⓐ The Montgolfier brothers were papermakers who became famous.
Ⓑ The Montgolfier brothers theorized that hot air can be used to propel a balloon into the air.
Ⓒ The Montgolfier brothers lost their jobs as papermakers because they were obsessed with their balloon.
Ⓓ The Montgolfier brothers liked to experiment.

Question 5 is based on the passage below.

The Emperor Penguin is the only penguin species that breeds during the Antarctic winter. It treks 31–75 miles over the ice to breeding colonies, which may include thousands of penguins. The female lays a single egg, which is then incubated by the male while the female returns to the sea to feed; parents subsequently take turns foraging at sea and caring for their chick in the colony. The average lifespan of the Emperor Penguin is 20 years, although observations suggest that some Emperor Penguins may live to 50 years of age.

5. What is the central idea of this passage?

Ⓐ The movie, Happy Feet was inspired by Emperor Penguins.
Ⓑ The male Emperor Penguin sits on the egg while the mother hunts for food.
Ⓒ Female Emperor penguins lay their eggs in the Antarctic and both male and female take turns caring for the egg until it hatches.
Ⓓ Emperor Penguins live over 50 years.

Question 6 and 7 are based on the passage below.

Archaeology is the study of past human life and culture through systematically examining and interpreting the material remains left behind. These material remains include archaeological sites (e.g., settlements, building features, graves), as well as cultural materials or artifacts such as tools and pottery. Through the interpretation and classification of archaeological materials, archaeologists work to understand past human behavior. In some countries, archaeology is often historical or art historical, with a strong emphasis on culture history, archaeological sites, and artifacts such as art objects. In the New World, archaeology can be either a part of history and classical studies or anthropology.

The exact origins of archaeology as a discipline are uncertain. Excavations of ancient monuments and the collection of antiquities have been taking place for thousands of years. It was only in the 19th century, however, that the systematic study of the past through its physical remains underwent professionalization, which meant it began to be carried out in a manner recognizable to modern students of archaeology.

6. What is the central idea of this passage?

Ⓐ the study of the origin of archaeology
Ⓑ the study of archaeology
Ⓒ the study of modern archaeology and anthropology
Ⓓ the study of the human past

7. What does the passage suggest about archaeologists?

Ⓐ They study past human life and culture by examining materials left by early humans.
Ⓑ They study humans and their interaction with their surroundings.
Ⓒ They study humans and their families by looking at the things they left behind.
Ⓓ They study art history.

Question 8 is based on the passage below.

Quinoa is a grain like seed. It is considered a whole grain and is cooked in much the same way as rice. Quinoa has many health benefits including nine essential amino acids and is cholesterol free. Additionally quinoa is gluten-free and kosher. Quinoa is a good source of protein and easily digestible.

8. What is the central idea of the passage above?

Ⓐ the health benefits of quinoa
Ⓑ how to cook quinoa
Ⓒ why people should eat quinoa
Ⓓ why people should cook quinoa

Question 9 is based on the passage below.

Cooking quinoa is much like cooking rice. Depending on the sort of quinoa you purchase, you may have to rinse the seed-like spores before cooking. Be sure to check the label. Boil two cups of water, vegetable stock, chicken broth or other liquid of your choice. Add one cup of raw (rinsed if necessary) quinoa and simmer for about twenty minutes. It doesn't take long for quinoa to cook up moist and tender.

9. What is the central idea of this passage?

Ⓐ the health benefits of quinoa
Ⓑ how to cook quinoa
Ⓒ quinoa as a meat replacement
Ⓓ none of the above

Question 10 is based on the passage below.

University of California Berkeley scientists confirmed that a cluster of fossilized bones found in Silicon Valley are likely the remains of a mammoth. The giant beast would have roamed the area between 10,000 and 40,000 years ago. A pair of elephant-like tusks, a huge pelvic bone and the animal's rib cage were found by an amateur naturalist who was walking a dog along a canal near San Jose's Guadalupe River. It could be the remains of a Columbian mammoth, according to paleontologists who expect to study the site.

10. What is the central idea of the above passage?

Ⓐ Mammoth fossils have been found in the Silicone Valley.
Ⓑ Fossils are in California.
Ⓒ Mammoths roamed North America.
Ⓓ Mammoths are roaming the Silicone Valley in California.

Question 11 is based on the passage below.

Marathon

Training for a marathon takes hard work and perseverance. It is not something you can do on the spur of the moment. Preparing for a marathon takes months, particularly if you have never run a marathon before. The official distance of a full marathon is 26.2 miles. In 2005, the average time to complete a marathon in the United States was 4 hours 32 minutes 8 seconds for men and 5 hours 6 minutes 8 seconds for women.

Most people who run marathons are not trying to win. Many runners try to beat their own best time. Some compare their time to other runners in the same gender and age group. Some people set time-oriented goals, such as finishing under four hours, while others try to complete the race without slowing to a walk. Many beginners simply hope to finish the marathon.

Trainers recommend that beginners maintain a consistent running schedule for six weeks prior to even starting a marathon training program. The purpose of this is to allow the body to adapt to the various physical demands of long-distance running. First-time marathon runners should train by running four days a week for at least four months, increasing distance by no more than ten percent weekly. As race day approaches, runners should taper their runs, reducing the strain on their bodies and resting before the marathon. It is important not to overexert yourself during training because that can lead to a lot of injuries. Most common injuries are spraining of the knees and ankles. These sprains can hinder the training.

Before the race, it is important to stretch in order to keep muscles limber. Staying hydrated is also important, but there is a danger in drinking too much water. If a runner drinks too much water, they may experience a dangerous condition called hyponatremia, a drop of sodium levels in the blood. So only drink water when you are thirsty. During the race, trainers recommend maintaining a steady pace. It is normal to feel sore after a marathon. Light exercise will help sore muscles heal faster.

Some people run marathons in pairs or groups. Training for and running a marathon with another person or group of people can make the experience more enjoyable and more rewarding. A running partner might be just the motivation you need to show up for an early morning run instead of rolling over to hit the snooze button. And, when you cross the finish line together, you can share the satisfaction of reaching your common goal.

Usually thousands of people sign up and run a marathon. Most people finish the race. The thrill of running a marathon for the first time is unbelievable. The training sessions are harder if you have never run before. But it is unbelievable what ones' body can do when one puts his/her mind to it. Having a good coach to support you makes all the difference in training for a marathon.

The daily runs are very important. Strength training and core training are also very important. The health benefits you gain from training are tremendous. Your core muscles grow stronger, and you will have tighter thighs and gluts. Your heart will be much stronger, and you can maintain lower cholesterol and blood sugar levels. Overall, you will look better and become healthier.

Nothing can explain how people feel when they reach that finish line at the end of the race. All the hard work and months of training feel worthwhile. The feeling of accomplishing something great overtakes you. It is great to run a marathon, but it is even greater to finish it.

11. Part A
How would you go about determining the central idea of this passage?

Ⓐ read the title
Ⓑ read the passage
Ⓒ pay attention to the details
Ⓓ all of the above

11. Part B
What is the central idea of the passage?

Ⓐ the health benefits of running of a marathon
Ⓑ how to run a marathon
Ⓒ what it takes to prepare for and run a marathon
Ⓓ none of the above

Question 12 is based on the passage below.

Learning how to ride a bike is no easy task. Most people learn as children and mount their first bicycle with training wheels mounted on the sides of the back tires. Those training wheels eventually come off. When that happens, usually someone runs behind the bicycle, holding the back of the seat as the rider learns to balance on two wheels. As the runner runs back and forth down the street, the rider eventually picks up on how to lean to stay up on two wheels. Eventually, the runner lets go of the seat, and the rider rides off on his or her own.

12. What is the central idea of this passage?
   Circle the correct answer choice.

Ⓐ Learning how to run behind a new rider.
Ⓑ How to take training wheels off a bicycle.
Ⓒ Learning how to ride a two wheel bicycle.
Ⓓ None of the above

Chapter 3

Lesson 3: Connections and Distinctions

Let us understand the concept with an example.

Redistricting State Legislative Districts

Redistricting refers to the periodic process individual states follow to designate voting districts for state legislators, municipal officeholders and municipal issues. Responsibility for managing redistricting is usually assigned in one of three ways: to the state legislature, to a commission made up of members of opposing political parties and to a politically independent commission. Let's examine each of these three methods.

To the state legislature: This is the most political and least transparent method. By transparency we mean the degree of openness of the process to review and influence by the citizens of the state. The discussions and decisions about assigning legislative districts are conducted in private within the legislature. Citizens have no direct involvement in the process; they can contact their state legislator.

To a commission made up of members of opposing parties: Each party has the same number of commission members. Because redistricting has a powerful influence on the party affiliations of voters in each district, which in turn determines which candidates for which party will be elected, you can imagine that there will be situations where the members are deadlocked on a decision. For this reason, there is a tiebreaker appointed who will cast the deciding vote to break a deadlock. There are also rules followed by some states that districts be contiguous (in close proximity), that a municipality be included in only one district (which is not always possible for a large city or a state in which each district must have approximately the same size population), and that the minority and majority parties and populations are given a fair representation within their districts.

This method is more transparent than the legislature, especially when both "sides" have review by the public. However, each party is motivated to seek legislative maps that favor its supporters.

Politically independent commission: This is the least political and most transparent method of redistricting. Theoretically, this commission can make decisions without the motivation to give one party an advantage over another. As a result, there could be maps drawn that encourage competition among candidates, thereby counteracting the advantage incumbents have in "safe" districts (districts designed to include a majority of voters in one party) and encouraging politicians to cooperate with the opposing party to get things done.

Your assignment: Show how the text makes connections among and distinctions among different ideas.

The text deals with one topic: redistricting of state legislative voting districts. It then goes into more detail, first by defining the term "redistricting", then describing how it is carried out by most states, and then comparing the methods by degree of transparency and extent to which each is influenced by political considerations. It also mentions rules that are designed to ensure fairness in representation for the voters in a district, and some favorable results from choosing the politically independent commission method of managing redistricting.

You can scan the QR code given below or use the url to access additional EdSearch resources including videos and mobile apps related to *Connections and Distinctions*.

URL	QR Code
http://www.lumoslearning.com/a/ri83	

1. What does it mean to make a distinction?

Ⓐ to find a similarity
Ⓑ to find a difference
Ⓒ to draw a conclusion
Ⓓ to point out a fact

2. What does it mean to make a connection?

Ⓐ to find a similarity
Ⓑ to find a difference
Ⓒ to draw a conclusion
Ⓓ to point out a fact

Question 3 and 4 are based on the passage below.

Archaeology is the study of past human life and culture through systematically examining and interpreting the material remains left behind. These material remains include archaeological sites (e.g., settlements, building features, graves), as well as cultural materials or artifacts such as tools and pottery. Through the interpretation and classification of archaeological materials, archaeologists work to understand past human behavior. In some countries, archaeology is often historical or art historical, with a strong emphasis on culture history, archaeological sites, and artifacts such as art objects. In the New World, archaeology can be either a part of history and classical studies or anthropology.

The exact origins of archaeology as a discipline are uncertain. Excavations of ancient monuments and the collection of antiquities have been taking place for thousands of years. It was only in the 19th century, however, that the systematic study of the past through its physical remains underwent professionalization, which meant it began to be carried out in a manner recognizable to modern students of archaeology.

3. What is similar between New World archaeology and archaeology of the past?

Ⓐ They both focus on history.
Ⓑ They both focus on art.
Ⓒ They both focus on culture.
Ⓓ all of the above

4. Based on the information in the article to examine archaeology which would be a good place?

Ⓐ online
Ⓑ at a museum
Ⓒ in a book
Ⓓ all of the above

148

Question 5 is based on the passage below.

Cooking quinoa is much like cooking rice. Depending on the sort of quinoa you purchase, you may have to rinse the seed-like spores before cooking. Be sure to check the label. Boil two cups of water, vegetable stock, chicken broth or other liquid of your choice. Add one cup of raw (rinsed if necessary) quinoa and simmer for about twenty minutes. It doesn't take long for quinoa to cook up moist and tender.

5. What is one distinction that the passage reminds you to take?

Ⓐ The type of quinoa you buy will determine if you have to rinse.
Ⓑ There are different types of quinoa that taste differently.
Ⓒ Always feel the quinoa before buying it.
Ⓓ The type of liquid to use is your choice.

Question 6 is based on the passage below.

Marathon

Training for a marathon takes hard work and perseverance. It is not something you can do on the spur of the moment. Preparing for a marathon takes months, particularly if you have never run a marathon before. The official distance of a full marathon is 26.2 miles. In 2005, the average time to complete a marathon in the United States was 4 hours 32 minutes 8 seconds for men and 5 hours 6 minutes 8 seconds for women.

Most people who run marathons are not trying to win. Many runners try to beat their own best time. Some compare their time to other runners in the same gender and age group. Some people set time-oriented goals, such as finishing under four hours, while others try to complete the race without slowing to a walk. Many beginners simply hope to finish the marathon.

Trainers recommend that beginners maintain a consistent running schedule for six weeks prior to even starting a marathon training program. The purpose of this is to allow the body to adapt to the various physical demands of long-distance running. First-time marathon runners should train by running four days a week for at least four months, increasing distance by no more than ten percent weekly. As race day approaches, runners should taper their runs, reducing the strain on their bodies and resting before the marathon. It is important not to overexert yourself during training because that can lead to a lot of injuries. Most common injuries are spraining of the knees and ankles. These sprains can hinder the training.

Before the race, it is important to stretch in order to keep muscles limber. Staying hydrated is also important, but there is a danger in drinking too much water. If a runner drinks too much water, they may experience a dangerous condition called hyponatremia, a drop of sodium levels in the blood. So only drink water when you are thirsty. During the race, trainers recommend maintaining a steady pace. It is normal to feel sore after a marathon. Light exercise will help sore muscles heal faster.

Some people run marathons in pairs or groups. Training for and running a marathon with another person or group of people can make the experience more enjoyable and more rewarding. A running partner might be just the motivation you need to show up for an early morning run instead of rolling over to hit the snooze button. And, when you cross the finish line together, you can share the satisfaction of reaching your common goal.

Usually, thousands of people sign up and run a marathon. Most people finish the race. The thrill of running a marathon for the first time is unbelievable. The training sessions are harder if you have never run before. But it is unbelievable what ones' body can do when one puts their mind to it. Having a good coach to support you makes all the difference in training for a marathon.

The daily runs are very important. Strength training and core training are also very important.

The health benefits you gain from training are tremendous. Your core muscles grow stronger, and you will have tighter thighs and gluts. Your heart will be much stronger, and you can maintain lower cholesterol and blood sugar levels. Overall, you will look better and become healthier.

Nothing can explain how people feel when they reach that finish line at the end of the race. All the hard work and months of training feel worthwhile. The feeling of accomplishing something great overtakes you. It is great to run a marathon, but it is even greater to finish it.

6. Part A
How is a marathon competition different than most competitions?

Ⓐ Runners compete against themselves to beat past times.
Ⓑ Runners do not compete against each other.
Ⓒ Runners set their own personal records.
Ⓓ All of the above

6. Part B
What makes marathon running similar to other competitive sports?

Ⓐ health benefits
Ⓑ trophies
Ⓒ winning
Ⓓ numbers of people

Question 7 is based on the passage below.

You read a research study that says eating a candy bar made of dark chocolate every day is good for your heart in the long run. The study followed the health of a large group of people over the course of ten years. You notice in fine print at the end of the research that the study was conducted by a major chocolate company.

7. What connection can you make with this study and other commercials you see on TV?

- Ⓐ The study must be true if it is published.
- Ⓑ Advertising agencies sometimes minimize major facts to help sell products.
- Ⓒ Studies in all commercials are conducted by one research company.
- Ⓓ Dark chocolate is good for your heart.

Question 8 and 9 are based on the passage below.

From Chapter 2 of **Bullets and Billets** by Bruce Bainsfather

I stood in a queue of Gordons, Seaforths, Worcesters, etc., slowly moving up one, until, finally arriving at the companion (nearly said staircase), I tobogganed down into the hold, and spent what was left of the night dealing out those rations. Having finished, at last, I came to the surface again, and now, as the transport glided along through the dirty waters of the river, and as I gazed at the motley collection of Frenchmen on the various wharves, and saw a variety of soldiery, and a host of other warlike "props," I felt acutely that now I was in the war at last—the real thing! For some time, I had been rehearsing in England; but that was over now, and here I was—in the common or garden vernacular—"in the soup."

8. Based on the context of the phrase "in the soup," what can you conclude the author is saying?

- Ⓐ He's happy he has reached his destination.
- Ⓑ He's hungry and ready to eat.
- Ⓒ He is entering a bad situation.
- Ⓓ He came to the surface and spent time.

9. What conclusion can you draw about this passage?

- Ⓐ The narrator is heading into war.
- Ⓑ The narrator is going on a trip.
- Ⓒ The narrator is frustrated about his journey.
- Ⓓ The narrator likes rivers.

Chapter 3

Lesson 4: Determining Meaning of Words

Let us understand the concept with an example.

In this text we define the words "technical," "figurative" and "connotative" that are in the standard and give examples of their usage. In the examples, key words whose meanings you need to determine are shown in bold type.

1. Technical: Technical words and phrases are used in connection with one specific subject or in one activity or job. Examples of technical words relating to baseball are: "inning," "pitch," "stolen base," and "line drive." Relating to computers are: "crashed" and "backed up."

Examples:

1. The announcer said: "Well it's the top of the ninth **inning**, the Lions have runners on first and third, two outs and they are down by one run. Jamison, the center fielder, steps up to the plate. Here's the **pitch** to Jamison. The runner on first goes, the catcher fumbles the ball, no time for a throw to second and it's a **stolen base**. The count is now 3 and 2. Here's the pitch. **Line drive** to center field, the runners are moving, it's a double, both runners will score and the Lions take the lead! Will the Lions pull this one out or collapse like a balloon punctured by a pin? My guess is the latter."

Comment: Of course you can determine the meanings of the words in bold text by using a printed or online dictionary. But you can also figure out their meanings from the context (other words and phrases) in which they are used. **Ninth inning** indicates a time period in a game, which you can figure is called an inning. The phrases "Jamison, the center fielder, steps up to the plate," and "Here's the **pitch** to Jamison," gives clues that there is someone throwing the ball to the hitter. "The runner on first goes, the catcher fumbles the ball, no time for a throw to second and it's a **stolen base**," gives clues that a base runner has advanced safely to second base. "Here's the pitch. **Line drive** to center field, the runners are moving, it's a double, both runners will score and the Lions take the lead!" is very descriptive and clearly indicates that the hitter has made a hit that has moved runners along.

Even though "double" and "pitch" can have other meanings, when considered in the context of the entire monologue by the announcer the listener knows they apply to baseball. The exclamation points after the words "lead" and "that" connote a tone of excitement in the announcer's voice.

2. When the computer appeared to **crash**, the person using it turned white as a sheet, and in a state of panic, called the help desk. The first question the technician asked was, "Have you **backed up** your data recently? I'll be right there." The technician turns to his help desk colleague and says "Guess what? It's our favorite personnel administrator again! As if I don't have enough to do!"

Comment: "Crash" indicates that something unexpected or uncontrollable happened (it connotes a tone of panic), especially considering that a crash may damage or destroy data stored in the computer and/or prevent access to it by a user. "Have you backed up your data recently?" gives you the clue that backing up refers to making a copy of the data and storing that copy on another device so that it is not destroyed or damaged by a crash on the originating computer. Asking the question about back up raises the emotional issue of whether a copy of the data was previously made (and can be accessed) or not, in which case it may be lost.

2. Figurative: Figurative language is a language where the meaning of a word or phrase is different from the literal (primary or strict or dictionary) meaning. Another way of defining figurative is using language that has another meaning besides its normal definition.

Examples of using similes as figurative language: The baseball announcer uses a simile when he speculates whether the Lions will "pull this one out or collapse like a balloon punctured by a pin". Another simile, "white as a sheet," occurs in the computer example. Obviously, the Lions are not a balloon and the computer user is not a sheet. These are just comparisons.

3. Connotative: Connotative meanings suggest that there is an associated or secondary meaning of a word or expression, in addition to its primary meaning, that the reader or listener will have to identify it himself/herself, since it is not stated in the text.

Examples: When the baseball announcer says "My guess is the latter," it connotes that he has seen the Lions lose the lead in several previous games, even though he does not actually say that. When the help desk technician says "Guess what? It's our favorite personnel administrator again! As if I don't have enough to do!" it connotes a sarcastic tone and contemptuous attitude toward the caller, and implies that the caller has had computer problems before.

You can scan the QR code given below or use the url to access additional EdSearch resources including videos and mobile apps related to *Determining Meaning of Words*.

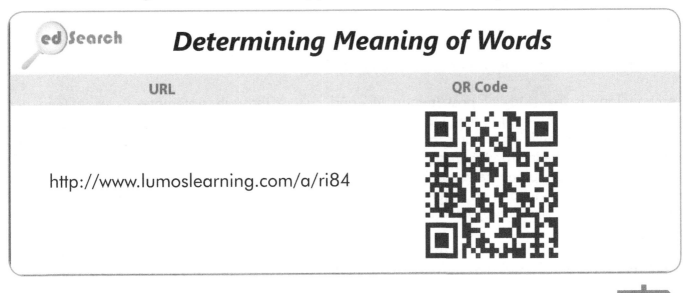

ed)Search

Determining Meaning of Words

URL	QR Code
http://www.lumoslearning.com/a/ri84	

1. What is connotation?

   Ⓐ A dictionary definition
   Ⓑ What a word means based on its context in a story
   Ⓒ A word with multiple meanings
   Ⓓ An opinion based on fact

2. What is denotation?

   Ⓐ A dictionary definition
   Ⓑ What a word means based on its context in a story
   Ⓒ A word that has a meaning that has changed over time
   Ⓓ An opinion based on fact

Question 3 is based on the passage below.

The Emperor Penguin is the only penguin species that breeds during the Antarctic winter. It treks 31–75 miles over the ice to breeding colonies, which may include thousands of penguins. The female lays a single egg, which is then incubated by the male while the female returns to the sea to feed; parents subsequently take turns foraging at sea and caring for their chick in the colony. The average lifespan of the Emperor Penguin is 20 years, although observations suggest that some Emperor Penguins may live to 50 years of age.

3. Based on how the word "trek" is used in the passage, determine its meaning.

   Ⓐ to fly a long-distance
   Ⓑ to circulate in a specific area
   Ⓒ to walk a long-distance
   Ⓓ to live a long life

Question 4 and 5 are based on the passage below.

Archaeology is the study of past human life and culture through <u>systematically</u> examining and interpreting the material remains left behind. These material remains include archaeological sites (e.g., settlements, building features, graves), as well as cultural materials or artifacts such as tools and pottery. Through the interpretation and classification of archaeological materials, archaeologists work to understand past human behavior. In some countries, archaeology is often historical or art historical, with a strong emphasis on culture history, archaeological sites, and artifacts such as art objects. In the New World, archaeology can be either a part of history and classical studies or anthropology.

The exact origins of archaeology as a discipline are uncertain. Excavations of ancient monuments and the collection of antiquities have been taking place for thousands of years. It was only in the

19th century, however, that the systematic study of the past through its physical remains underwent _professionalization_, which meant it began to be carried out in a manner recognizable to modern students of archaeology.

4. What does the underlined word "professionalization" mean?

Ⓐ the way a field of study turns into a professional job
Ⓑ the way an artifact turns into a noted antique
Ⓒ the way a civilization is recovered and displayed
Ⓓ to study art history

5. What does it mean to do something "systematically"?

Ⓐ to follow very specific instructions
Ⓑ to use the scientific method of trial and error
Ⓒ to record the process you followed to do something
Ⓓ none of the above

Question 6 and 7 are based on the passage below.

Marathon

Training for a marathon takes hard work and perseverance. It is not something you can do on the spur of the moment. Preparing for a marathon takes months, particularly if you have never run a marathon before. The official distance of a full marathon is 26.2 miles. In 2005, the average time to complete a marathon in the United States was 4 hours 32 minutes 8 seconds for men and 5 hours 6 minutes 8 seconds for women.

Most people who run marathons are not trying to win. Many runners try to beat their own best time. Some compare their time to other runners in the same gender and age group. Some people set time-oriented goals, such as finishing under four hours, while others try to complete the race without slowing to a walk. Many beginners simply hope to finish the marathon.

Trainers recommend that beginners maintain a consistent running schedule for six weeks prior to even starting a marathon training program. The purpose of this is to allow the body to adapt to the various physical demands of long-distance running. First-time marathon runners should train by running four days a week for at least four months, increasing distance by no more than ten percent weekly. As race day approaches, runners should taper their runs, reducing the strain on their bodies and resting before the marathon. It is important not to overexert yourself during training because that can lead to a lot of injuries. Most common injuries are spraining of the knees and ankles. These sprains can hinder the training.

Before the race, it is important to stretch in order to keep muscles limber. Staying hydrated is also important, but there is a danger in drinking too much water. If a runner drinks too much water, they may experience a dangerous condition called hyponatremia, a drop of sodium levels in the blood. So only drink water when you are thirsty. During the race, trainers recommend maintaining a steady pace. It is normal to feel sore after a marathon. Light exercise will help sore muscles heal faster.

Some people run marathons in pairs or groups. Training for and running a marathon with another person or group of people can make the experience more enjoyable and more rewarding. A running partner might be just the motivation you need to show up for an early morning run instead of rolling over to hit the snooze button. And, when you cross the finish line together, you can share the satisfaction of reaching your common goal.

Usually, thousands of people sign up and run a marathon. Most people finish the race. The thrill of running a marathon for the first time is unbelievable. The training sessions are harder if you have never run before. But it is unbelievable what ones' body can do when one puts their mind to it. Having a good coach to support you makes all the difference in training for a marathon.

The daily runs are very important. Strength training and core training are also very important.

The health benefits you gain from training are tremendous. Your core muscles grow stronger, and you will have tighter thighs and gluts. Your heart will be much stronger, and you can maintain lower cholesterol and blood sugar levels. Overall, you will look better and become healthier.

Nothing can explain how people feel when they reach that finish line at the end of the race. All the hard work and months of training feel worthwhile. The feeling of accomplishing something great overtakes you. It is great to run a marathon, but it is even greater to finish it.

6. Part A
What does the phrase "overexert" (third paragraph) mean?

- Ⓐ go over the amount of time you need to run
- Ⓑ go over the distance you need to run
- Ⓒ do more than your body can handle
- Ⓓ drink too much water

6. Part B
What does the phrase "spur of the moment" (first paragraph) mean?

- Ⓐ in the moment, without thinking
- Ⓑ at the last minute
- Ⓒ on a horse wearing spurs
- Ⓓ taking time to train

7. How does the phrase "spur of the moment" add to the tone of the passage?

Ⓐ It creates a humorous tone so the readers laugh and enjoy the piece.
Ⓑ It creates a serious tone necessary to show how hard running a marathon is.
Ⓒ It creates a factual tone so readers can study before training.
Ⓓ It creates a reminder of how important training is.

Question 8 is based on the passage below.

From Chapter 2 of **Bullets and Billets** by Bruce Bainsfather

I stood in a queue of Gordons, Seaforths, Worcesters, etc., slowly moving up one, until, finally arriving at the companion (nearly said staircase), I tobogganed down into the hold, and spent what was left of the night dealing out those rations. Having finished, at last, I came to the surface again, and now, as the transport glided along through the dirty waters of the river, and as I gazed at the motley collection of Frenchmen on the various wharves, and saw a variety of soldiery, and a host of other warlike "props," I felt acutely that now I was in the war at last—the real thing! For some time, I had been rehearsing in England; but that was over now, and here I was—in the common or garden vernacular—"in the soup."

8. Part A
Based on how they are used to begin the passage, what are "Gordons, Seaforths, and Worcesters?

Ⓐ Ranks in an army
Ⓑ Types of holding facilities on a ship
Ⓒ Different destinations on the journey
Ⓓ None of the above

8. Part B
The author is using what type of figurative language to compare war to a theater in the above passage.

Ⓐ implied metaphor
Ⓑ simile
Ⓒ imagery
Ⓓ allusion

Chapter 3

Lesson 5: Analyzing Structures in Text

Let us understand the concept with an example.

The issue: The Board of Education in our town wants to decide whether or not students should be allowed to have their own smartphones and tablets with them and available for use during class time during the school day. They are seeking feedback from parents, teachers, administrators and students.

A student's response:

Dear Board of Education:

My name is Jennifer and I am an eighth grade-student. I am offering my opinion on whether to allow students to have their own smartphones and tablets available during class time. This is not a good idea. It provides too great an opportunity for students to use their tablets or smartphones to play games or login to social media to conduct personal communications with their friends, instead of focusing on performing assigned work. There are enough desktop school computers available to each student to use for class work, and these computers are programmed to allow access to only those websites assigned by the teachers. Otherwise the classroom teacher will have to spend time walking around the classroom checking each student's screen to see that they are only looking at what was assigned. As far as parents being able to reach students during school hours, the school office will be able to pass messages on to the student, allow them to use a school phone to speak with their parents, or provide access to computers that are not restricted to specific websites.

I hope you will agree with my position in making your decision.

Sincerely yours,
Jennifer Monroe

Your Assignment: Analyze the structure of the sample paragraphs.

Here is what you might write (after researching the topic "paragraph structure.")

A paragraph is a collection of related sentences dealing with a single topic. Jennifer's paragraphs deal only with her response to the Board of Education about the issue of whether students should have their tablets or smartphones available during class time.

In her first paragraph, her second and third sentences are topic sentences. A topic sentence is general, there are not many specific details in the sentence, but the sentence introduces the main idea that

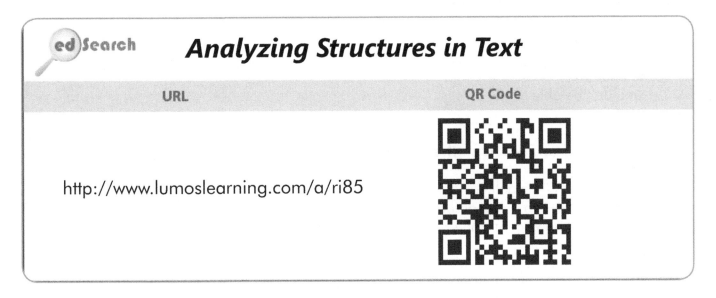

she is writing about and what it is that she wants to prove or support in her response. In her second paragraph, its only sentence is her topic sentence.

Following the topic sentence are usually supporting sentences that provide specific detail and discussion of claims. Claims attempt to "prove" the idea in the topic sentence. In her first paragraph, every sentence that follows Jennifer's topic sentences are claims that support her main topic sentence "This is not a good idea."

Following the topic sentence and claims is usually a concluding sentence. It should explain why the evidence supports the main idea(s) in your paper. It is more convincing if it is expressed as your own opinion instead of containing more evidence or giving someone else's opinion. Jennifer's last sentence is a concluding sentence, and it is clearly a personal statement from her stating what her desired outcome is from the Board.

You can scan the QR code given below or use the url to access additional EdSearch resources including videos and mobile apps related to *Analyzing Structures in Text*.

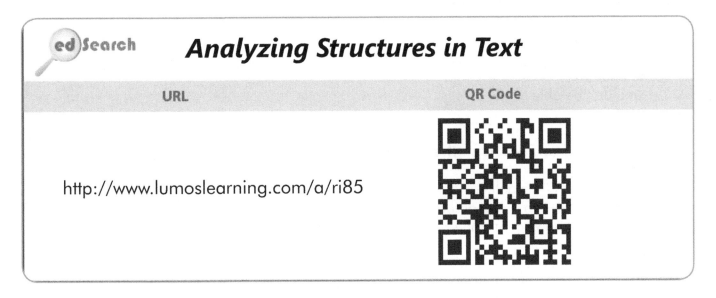

ed Search	**Analyzing Structures in Text**
URL	QR Code
http://www.lumoslearning.com/a/ri85	

1. **What should you look at when analyzing the structure of a piece of text?**

   Ⓐ the genre of writing
   Ⓑ the author's purpose
   Ⓒ the types of transition words that are being used
   Ⓓ all of the above

2. **What type of writing has the following literary elements: characters, conflict, setting, and plot?**

   Ⓐ nonfiction
   Ⓑ fiction
   Ⓒ technical
   Ⓓ poetry

3. **If you saw words such as, "unlike", "as well as", "on the other hand", and "in contrast", what would you think the author's purpose was?**

   Ⓐ to persuade
   Ⓑ to compare
   Ⓒ to entertain
   Ⓓ wouldn't be able to tell

Question 4 and 5 are based on the passage below.

Stephen and Joseph Montgolfier were papermakers, but they had been interested in flying for many years. One night, in 1782, Joseph noticed something that gave him an idea. He was sitting in front of the fire when he saw some small pieces of scorched paper being carried up the chimney.

Soon afterwards, the brothers conducted an experiment. They lit a fire under a small silk bag, which was open at the bottom; at once, the bag rose to the ceiling. After this, Stephen and Joseph conducted many more experiments, both indoors and in the open air. Eventually, they built a huge balloon of linen and paper. On June 5th, 1783, they launched their balloon in the village of Annonay.

4. **What would change this passage into an essay?**

   Ⓐ Adding an introductory paragraph and a conclusion.
   Ⓑ Adding more details to the experiments.
   Ⓒ Adding nothing, it is already an essay.
   Ⓓ Rewriting it as a personal narrative.

5. What type of text structure is used in this passage?

A. sequence
B. compare/contrast
C. cause/effect
D. description

Question 6 is based on the passage below.

The Emperor Penguin is the only penguin species that breeds during the Antarctic winter. It treks 31–75 miles over the ice to breeding colonies, which may include thousands of penguins. The female lays a single egg, which is then incubated by the male while the female returns to the sea to feed; parents subsequently take turns foraging at sea and caring for their chick in the colony. The average lifespan of the Emperor Penguin is 20 years, although observations suggest that some Emperor Penguins may live to 50 years of age.

6. What type of text structure is used in the passage above?

A. sequence
B. compare/contrast
C. description
D. cause/effect

Question 7 is based on the passage below.

Archaeology is the study of past human life and culture through systematically examining and interpreting the material remains left behind. These material remains include archaeological sites (e.g., settlements, building features, graves), as well as cultural materials or artifacts such as tools and pottery. Through the interpretation and classification of archaeological materials, archaeologists work to understand past human behavior. In some countries, archaeology is often historical or art historical, with a strong emphasis on culture history, archaeological sites, and artifacts such as art objects. In the New World, archaeology can be either a part of history and classical studies or anthropology.

The exact origins of archaeology as a discipline are uncertain. Excavations of ancient monuments and the collection of antiquities have been taking place for thousands of years. It was only in the 19th century, however, that the systematic study of the past through its physical remains underwent professionalization, which meant it began to be carried out in a manner recognizable to modern students of archaeology.

"Archaeology is the study of past human life and culture through systematically examining and interpreting the material remains left behind."

7. The author uses this as the opening line to his article in order to:

Ⓐ give the reader a base to build their understanding of archaeology
Ⓑ tell why archaeology is important
Ⓒ give the reader an idea of what the article is going to be about
Ⓓ both A and C

Question 8 is based on the sentence below.

"Through the interpretation and classification of archaeological materials, archaeologists work to understand past human behavior."

8. Why is this sentence included?

Ⓐ to give an example of why archaeology is important
Ⓑ to show the technical side of archaeology
Ⓒ to show the process of archaeology
Ⓓ to show how archaeology has changed

Question 9 is based on the sentence below.

"Excavations of ancient monuments and the collection of antiquities have been taking place for thousands of years."

9. Why was this sentence included?

Ⓐ to clarify what archaeology is
Ⓑ to show that archaeology is not something that was supported long ago
Ⓒ to show that archaeology is a fairly modern concept
Ⓓ to explain that some form of archaeology has been happening for a very long time

Question 10 is based on the passage below.

Marathon

Training for a marathon takes hard work and perseverance. It is not something you can do on the spur of the moment. Preparing for a marathon takes months, particularly if you have never run a marathon before. The official distance of a full marathon is 26.2 miles. In 2005, the average time to complete a marathon in the United States was 4 hours 32 minutes 8 seconds for men and 5 hours 6 minutes 8 seconds for women.

Most people who run marathons are not trying to win. Many runners try to beat their own best time. Some compare their time to other runners in the same gender and age group. Some people set time-oriented goals, such as finishing under four hours, while others try to complete the race without slowing to a walk. Many beginners simply hope to finish the marathon.

Trainers recommend that beginners maintain a consistent running schedule for six weeks prior to even starting a marathon training program. The purpose of this is to allow the body to adapt to the various physical demands of long-distance running. First-time marathon runners should train by running four days a week for at least four months, increasing distance by no more than ten percent weekly. As race day approaches, runners should taper their runs, reducing the strain on their bodies and resting before the marathon. It is important not to overexert yourself during training because that can lead to a lot of injuries. Most common injuries are spraining of the knees and ankles. These sprains can hinder the training.

Before the race, it is important to stretch in order to keep muscles limber. Staying hydrated is also important, but there is a danger in drinking too much water. If a runner drinks too much water, they may experience a dangerous condition called hyponatremia, a drop of sodium levels in the blood. So only drink water when you are thirsty. During the race, trainers recommend maintaining a steady pace. It is normal to feel sore after a marathon. Light exercise will help sore muscles heal faster.

Some people run marathons in pairs or groups. Training for and running a marathon with another person or group of people can make the experience more enjoyable and more rewarding. A running partner might be just the motivation you need to show up for an early morning run instead of rolling over to hit the snooze button. And, when you cross the finish line together, you can share the satisfaction of reaching your common goal.

Usually, thousands of people sign up and run a marathon. Most people finish the race. The thrill of running a marathon for the first time is unbelievable. The training sessions are harder if you have never run before. But it is unbelievable what ones' body can do when one puts their mind to it. Having a good coach to support you makes all the difference in training for a marathon.

The daily runs are very important. Strength training and core training are also very important.

The health benefits you gain from training are tremendous. Your core muscles grow stronger, and you will have tighter thighs and gluts. Your heart will be much stronger, and you can maintain lower cholesterol and blood sugar levels. Overall, you will look better and become healthier.

Nothing can explain how people feel when they reach that finish line at the end of the race. All the hard work and months of training feel worthwhile. The feeling of accomplishing something great overtakes you. It is great to run a marathon, but it is even greater to finish it.

"Nothing can explain how people feel when they reach that finish line at the end of the race. All the hard work and months of training feel worthwhile."

10. Why are these two sentences included in the conclusion?

Ⓐ leave the reader with a positive reason to run a marathon
Ⓑ persuade the reader that anyone can run a marathon
Ⓒ show the reader that running a marathon is not difficult
Ⓓ change the tone of the article

Question 11 is based on the passages below.

The Eagle	First Flight
Far from the habitations of humans and their petty quarrels, there once lived on top of a rugged hill, an old eagle. When the fragrant morning breeze blew through his nest, the eagle would shake his feathers and spread out his wings. When the sun rose high and the world below engaged itself in its unceasing fight for survival, the eagle would take off from the hilltop and circle majestically over the valley and its dwellers, the fields and the running brooks. If he saw something worthwhile, such as a hare or a rat, a pigeon or a chick, he would swoop down on it like lightning, fetch it to his nest, and devour it. He would then inspect the surroundings once again.	The young seagull was alone on his ledge.His two brothers and his sister had already flown away the day before. He had afraid to fly with them. Somehow, when he had taken a little run forward to the brink of the ledge and attempted to flap his wings he became afraid. The great expanse of sea stretched down beneath, and it was such a long way down - miles down. He felt certain that his wings would never support him; so he bent his head and ran away, back to the little hole under the ledge where he slept at night. Even when each of his brothers and his little sister, whose wings were far shorter than his own, ran to the brink, flapped their wings, and flew away, he failed to muster up courage to take that plunge, which appeared to him so desperate. His father and mother had come around calling to him shrilly, upbraiding him, and threatening to let him starve on his ledge unless he flew away; but for the life of him he could not move.

11. Part A
After reading the two passages, what contrast can be made?

Ⓐ Passage one is about an eagle and passage two is about a seagull.
Ⓑ The eagle is old and the seagull is young.
Ⓒ The old eagle has mastered flying where as the young seagull is afraid of flying.
Ⓓ all of the above

11. Part B

While the eagle is a confident flyer, the seagull is _____.

(A) afraid to fly.
(B) also a confident flyer.
(C) a smaller bird.
(D) excited to fly.

11. Part C

The process of learning how to fly is discussed in _____.

(A) both passages.
(B) neither passage.
(C) "The Eagle"
(D) "First Flight"

Question 12 is based on the passages below.

Archaeology	History of Mankind
Archaeology is the study of past human life and culture through systematically examining and interpreting the material remains left behind. These material remains include archaeological sites (e.g., settlements, building features, graves), as well as cultural materials or artifacts such as tools and pottery. Through the interpretation and classification of archaeological materials, archaeologists work to understand past human behavior. In some countries, archaeology is often historical or art historical, with a strong emphasis on cultural history, archaeological sites, and artifacts such as art objects. In the New World, archaeology can be either a part of history and classical studies or anthropology. The exact origins of archaeology as a discipline are uncertain. Excavations of ancient monuments and the collection of antiquities have been taking place for thousands of years. It was only in the 19th century, however, that the systematic study of the past through its physical remains began to be carried out in a manner recognizable to modern students of archaeology.	History is about events that happened in the past. It is like an interesting and exciting series of stories. However, these stories are not like the many fairy tales you may have read. These stories are about real people and events that have really happened. It tells us about the lives of great men_ Some were great rulers who fought battles and conquered lands. Some were famous teachers, writers, explorers, scientists, artists, and musicians. They performed great deeds and showed people how to lead productive lives. History tells us how early civilization began. It describes how those people lived, how they got their food, and how they built their villages and cities. How do we have a record of events from long ago? In recent years. People have excavated ruins of old cities that were buried deep beneath the ground. We can learn about the people who lived in the lost cities by carefully examining artifacts found in these sites. Some of the items include sharp stones used for hunting, pots, and pans used for cooking and beads and necklaces used as jewelry. These items offer some clues about the life of people who lived during that time.

12. Part A
Both passages focus on _____.

Ⓐ the method of finding artifacts.
Ⓑ learning more about the past.
Ⓒ why history is taught in school.
Ⓓ events in history.

12. Part B
What comparison can be made between the two passages?

Ⓐ Both passages are about human life in the past.
Ⓑ Both passages are about mummies.
Ⓒ Both A and B.
Ⓓ None of the above.

Lesson 6: Author's Point of View

Let us understand the concept with an example.

The issue: The Board of Education in our town wants to decide whether or not students should be allowed to have their own smartphones and tablets with them and available for use during class time during the school day. They are seeking feedback from parents, teachers, administrators and students.

A student's response:

Dear Board of Education:

My name is Jennifer and I am an eighth-grade student. I am offering my opinion on whether to allow students to have their own smartphones and tablets available during class time. This is not a good idea. It provides too great an opportunity for students to use their tablets or smartphones to play games or login to social media to conduct personal communications with their friends, instead of focusing on performing assigned work. I think there are enough desktop school computers available to each student to use for class work, and these computers are programmed to allow access to only those websites assigned by the teachers. Otherwise the classroom teacher will have to spend time walking around the classroom checking each student's screen to see that they are only looking at what was assigned. As far as parents being able to reach students during school hours, the school office will be able to pass messages on to the student, allow them to use a school phone to speak with their parents, or provide access to computers that are not restricted to specific websites.

You will probably hear from students who are in favor of having their tablets and smartphones available during class time. They may argue that it allows each student to work on a different assignment and/or to progress at their own pace. The school desktop computers will also allow this. They may also argue that because the school desktop computers are not available outside of school hours that they cannot perform assignments when they are home. This is not true because teachers have software that allows them to create assignments on the school website that students can access at any time from any location that provides internet access. I will concede that not all rooms used for study halls have computers, but I believe that the other advantages I have pointed out outweigh this disadvantage.

I hope you will agree with my position in making your decision.

Sincerely yours,
Jennifer Monroe

Your Assignment:

1. Determine the author's point of view or purpose.

Jennifer's purpose in writing her letter is to provide feedback to the Board of Education on the issue of whether to allow students to have their own smartphones and tablets available during class time. Her point of view is her statement "This is not a good idea."

2. Analyze how the author acknowledges and responds to conflicting evidence or viewpoints.

Jennifer writes a second paragraph acknowledging what she thinks will be reasons given to the Board by those who oppose her position; that is by those who favor students having their tablets or smartphones available during class time. She has taken the time to prepare this paragraph to influence the Board with reasons why they should oppose those in favor of students having their tablets or smartphones available during class time. This is a supplement to her statements as to why the Board should support her position.

You can scan the QR code given below or use the url to access additional EdSearch resources including videos and mobile apps related to *Author's Point of View.*

ed)Search	**Author's Point of View**	
URL		**QR Code**
http://www.lumoslearning.com/a/ri86		

1. What is point of view?

Ⓐ a character's view of the action in a story
Ⓑ the perspective from which a story is told
Ⓒ where the author is when writing a story
Ⓓ the view of the character in the story

2. Which type of point of view uses the pronouns "I, me, and my"?

Ⓐ first person
Ⓑ third person omniscient
Ⓒ third person limited
Ⓓ second person

3. When the narrator is one of the characters in the story, what point of view is the story being told from?

Ⓐ First person
Ⓑ Third person omniscient
Ⓒ Third person limited
Ⓓ second person

4. Which of the following is true of the point of view known as third person omniscient?

Ⓐ The narrator is not a character in the story.
Ⓑ The narrator is a character in the story.
Ⓒ The narrator only knows that which he or she sees and hears.
Ⓓ The narrator is talking about himself

5. Which of the following is true of the point of view known as third person limited?

Ⓐ The narrator is not a character in the story.
Ⓑ The narrator is a character in the story.
Ⓒ The narrator only knows that which he or she sees and hears.
Ⓓ The narrator knows everything about all of the characters.

6. Which type of narrator is the most reliable?

Ⓐ first person
Ⓑ third person limited
Ⓒ third person omniscient
Ⓓ second person

Question 7 is based on the passage below.

Marathon

Training for a marathon takes hard work and perseverance. It is not something you can do on the spur of the moment. Preparing for a marathon takes months, particularly if you have never run a marathon before. The official distance of a full marathon is 26.2 miles. In 2005, the average time to complete a marathon in the United States was 4 hours 32 minutes 8 seconds for men and 5 hours 6 minutes 8 seconds for women.

Most people who run marathons are not trying to win. Many runners try to beat their own best time. Some compare their time to other runners in the same gender and age group. Some people set time-oriented goals, such as finishing under four hours, while others try to complete the race without slowing to a walk. Many beginners simply hope to finish the marathon.

Trainers recommend that beginners maintain a consistent running schedule for six weeks prior to even starting a marathon training program. The purpose of this is to allow the body to adapt to the various physical demands of long-distance running. First-time marathon runners should train by running four days a week for at least four months, increasing distance by no more than ten percent weekly. As race day approaches, runners should taper their runs, reducing the strain on their bodies and resting before the marathon. It is important not to overexert yourself during training because that can lead to a lot of injuries. Most common injuries are spraining of the knees and ankles. These sprains can hinder the training.

Before the race, it is important to stretch in order to keep muscles limber. Staying hydrated is also important, but there is a danger in drinking too much water. If a runner drinks too much water, they may experience a dangerous condition called hyponatremia, a drop of sodium levels in the blood. So only drink water when you are thirsty. During the race, trainers recommend maintaining a steady pace. It is normal to feel sore after a marathon. Light exercise will help sore muscles heal faster.

Some people run marathons in pairs or groups. Training for and running a marathon with another person or group of people can make the experience more enjoyable and more rewarding. A running partner might be just the motivation you need to show up for an early morning run instead of rolling over to hit the snooze button. And, when you cross the finish line together, you can share the satisfaction of reaching your common goal.

Usually, thousands of people sign up and run a marathon. Most people finish the race. The thrill of running a marathon for the first time is unbelievable. The training sessions are harder if you have never run before. But it is unbelievable what ones' body can do when one puts their mind to it. Having a good coach to support you makes all the difference in training for a marathon.

The daily runs are very important. Strength training and core training are also very important. The health benefits you gain from training are tremendous. Your core muscles grow stronger, and you will have tighter thighs and gluts. Your heart will be much stronger, and you can maintain lower cholesterol and blood sugar levels. Overall, you will look better and become healthier.

170

Nothing can explain how people feel when they reach that finish line at the end of the race. All the hard work and months of training feel worthwhile. The feeling of accomplishing something great overtakes you. It is great to run a marathon, but it is even greater to finish it.

7. In what point of view is the below sentence said?
Many runners try to beat their own best time.

- (A) first person
- (B) second person
- (C) third person omniscient
- (D) third person limited

8. Which point of view is the following excerpt told from?

From Chapter 2 of **Bullets and Billets** by Bruce Bainsfather

I stood in a queue of Gordons, Seaforths, Worcesters, etc., slowly moving up one, until, finally arriving at the companion (nearly said staircase), I tobogganed down into the hold, and spent what was left of the night dealing out those rations. Having finished, at last, I came to the surface again, and now, as the transport glided along through the dirty waters of the river, and as I gazed at the motley collection of Frenchmen on the various wharves, and saw a variety of soldiery, and a host of other warlike "props," I felt acutely that now I was in the war at last—the real thing! For some time, I had been rehearsing in England; but that was over now, and here I was—in the common or garden vernacular—"in the soup."

- (A) first person
- (B) third person omniscient
- (C) third person limited
- (D) second person

Question 9 is based on the passage below.

You read a research study that says eating a candy bar made of dark chocolate every day is good for your heart in the long run. The study followed the health of a large group of people over the course of ten years. You notice in fine print at the end of the research that the study was conducted by a major chocolate company.

9. What might you, as a critical reader, take away from this? Circle the correct answer choice.

- (A) The study must be true if it is published.
- (B) The conductors of the study benefit from the findings of this claim.
- (C) Before believing this to be true, more studies need to be done by people who don't have stakes in the particular market.
- (D) both B and C

10. What is the author's purpose for writing the statement below?

If you are thinking about buying a new car, Bruce's on Route 12 has the best deals in town.

(A) to inform
(B) to instruct
(C) to sell
(D) to entertain

11. "Often when reading a magazine you will come across advertisements. These advertisements are meant to:

Circle the correct answer choice."

(A) show the reader a product
(B) persuade the reader to buy the product
(C) introduce the reader to the product
(D) provide the reader with a break from stories

Chapter 3

Lesson 7: Publishing Mediums

Let us understand the concept with an example.

Definitions:
1. Evaluate means to assess or judge the significance, worth or value of something.
2. Note: Media, not mediums, is the plural of medium.
Media are the means of communication, such as radio and television, newspapers, magazines, and the Internet, that reach or influence people widely.

Here are descriptions of the last few seconds of a basketball game, presented using three different media. First, as if you were reading about it in a newspaper. Second, as if you are seeing it broadcast live on TV. Third as if you were listening to a live radio broadcast. After reading these descriptions, see the example below of how you might compare the advantages and disadvantages of each medium.

Article in a newspaper
There would be a headline and a still photo from the game. There might also be a web address for further information and the writer's contact information. In the article would be a written description of the last few seconds of the game including the slam dunk by Hendricks that won the game.

Broadcast live on TV
Imagine this as a continuous stream of live action pictures with live commentary by the sportscaster.

Sportscaster's commentary:
"Rebound Jackson, pass to Jacovik, closing seconds, pass to Hendricks...a slam dunk, there's the buzzer, AND THE TIGERS WIN IT!! What a comeback! One for the record books! And what a slam dunk – did you ever see anything like it?"

Broadcast live on the radio

Sportscaster's commentary: "Rebound Jackson, he fakes a dribble, passes to his right to Jacovik, Jacovik drives to the right of the key, closely guarded by Sosnowska, fakes a jump shot and passes to Hendricks slanting into the center of the key...slam dunk by Hendricks, there's the buzzer, THE TIGERS WIN IT!! Hendricks must have leaped four feet in the air, and sailed most of the way from the foul line to the basket! An amazing slam dunk! What athleticism!"

Example: Here is an example of what you might write to compare the advantages and disadvantages of each of the three media. What you might write should be influenced by your personal observations and opinions from reading sports news in a newspaper, watching a live broadcast of a sporting event, or listening to live coverage of a sporting event on the radio.

The newspaper reporter is facing a disadvantage compared with the sportscasters. The reporter is writing after the event, and through his/her creative use of words, will try to create interest and emotions with details about the game, but will probably not match the excitement experienced by someone watching or listening to a live broadcast. On the other hand, the reporter has more time to create a write-up of the game, to think up more creative use of language to describe it, and to carefully select which details he/she will report on (something a sportscaster may not have much time to do), and to write related articles such as articles about the league that the Tigers play in and tables of stats that readers can take the time to study. The reporter can also add one or more still photos to enhance the article.

In the past, before television was available, if you could not attend the game or listen on the radio, the newspaper was the only other source of information. Today, however, with rebroadcast options and VCR capabilities, you can see the game live after the event is over.

For those Tiger fans unable to attend the game, the television sportscaster probably has the best advantage in attracting their attention. The TV sportscaster has the advantage of live video coverage of the game while also injecting his/her commentary. Because viewers can see the action, the TV sportscaster will probably use fewer words to describe it than a radio sportscaster, whose audience needs a more descriptive narrative to paint a picture of the action in their minds, since they cannot actually see it. The TV sportscaster can also conduct live interviews of coaches and players during pregame and postgame time periods. Also, he/she can capture crowd noise and any entertainment provided by the venue. But similar to the newspaper reporter and radio broadcaster, he/she will likely research the teams, players and stats relating to the teams before the broadcast or the writing of the article. In my opinion, the second most interesting media coverage is the radio broadcast. While it lacks the excitement of live or recorded video, it has the excitement of live action commentary, with time for pregame and postgame interviews.

One characteristic of sports casting jobs is having the ability to think on your feet and react professionally to unexpected situations that can occur during live coverage of a game. This is more pressure that a newspaper reporter will likely have.

You can scan the QR code given below or use the url to access additional EdSearch resources including videos and mobile apps related to *Publishing Mediums.*

ed Search   **Publishing Mediums**

URL	QR Code
http://www.lumoslearning.com/a/ri87	

1. **Which of the following is important to consider when reading a text online?**

   Ⓐ evaluate the background of the source
   Ⓑ look for why the information is being provided
   Ⓒ check the date of the source
   Ⓓ all of the above

2. **You want to write a short piece that people can respond to immediately and publicly. What is the best place to do this?**

   Ⓐ a web page
   Ⓑ the local newspaper
   Ⓒ the national newspaper
   Ⓓ a magazine

3. **You are writing an article about the stresses involved in being a high school student and what to do about them. What is the best medium/media of publication?**

   Ⓐ a magazine for teenagers
   Ⓑ a website aimed at teenagers
   Ⓒ a national newspaper
   Ⓓ both A and B

4. **What is the best way to learn about WWII?**

   Ⓐ to watch movies
   Ⓑ read nonfiction texts
   Ⓒ read first-hand accounts published online
   Ⓓ all of the above

5. **You want to create a literary analysis of two novels. What is the best way to present this information?**

   Ⓐ in print
   Ⓑ electronically
   Ⓒ with pictures
   Ⓓ online

6. Your teacher tells you that you must show a visual representation of a scene from a popular book. What is the best way to do this?

   Ⓐ a movie
   Ⓑ a play
   Ⓒ an article
   Ⓓ both A and B

7. You want to ensure you will have as few problems as possible when presenting information for your final project. What medium of publication would be best to use?

   Ⓐ use print
   Ⓑ use electronics
   Ⓒ with pictures
   Ⓓ power point

8. You are writing a piece on your family's history that you would like your family in the country and in Europe to read and respond to as quickly as possible. What is the best way to do this?

   Ⓐ to write them letters and enclose the information in the letter
   Ⓑ to create a webpage for them to visit
   Ⓒ to write the history electronically and email it to them
   Ⓓ either B or C

9. You want to persuade students in your school to vote for you in the upcoming student government elections. What medium of publication would be best to do this?

   Ⓐ in your school newspaper
   Ⓑ in your local newspaper
   Ⓒ on a website
   Ⓓ through a slide show

10. What is the best place to search for a specific recipe you need in a hurry?

Circle the correct answer choice.

   Ⓐ Internet
   Ⓑ magazine
   Ⓒ newspaper
   Ⓓ recipe books

11. If your dad wants to learn how to operate a paint sprayer correctly, where is the best place to look?

(A) magazines
(B) Internet
(C) book
(D) none of these.

Chapter 3

Lesson 8: Evaluating Authors Claims

Let us understand the concept with an example.

Definitions:
1. Delineate means to portray or represent something in words. Describe with precision.
2. Evaluate means to assess or judge the significance, worth or value of something.

The Obesity Epidemic

In the United States population, 30% of adults and 17% of children are obese, according to the American Heart Association. And by 2020, 83% of men and 72% of women are expected to be overweight or obese, according to research presented at the Heart Association's scientific meeting in 2011. More than one-third (36.5%) of U.S. adults have obesity, states the Centers for Disease Control and Prevention.

Being obese has negative health and health expense disadvantages. According to the Centers for Disease Control and Prevention:

- Obesity-related conditions include heart disease, stroke, type 2 diabetes, high blood pressure, arthritis and certain types of cancer, some of the leading causes of preventable death.
- The estimated annual medical cost of obesity in the U.S. was $147 billion in 2008 U.S. dollars; the medical costs for people who are obese were $1,429 higher than those of normal weight.

What is causing so many people to be obese? More sedentary lifestyles are one factor. Sitting and watching television, driving instead of walking, not exercising enough. Nutrition is another. So much of our food is processed, which means fat and sugar are added. Also, we frequently eat portions larger than our bodies need, and we often snack between meals.

What can people do about reducing their obesity?

- Exercise: The Centers for Disease Control (CDC) recommends 2.5 hours of moderate aerobic exercise per week, along with 2 days of strength training. Americans are clearly not abiding by these minimum recommendations. But diet can have more effect on weight loss than exercise, although both are important solutions.
- An article in a fitness newsletter, published by a leading chain of physical fitness centers, emphasizes participating daily in their fitness plans that will result in losing weight, and building endurance and muscle tone.
- Nutrition: Controlling the intake of carbohydrates is one important action. Also, eating less processed food, less refined grains and bread and more vegetables are also important. You need to add lean protein to every meal and every snack, along with moderate amounts of healthy fats.

Your assignment: Write text that meets the requirements of the standard.

Here is what you might write.

The authors state the argument that there is an obesity epidemic today among adults and children in America. They cite statistics from the American Heart Association and the Centers for Disease Control and Prevention as proof. Because these two organizations are reputable and trustworthy, I believe that their arguments are relevant and accurate.

The authors also state that being obese has negative health and health expense disadvantages, and list diseases associated with obesity and the medical costs incurred by obese people. These facts were also provided by the Centers for Disease Control and Prevention. I checked with two family doctors and both agreed with the list of diseases.

Therefore, I support these facts as accurate.

The authors also speculate on the causes of the obesity epidemic, citing a more sedentary lifestyle, insufficient exercise and dietary factors. I have observed many fellow students, and the lifestyles of most fit these three causes of obesity. My parents also subscribe to a newsletter edited by a nutritionist, and it cites the same conclusions about the causes of obesity.

Lastly, the authors state what can be done to reduce obesity, citing suggestions for exercise and nutrition. These suggestions are also in line with the newsletter and with the recommendations of two trainers at my parent's physical fitness center. However, the citing of newsletter recommendations by a for-profit commercial company is not on a par with the quality of the other sources of information provided and is not specific in its detail and therefore its accuracy and relevancy cannot be easily verified.

You can scan the QR code given below or use the url to access additional EdSearch resources including videos and mobile apps related to *Evaluating Authors Claims*.

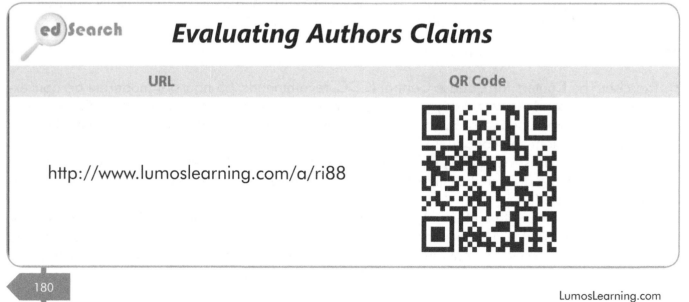

ed)Search	***Evaluating Authors Claims***
URL	**QR Code**
http://www.lumoslearning.com/a/ri88	

1. What is an author's claim?

Ⓐ his or her argument
Ⓑ the support for his or her argument
Ⓒ his or her opinion
Ⓓ the facts for the argument

2. What evidence must you look at in evaluating an author's claim?

Ⓐ the argument itself
Ⓑ the support that the author provides to back up his or her argument
Ⓒ the author's opinion about that which he or she is arguing
Ⓓ how many people support the argument.

3. What is the best way to determine the accuracy of evidence provided by the author?

Ⓐ ask somebody
Ⓑ personal experience
Ⓒ look it up on the computer, any site will do
Ⓓ do your own research

4. Which of the following is the least acceptable piece of evidence?

Ⓐ statistics
Ⓑ quotes taken from a reliable source
Ⓒ opinion
Ⓓ facts

5. Emotional appeals (appealing to the reader's emotions) should...

Ⓐ never be used
Ⓑ be used sometimes
Ⓒ should always be used
Ⓓ are never appropriate

6. The author's evidence must...

Ⓐ partially support the author's claims
Ⓑ always be taken from a primary source
Ⓒ directly support the author's claims
Ⓓ all of the above

7. Which of the following should you look at when examining the author's claim?

Ⓐ What is the author's purpose?
Ⓑ What are the sources that the author has cited?
Ⓒ Does the author provide evidence several times in the passage to strengthen his claim?
Ⓓ What is the purpose of the evidence?

Question 8-10 are based on the passage below.

The Necessity of Exercise

(1) 58 million Americans are overweight (getfitamerica.com). (2) This number is and has been on a steady rise. More and more Americans are exercising less and less. (3) The Center for Disease Control recommends 2.5 hours of moderate aerobic activity each week, along with 2 days of strength training. (4) Americans are clearly not abiding by these minimum recommendations as the numbers prove. (5) It is necessary for Americans to get more exercise in order to lead healthy lives. (6) There is no good reason for healthy people not to exercise, but there are many benefits, including maintaining a healthy weight, relieving everyday stress and lowering one's chances for certain diseases.

8. Which of the sentences above includes the author's argument?

Ⓐ 3
Ⓑ 4
Ⓒ 5
Ⓓ 6

9. According to the author's introduction, what are the points that provide evidence?

Ⓐ how much exercise people need
Ⓑ how much exercise one needs to maintain a healthy weight
Ⓒ how exercise raises everyday stress
Ⓓ how exercise increases risk for certain diseases

10. Which of the author's statements provides evidence?

Ⓐ 1
Ⓑ 2
Ⓒ 3
Ⓓ 4
Ⓔ 5

11. Determine whether the following statement is a fact, supported opinion, or unsupported opinion:

Texas is the hottest state in the United States.

Write your answer in the box given below.

```




```

12. Determine whether the following statement is a fact, supported opinion, or unsupported opinion.

Smoking should not be allowed in public places because second hand smoke is dangerous.

Write your answer in the box given below.

```




```

Chapter 3

Lesson 9: Conflicting Information

Let us understand the concept with an example.

The president of the local voter organization's point of view:

Dear members: I attended the recent town meeting organized by a local candidate for Mayor Brian Jones. As you know, he is a newcomer to local politics but is considered a threat by the current mayor and his administration because he has been criticizing them for excessive spending and a lack of cost controls. This administration has been in office for many years and is well connected in this city.

When Mr. Jones scheduled a town hall meeting here, he publicized it with posters; we also publicized it but the local paper would not. The meeting was well attended and Mr. Jones explained the plans and programs he would present to the town council for approval. That part went according to plan. But during the question and answer period, several of those in attendance, who I recognized as friends and supporters of the mayor, asked loaded questions designed to make Mr. Jones look bad; some of the questions implied actions or views on his part that I recognized were false. When any-one tried to criticize their questions, and especially tried to defend him, they were shouted down by the mayor's friends. Emotions on both sides flared to the point that a couple of fist fights started but were quickly broken up by police officers serving as security at the meeting. They disbursed the crowd but arrested a couple of Mr. Jones's friends for disturbing the peace, even though it was the mayor's friends who provoked them and started the fights.

I am appalled by the biased article by the reporter who covered this meeting for the local newspaper. I wrote a letter criticizing the article and sent it to the newspaper, but of course it was not published. The Newspaper Reporter's Point of View: Here is the article published in the paper.

Headline: *Riot erupts at Jones's town hall meeting*

Mayoral candidate Brian Jones held a town hall meeting last night that ended when police were called to quell a riot. After Jones made a speech about his political platform, a question and answer period followed. Jones either refused to answer some questions or provided answers that antago-nized members of the audience, especially answers which criticized the mayor and his administra-tion. Rather than try to maintain calm, Jones continued on with inflammatory comments that caused heated arguments between his supporters and detractors which led to several fist fights and the ar-rival of police. This is in contrast to a town hall held by the mayor two weeks ago that was conducted in a professional manner.

Publisher's Note: This example shows how different two points of view about the same event can be, depending on the outlook/biases/intents of the people telling or writing about the event. The

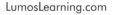

newspaper reporter and the newspaper itself had a strong negative bias toward this candidate and a strong positive bias toward the mayor. The candidate had a positive bias toward his political platform and a negative bias toward the newspaper, the mayor and the mayor's friends who attended the meeting.

Your assignment: Analyze the newspaper article and letter from the president of the local voter organization to identify conflicting information and disagreement on the facts about the town hall meeting and their interpretation by these two writers.

Here is what you might write: Besides reading the newspaper article and the letter, I obtained a recording of the meeting and used it to form the opinions in this write-up.

To meet his goal of trying to portray Mr. Jones in a negative light, the reporter used fairly accurate but highly biased reasoning in the content of his article. He chose the wording of the headline to include the word "riot" which portrayed the most negative part of the meeting; he classified what were a couple of fist fights as a riot; he inaccurately mentioned "the arrival of police" when in fact Mr. Jones had requested their presence to provide security; he characterized Mr. Jones's attempts to answer questions as evasive or antagonistic; and he accused Mr. Jones of purposely continuing these inflammatory remarks thereby causing the fistfights to occur.

No doubt those who were friends and/or supporters of the mayor thought the newspaper article was accurate and fair. But anyone else who attended and had any sense of fairness would have resented the biased slant and comments of the reporter. My conclusions about the question and answer session are the same as the president of the local voter organization. The president's views represented sound reasoning and are a much fairer, accurate and complete documentation of the meeting. The opinions of the reporter avoid mentioning the actual questions and answers discussed, which reflected the real purpose of the meeting, and therefore are less important in a reasonable discussion of the meeting.

You can scan the QR code given below or use the url to access additional EdSearch resources including videos and mobile apps related to *Conflicting Information*.

Conflicting Information

URL	QR Code
http://www.lumoslearning.com/a/ri89	

1. When you come across two conflicting viewpoints, what should you do?

Ⓐ research other sources to find out which fact is correct
Ⓑ look to see if the fact may have changed
Ⓒ examine the reliability of both writers
Ⓓ all of the above

2. Determine whether the writers are presenting conflicting information based on fact or interpretation.

Writer One: Geology is a branch of science.
Writer Two: Geology is a branch of math.

Ⓐ fact
Ⓑ opinion

3. Determine whether the writers are presenting conflicting information based on fact or interpretation.

Writer One: The president's sweater was too small.
Writer Two: The president's sweater fit him well.

Ⓐ fact
Ⓑ opinion

4. Determine whether the writers are presenting conflicting information based on fact or interpretation.

Writer One: The worst storm of the season passed through Seattle yesterday.
Writer Two: A moderate storm passed through Seattle yesterday.

Ⓐ fact
Ⓑ opinion

5. Which of the following is an example of a fact that could change?

Ⓐ someone's name
Ⓑ the location of a store
Ⓒ the area of a park
Ⓓ all of the above

6. Determine whether the conflicting information presented by the two authors is fact or interpretation.

Einstein
Albert Einstein was born on March 14th, 1879, in the German city of Ulm, without any indication that he was destined for greatness.

Einstein
Albert Einstein was born on March 15, 1879, in the city of Ulm. When he was born, people did not think he was going to be anything special.

Ⓐ fact
Ⓑ interpretation

7. Determine whether the following is fact or opinion.

Bailey is wearing blue shoes.

Write your answer in the box given below.

```



```

8. Determine whether the following is fact or opinion.

Dr. Blair studied at the most prestigious of schools, Harvard University.

Write your answer in the box given below.

```



```

9. Which of the following is not a reason for the differing interpretations between texts?

Ⓐ The authors are trying to prove different points.
Ⓑ One or both of the authors may be trying to persuade the reader to believe one way.
Ⓒ The authors are both trying to be objective.
Ⓓ Subjectivity is often apparent in writing.

10. Determine whether the following is fact or opinion.

The atrocious painting sold for $1,000,000.

Ⓐ fact
Ⓑ opinion
Ⓒ both

End of Reading: Informational Text

Answer Key and
Detailed Explanations

Chapter 3
Reading: Informational Text

Lesson 1: Making Inferences Based on Textual Evidence

Question No.	Answer	Detailed Explanations
1.	B	Answer choice B is correct. It is the definition of inference.
2.	C	Answer choice C is correct. The proper way to cite evidence from a text is to put it in quotes.
3.	D	Answer D is the correct choice. All three methods are acceptable ways of citing evidence.
4.	A	Answer choice A is correct because it asked about the discovery, not actually trying to create. Answers B and C both have to do with experimenting, not discovering.
5.	B	Answer choice B is correct because it talks about the success of the experiment. Answer choice A is about the discovery of the idea, and answer choice C is about the trial and error of the experiment.
6.	C	Answer choice C is correct because it talks about how they tried "many more experiments".
7. Part A	D	Answer choice D is correct because it describes the first experiment the Montgolfier brothers did with a silk bag and fire. Answer choice A is incorrect because it provides information about the brothers' interests. Answer choice B is incorrect because it explains how Joseph Montgolfier conceived the idea of using hot air to propel an object. The idea came from an observation, not an experiment. Answer choice C is incorrect because it refers to other experiments, not the first one.
7. Part B	B	Answer choice B is correct because it shows how Joseph observed something as small as pieces of paper floating up the chimney. Answer choice A is incorrect because it describes the materials used to build the balloon. Answer choice C is incorrect because there is no text evidence to support this answer. The passage does not indicate that the Montgolfier's village was the best place to launch their balloon. Answer choice D is incorrect because it simply gives the reader information about Josepeh Montgolfier's interest in flying.

Question No.	Answer	Detailed Explanations
8 Part A	A	Answer choice A is correct. Text evidence can be found in the last paragraph. Answer choices B, C and D are incorrect because none of these are an important aspect of terrorism. It is important here to look at connotation of each of the answer choices. Answer choice A, violence, has a negative connotation. Answer choices B, C and D all have positive connotations. The key word in the question, terrorism, has a negative connotation, so it stands to reason that the answer choice should also have a negative connotation.
8 Part B	D	Answer choice D is correct. Both choices tell the reader that terrorism is a crime against humanity or human beings. Answer choice A is incorrect because it does not explain who is targeted.
9.	C	Answer choice C is correct because it says the parents take turns, which leads readers to believe they are sharing responsibility.
10.	C	Answer C is correct. There is nothing in the text that suggests what the penguins do for survival after the chick is born.
11.	A	Answer choice A is the correct answer because the text states that, "He seemed always to be laughing..." and continued to discuss how he engaged happily with the children. Answers B and C are incorrect because there is no evidence to support those conclusions.
12.	C	Answer C is correct because the text implies that the author met the captain before the civil war began.

Lesson 2: Central Idea

Question No.	Answer	Detailed Explanations
1.	D	Answer choice D is correct. The central idea is the main idea in a piece of informational text. Answer choice A is incorrect because the central idea may not be easily located in the topic sentence. Answer choice B is incorrect because a central idea is located in informational text rather than literature which is generally fiction. Answer choice C is incorrect because an informational piece may not be about a person.
2.	D	Answer choice D is correct. The central idea is supported by details in the text; It can sometimes be found in the title of the text, and covers the whole text.
3.	D	Answer choice D is correct. When determining the main idea, it is important not to confuse the main idea with the topic (what the passage is about) and the supporting details. The supporting details work to support the main idea.
4.	B	Answer choice B is correct. The Montgolfier brothers theorized that hot air would make a balloon rise and conducted an experiment to prove their theory. Answer choice A is incorrect because the central idea is what the brothers did. It is not about why they were famous. Answer choice C is incorrect because there is nothing in the passage about the brothers losing their jobs.
5.	C	Answer choice C is correct. Emperor penguins lay their eggs in the Antarctic and take turns caring for the egg until it hatches. Answer choice A is incorrect because it is not the central idea of the text. Answer choice B is incorrect because the central idea includes both the location and caring of the egg. Answer choice D is a detail.
6.	B	Answer choice B is correct. The central idea of this piece of informational text is the study of archaeology. Answer choice A is incorrect because the central idea is not the origin of archaeology as the origins are uncertain. Answer choice C is incorrect because the text is not at all about anthropology. Answer choice D is incorrect because the text is not only about the study of the human past.
7.	A	Answer choice A is correct. Archaeologists study past human life and culture by examining the things left behind by early humans. Answer choice B is incorrect because archaeologists study humans and their culture. Answer choice C is incorrect because archaeologists study not only humans and possibly their families, but also their culture.

Question No.	Answer	Detailed Explanations
8.	A	Answer choice A is correct. The passage is mainly about the health benefits of quinoa.
9.	B	Answer choice B is correct. The central idea of the passage is about how to cook quinoa. All the details support this central idea.
10.	A	Answer choice A is correct. The main or central idea of the text is located in the first sentence. Mammoth fossils have been found in the Silicone Valley which means they roamed the area.
11. Part A	D	Answer choice D is correct. When trying to determine the central idea of a passage, it is important to read the title, to read the passage, and pay close attention to the details which should support the central idea.
11. Part B	C	Answer choice C is correct. The passage is mainly about what it takes to prepare for and run a marathon. Most of the details support the central idea of preparing for and running a marathon.
12	C	Answer choice C is correct. This passage is mainly about learning how to ride a two wheel bike. It does not give instructions, but rather describes the process.

Lesson 3: Connections and Distinctions

Question No.	Answer	Detailed Explanations
1.	B	Answer B is correct. To find distinctions is to find differences.
2.	A	Answer choice A is correct. A connection is a similarity between the reader and something he understands.
3.	D	Answer choice D is correct. They both focus on all of the above.
4.	B	Answer choice B is correct. While it can be studied in all the places, a museum is the best place to see the many different examples of it.
5.	A	Answer choice A is correct because the text points out one distinction between the types of quinoa.
6. Part A	D	Answer D is correct. There are many ways that marathons are different than other competitions.
6. Part B	A	Answer A is correct. The article mentions in the beginning that it's not competitive; therefore, answers B and C are incorrect.
7.	B	Answer B is correct. The similarity between this ad and many other ads is the small print.
8.	C	Answer C is correct. The idiom "in the soup" means in a bad situation.
9.	A	Answer A is the correct answer because the narrator says he has arrived at the war.

LumosLearning.com

Lesson 4: Determining Meaning of Words

Question No.	Answer	Detailed Explanations
1.	B	Answer choice B is correct. A connotation is the meaning of the word with regard to its use in context.
2.	A	Denotation means the actual meaning of a word. In other words, it is the dictionary definition of the word. Hence, answer choice A is correct.
3.	C	Answer choice C is correct. To trek means to walk a long-distance.
4.	A	Answer choice A is correct. The way a field turns into a profession is professionalization.
5.	A	Answer choice A is correct. When one does something systematically, he follows a very specific procedure.
6. Part A	C	Answer choice C is correct. To overexert means to do more than your body can handle.
6. Part B	A	Answer choice A is correct. In the spur of moment means taking immediate decisions without thinking. In this context also it means that training for marathon requires determination, hard work and commitment and it cannot be something that can be done instantaneously.
7.	B	Answer choice B is correct. The phrase is meant to set up a serious tone so readers understand the complexity of running a marathon.
8. Part A	A	Answer choice A is correct. Readers can assume they are ranks in the military because the narrator is on a military ship traveling to a battle.
8. Part B	A	Answer choice A is the correct answer. The various references to the theater imply that he is comparing a theater to war. Hence, it is an implied metaphor.

Lesson 5: Analyzing Structures in Text

Question No.	Answer	Detailed Explanations
1.	D	Answer choice D is correct. When trying to determine the structure of a piece of text, it is important to look at the genre of writing, the author's purpose and the types of transition words use.
2.	B	Answer choice B is correct. Unlike nonfiction, a fictional story will have a plot.
3.	B	Answer choice B is correct. Words such as "unlike", "as well as", "on the other hand", and "in contrast", are all indicative of a comparison.
4.	A	Answer choice A is correct. Adding an introductory and concluding paragraph would turn this passage into an essay. Remember an essay must have an introduction, body, and conclusion.
5.	A	Answer choice A is correct. The key words are first, soon afterwards, after this, and eventually. These words indicate a sequence of event.
6.	C	Answer choice C is correct. The passage was written to describe the egg laying routine of the Emperor Penguin. There are no clue words to lead the reader to believe there is any sequencing, comparing/contrasting, or cause/effect included in the passage.
7.	D	Answer choice D is correct. The author uses this introductory sentence to give the reader some background information on archaeology and what the article is about.
8.	A	Answer choice A is correct. This sentence is included to inform the reader why archaeology is important. It is important to note that authors have a reason for every piece of text they include in any piece of writing.
9.	D	Answer choice D is correct. This sentence is included so that readers will understand that archaeology has been happening for a very long time.
10.	A	Answer choice A is correct. These two sentences have a positive connotation in an effort to leave the reader with a positive opinion about running.
11. Part A	D	Answer choice D is correct. All three statements reflect differences, or contrasts, in the text.
11. Part B	A	Answer choice A is correct. The eagle is a confident flyer, but the seagull is afraid to leave the ledge. Answer choices B, C, and D are incorrect.
11. Part C	B	Answer choice B is correct. Neither passage discusses the process of flying.

Question No.	Answer	Detailed Explanations
12. Part A	B	Answer choice B is correct. Both passages are about learning more about the past. Answer choices A, C, and D are incorrect.
12. Part B	A	Answer choice A is correct. Both passages discuss human life in the past. "Archaeology" is about the study of past life and "History of Mankind" is about the events in history and how we learn about them today. Answer choices B, C, and D are incorrect.

Lesson 6: Author's Point of View

Question No.	Answer	Detailed Explanations
1.	B	Answer choice B is correct. Point of view is the perspective from which the story or text is written.
2.	A	Answer choice A is correct. First person point of view is written from the narrator's point of view and will include personal pronouns.
3.	A	Answer choice A is correct. When the narrator is in the story, in other words, he or she is telling the story, the story is being told from the first person point of view.
4.	A	Answer choice A is correct. A third person omniscient narrator is not included as a character in the story. The third person omniscient narrator knows the thoughts and feelings of all the characters in the story.
5.	A	Answer choice A is correct. A third person limited narrator is not a character in the story. The third person limited narrator only knows the thoughts and feelings of one character. This is unlike the third person omniscient narrator who knows the thoughts and feelings of all the characters.
6.	C	Answer choice C is correct. The most reliable narrator is the third person omniscient narrator because he or she knows the thoughts and feelings of all the characters.
7.	A	Answer choice A is correct. When the narrator is in the story, in other words, he or she is telling the story, the story is being told from the first person point of view.
8.	A	Answer choice A is correct. This excerpt is written in first person point of view. Note the use of the personal pronoun "I."
9.	D	Answer choice D is correct. If the research was done by a company with ties to chocolate, chances are the data was collected or interpreted in a way to make it appear that eating chocolate is beneficial. It is best to rely on research conducted by independent research facilities.
10.	C	Answer choice C is correct. This statement was written to convince a reader that the best place to buy a car is at Bruce's on Route 12. It is likely that someone who works for or was contracted with Bruce's wrote this statement.
11.	B	Answer choice B is correct. Advertisements are created to convince readers or viewers to purchase the item or items being advertised.

Lesson 7: Publishing Mediums

Question No.	Answer	Detailed Explanations
1.	D	Answer choice D is correct. When reading text online, it is important to evaluate the source of the information, author's purpose, and date of the source.
2.	A	Answer choice A is correct. The fastest place to publish and get public responses is on a webpage on the internet.
3.	D	Answer choice D is correct. The best place, and likeliest to reach the most readers, is via a teen magazine AND a website targeting teen audiences.
4.	D	Answer choice D is correct. Remember, though, that movies will take liberties with facts. Primary sources will give accurate information, but you should incorporate nonfiction text in with your research, as well. Using as many data sources as possible in research will allow for a more thorough paper.
5.	A	Answer choice A is correct. The best way to present a literary analysis is in print, like an essay.
6.	D	Answer choice D is correct. The best way to show a visual representation of a book is via a short movie you film yourself or a play you create yourself.
7.	A	Answer choice A is correct. Using electronics when presenting means always having to depend on something electronic to work. A paper presentation never fails to load or suffer from an unavoidable systems crash.
8.	D	Answer choice D is correct. Creating something online would be the fastest way to disseminate the information. Writing a letter and mailing it would be more personal, but if time is of the essence, then using the electronic route is by far less time consuming.
9.	A	Answer choice A is correct. The best place to campaign for a school office is in the school newspaper.
10.	A	Answer choice A is correct. If you need a specific recipe in a hurry, the fastest place to get the information is by doing a web search on the Internet. You can use specific terms which should then navigate you to the appropriate sites.
11.	B	Answer choice B is correct. To get immediate information or feedback, the Internet is the best resource. However, it is important to always check the source of your search to ensure what you are reading or watching is accurate. Remember anyone can put anything on the Internet.

Lesson 8: Evaluating Authors Claims

Question No.	Answer	Detailed Explanations
1.	A	Answer choice A is correct. An author's claim is something an author is trying to convince you of that hasn't been proven. Once proven, it becomes a fact.
2.	B	Answer choice B is correct. When evaluating an author's claim, you must be a careful reader of the support he or she provides for the claim.
3.	D	Answer choice D is correct. If you are in doubt of an author's claim, do some research on your own. Look up information on the internet using sites that are dependable or use other research tools such as books and encyclopedias.
4.	C	Answer choice C is correct. An author who bases his or her claim primarily on opinion does not provide acceptable proof. Opinions are the least acceptable tools to use when making a claim.
5.	B	Answer choice B is correct. Emotional appeals should be used sparingly because, while they can be effective, they tend to be weak.
6.	C	Answer choice C is correct. Evidence used to support an author's claim should always be supportive of the claim.
7.	D	Answer choice D is correct. When examining an author's claim, you should always try to determine his/her purpose and validity of the sources cited. Is the author trying to sell you something or simply provide information? Be a careful reader.
8.	D	Answer choice D is correct. The author's claim is at the end of the paragraph.
9.	B	Answer choice B is correct. Based on the introduction, sentence one and two, the reader should expect to read about how much exercise is needed to maintain a healthy weight.
10.	A	Answer choice A is correct. This is statistical evidence. As a careful reader, you should consider navigating to the website mentioned to verify this statistic. Additionally, a careful reader will check the sources used to gather this data.
11	Unsupported opinion	While people who live in Texas may claim this to be true, this is an unsupported opinion.
12	Supported opinion	This is supported opinion as there is data to back up the claim.

Lesson 9: Conflicting Information

Question No.	Answer	Detailed Explanations
1.	D	Answer choice D is correct. When faced with conflicting information, it is a good idea to do further research. Remember, facts can sometimes change. For example, advances in medicine can change what we believe are facts about health. Additionally, checking the credibility of the authors is a good idea.
2.	A	Answer choice A is correct. Geology is a science and this can be verified or proven.
3.	B	Answer choice B is correct. Whether or not the president's sweater is too small is an opinion. Some people may prefer a snugger fit than others. The conflicting information is based on opinion.
4.	B	Answer choice B is correct. The ferocity of a storm is an opinion; therefore, the conflicting interpretation is opinion.
5.	D	Answer choice D is correct. All three choices could be proven, but could also change. When a woman gets married, she may choose to take her husband's last name; thus, her name changes. If a store chooses not to renew its lease and moves to a cheaper location, it's former location, which could be proven, is no longer valid. The same goes for a park. If a park's original location isn't large enough to accommodate an extension, its location may be moved.
6.	A	Answer choice A is correct. Birthdates are verifiable; therefore, the conflicting information is based on fact. Additionally, the statements of what a Einstein might be is documented fact.
7.	Fact	The color of Bailey's shoes can be proven.
8.	Both fact and opinion	There is both a fact and an opinion in the statement. Dr. Blair's university training can be verified, therefore, it is a fact. Whether or not Harvard is the most prestigious university is an opinion. Be careful you do not let a sentence with mixed information misguide you. Even in nonfiction, authors have bias.
9.	C	Answer choice C is correct. When authors write, they have a purpose in mind. Many times their interpretation of data is skewed to fit the intentions of the author.
10.	C	Answer choice C is correct. Evidently the person who purchased the painting for $1,000,000 (which is verifiable) did not believe the painting to be atrocious. Therefore, the statement included both a fact and an opinion.

Chapter 4 - Language

The objective of the Language standards is to ensure that the student is able to accurately use grade appropriate general academic and domain specific words and phrases related to Grade 8.

To help student master the necessary skills, we encourage the student to go through the resources available online on EdSearch to gain an in depth understanding of these concepts. EdSearch page for each lesson can be accessed with the help of the url or the QR code provided.

Chapter 4

Lesson 1: Adjectives and Adverbs

You can scan the QR code given below or use the url to access additional EdSearch resources including videos and mobile apps related to *Adjectives and Adverbs*.

---

ed Search

Adjectives and Adverbs

URL	QR Code
http://www.lumoslearning.com/a/l81	

---

1. What is an adjective?

Ⓐ a word that modifies (describes) a verb
Ⓑ a word that modifies (describes) a noun in a sentence
Ⓒ a word that modifies (describes) a sentence
Ⓓ a word that modifies (describes) descriptive words

2. What is an adverb?

Ⓐ a word that modifies (describes) adjectives
Ⓑ a word that modifies (describes) verbs
Ⓒ a word that modifies (describes) adverbs
Ⓓ a word that modifies (describes) descriptive words

3. A lot of people have trouble with the words "good" and "well". See if you can use them correctly in the following sentences by choosing the correct words in correct sequence.

a) I am _____.
b) Dinner was really _____ .
c) They are _____ baseball players.
d) You play really_____.

Ⓐ well, well, good, good
Ⓑ well, good, well, good
Ⓒ well, good, good, good
Ⓓ well, good, good, well

4. Choose the correct adjective/ adverb sequence for the following sentences.

a) I stayed home from school because when I woke up this morning I felt (bad/ badly).
b) I did (good/ well) on my science test.
c) I answered the question as (honest/ honestly) as I could.

Ⓐ bad, good, honest
Ⓑ badly, well, honestly
Ⓒ bad, well, honestly
Ⓓ badly, well, honestly

5. Which choice is the adverb that correctly completes the following sentence?

I am very fond of Miss Jenkins; she teaches very _____.

Ⓐ patiently
Ⓑ patient
Ⓒ patience
Ⓓ patiented

6. Which word is the adverb in the following sentence?

She picked up the sweet baby very carefully.

Ⓐ sweet
Ⓑ very
Ⓒ carefully
Ⓓ both B and C

7. Which word in the following sentence is an adjective?

After a long afternoon at practice, I am tired, hungry, and dirty.

Ⓐ tired
Ⓑ hungry
Ⓒ dirty
Ⓓ all of the above

8. What is the adjective in the following sentence?

The pretty girl brushed her hair before she went to bed.

Ⓐ pretty
Ⓑ girl
Ⓒ brushed
Ⓓ hair

9. What is the adverb in the following sentence?

He slowly walked towards the elevator on his floor.

Ⓐ slowly
Ⓑ elevator
Ⓒ floor
Ⓓ walked

10. What is the adverb in the following sentence?

Jimmy sadly walked away after having lost a tough game of baseball.

- Ⓐ sadly
- Ⓑ lost
- Ⓒ tough
- Ⓓ baseball

11. What is the adjective in the following sentence?

Greg bounced around the playground, happily playing on his new slide.

Write your answer in the box given below.

```
┌─────────────────────────────────────────┐
│                                          │
│                                          │
│                                          │
└─────────────────────────────────────────┘
```

12. What is the adverb in the following sentence?

Greg bounced around the playground, happily playing on his new slide.

Write your answer in the box given below.

```
┌─────────────────────────────────────────┐
│                                          │
│                                          │
│                                          │
└─────────────────────────────────────────┘
```

13. What is the adjective in the following sentence?

Bob's mother laughed when she saw her blonde son lazily lounging by the pool.

Write your answer in the box given below.

```
┌─────────────────────────────────────────┐
│                                          │
│                                          │
│                                          │
└─────────────────────────────────────────┘
```

14. What is the adverb in the following sentence?

Bob's mother laughed when she saw her blonde son lazily lounging by the pool.

Write your answer in the box given below.

15. What is the adjective in the following sentence?

Although her husband claims their dog is one of the smartest breeds, Caroline was fairly certain he is mistaken.

Write your answer in the box given below.

16. What is the adverb in the following sentence?

Although her husband claims their dog is one of the smartest breeds, Caroline was fairly certain he is mistaken.

Write your answer in the box given below.

Chapter 4

Lesson 2: Subject-Verb Agreement

You can scan the QR code given below or use the url to access additional EdSearch resources including videos and mobile apps related to *Subject-Verb Agreement*.

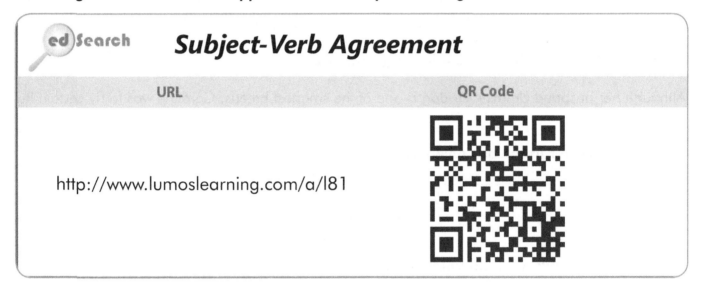

URL	QR Code
http://www.lumoslearning.com/a/l81	

1. Select the correct verb form to agree with the subject in the following sentence.

Either the teacher or the principal _____ going to contact you.

    Ⓐ are
    Ⓑ is
    Ⓒ not
    Ⓓ never

2. Which sentence shows the correct subject-verb agreement?

a) Neither the cat nor the dogs have been fed.
b) Neither the cat nor the dogs has been fed.

    Ⓐ a
    Ⓑ b

3. Select the correct verb form to agree with the subject in the following sentence.

_____ my sister or my parents going to pick me up?

    Ⓐ Is
    Ⓑ Are
    Ⓒ you're
    Ⓓ watching

4. Select the correct verb form to agree with the subject in the following sentence.

Some of the answers _____ to have been wrong.

    Ⓐ seems
    Ⓑ seem
    Ⓒ just
    Ⓓ really

5. Select the correct verb form to agree with the subject in the following sentence.

Mary and Joe _____ going to the dance together.

    Ⓐ is
    Ⓑ are
    Ⓒ wouldn't
    Ⓓ walking

6. Select the correct verb form to agree with the subject in the following sentence.

The highlighter or the marker _____ in the side drawer.

    Ⓐ is
    Ⓑ are
    Ⓒ rolling
    Ⓓ writing

7. Select the correct verb form to agree with the subject in the following sentence.

The student, along with his parents, _____ coming to the talent show.

    Ⓐ is
    Ⓑ are
    Ⓒ never
    Ⓓ walking

8. Select the correct verb form to agree with the subject in the following sentence.

Neither the tomatoes nor the mint in my garden _____ begun to grow.

    Ⓐ has
    Ⓑ have
    Ⓒ it doesn't matter which verb form is used

9. Identify the subject(s) in the following sentence.

Some of the food is spoiled because it was sitting in the sun too long.

    Ⓐ The food
    Ⓑ some and food
    Ⓒ sitting in the sun
    Ⓓ food is spoiled

10. Identify the subject(s) in the following sentence.

Either the teacher or the principal is going to contact you regarding your grades.

    Ⓐ either the teacher
    Ⓑ contact you
    Ⓒ Either the teacher or the principal
    Ⓓ regarding your grades

11. Fill in the blank with the correct verb.

The boys and girls _____ very excited about the trip next week.

12. Fill in the blank with the correct verb.

The boys and Sally _____ going skiing together.

Chapter 4

Lesson 3: Pronouns

You can scan the QR code given below or use the url to access additional EdSearch resources including videos and mobile apps related to *Pronouns*.

ed Search   *Pronouns*

URL	QR Code
http://www.lumoslearning.com/a/l81	

1. Select the pronoun that will best fit into the following sentence.

The instructor put _____ students at ease when he said no one would fail.

- Ⓐ we
- Ⓑ his
- Ⓒ their
- Ⓓ them

2. Select the pronoun that will best fit into the following sentence.

My grandmother and _____ enjoyed spending the day together at the fair.

- Ⓐ I
- Ⓑ myself
- Ⓒ me
- Ⓓ my

3. Select the pronoun that will best fit into the following sentence.

_____ students laughed so loudly that the class next door was distracted from their lesson.

- Ⓐ They
- Ⓑ Us
- Ⓒ Them
- Ⓓ Those

4. To what does the demonstrative pronoun "that" refer to in the following sentences?

I saw a terrible skateboarding accident down the street. That was awful.

- Ⓐ The skateboarding accident
- Ⓑ Being in the street
- Ⓒ Seeing the skateboard down the street
- Ⓓ The awful thing

5. Choose the correct pronoun in the sentence below.

The woman (who/whom) is wearing the red dress would like to make a reservation.

- Ⓐ who
- Ⓑ whom

6. Choose the correct pronoun in the sentence below.

With (who/whom) were you speaking?

Ⓐ who
Ⓑ whom

7. Choose the correct pronoun in the sentence below.

(Who/whom) can you send to help us?

Ⓐ who
Ⓑ whom

8. Identify the pronoun in the following sentence.

Martha's sister wanted her siblings to give her something exciting for her birthday.

Ⓐ Martha
Ⓑ sister
Ⓒ birthday
Ⓓ her

9. To what does the demonstrative pronoun "those" refer to in the following sentences?

Since I was going to be carting furniture up and downstairs, I put on my favorite pair of shoes. My daughter looked me over once and said, "You're wearing those?"

Ⓐ the shirt
Ⓑ the shoes
Ⓒ the shorts
Ⓓ the whole look

10. Identify the pronoun in the following sentence.

Mike's mother told him that the trash needed to be taken out sooner rather than later.

Ⓐ Mike
Ⓑ mother
Ⓒ him
Ⓓ trash

11. Fill in the blank with the correct pronoun:

Julie couldn't believe _____ friend didn't listen to _____ advice.

12. Fill in the blank with the correct pronouns:

Michael noticed that _____ buddy was wearing the same shirt as _____.

Lesson 4: Phrases and Clauses

You can scan the QR code given below or use the url to access additional EdSearch resources including videos and mobile apps related to *Phrases and Clauses.*

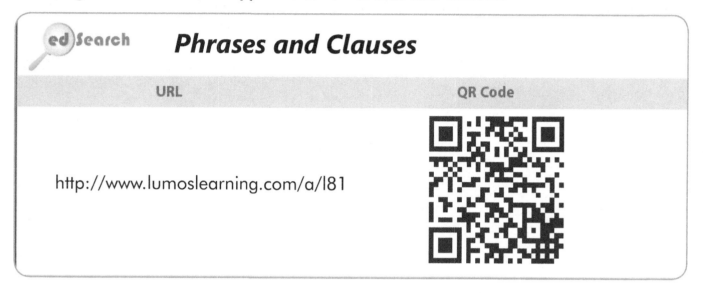

ed)Search

Phrases and Clauses

URL	QR Code
http://www.lumoslearning.com/a/l81	

1. Which of the following sentences is an infinitive phrase?

Ⓐ To make my birthday special, my family threw me a surprise party.
Ⓑ My teacher, the one wearing the blue dress, gave us our final yesterday.
Ⓒ Mary waited at the bus stop, hoping another would come by.
Ⓓ On the side of the road, we saw a perfectly good couch.

2. Identify whether the following is an independent or subordinate clause.

The boy cried.

3. Identify whether the following is an independent or subordinate clause.

When I jumped down

Ⓐ independent
Ⓑ subordinate

4. Identify whether the following is an independent or subordinate clause.

He stopped.

Ⓐ independent
Ⓑ subordinate

5. Identify whether the following is an independent or subordinate clause:

If he had run

Ⓐ independent
Ⓑ subordinate

6. What is an independent clause?

Ⓐ It has a subject and verb and can be a complete sentence by itself.
Ⓑ It has a subject and a verb but cannot stand by itself as a complete sentence.
Ⓒ It is only part of a sentence.
Ⓓ It does not have either a subject or a verb and is therefore not a sentence.

7. What is a subordinate clause?

Ⓐ It has a subject and verb and can be a complete sentence by itself.
Ⓑ It has a subject and a verb but cannot stand by itself as a complete sentence.
Ⓒ It is only two words.
Ⓓ It does not have either a subject or a verb and is therefore not a sentence.

8. What is an adjective phrase?

Ⓐ It modifies a noun.
Ⓑ It modifies a verb, adverb, or adjective.
Ⓒ It tells "what kind" or "which one".
Ⓓ both A and C

9. What does the following sentence contain?

The dog with the bright blue collar jumped on me.

Ⓐ an adverb phrase
Ⓑ an adjective phrase

10. Identify the type of phrase in the following sentence?

Because she did not clean her room, Bethany lost her iPad privileges for the weekend.

Ⓐ adjective
Ⓑ adverb
Ⓒ gerund
Ⓓ noun

11. Is the clause in the following sentence independent or subordinate?

My son, an accomplished fisherman, caught the largest fish in the tournament.

Chapter 4

Lesson 5: Verbals

You can scan the QR code given below or use the url to access additional EdSearch resources including videos and mobile apps related to *Verbals*.

ed Search **Verbals**

URL	QR Code
http://www.lumoslearning.com/a/l81	

1. What is the definition of a verbal?

   Ⓐ a spoken form of communication
   Ⓑ forms of verbs that function as other parts of speech
   Ⓒ a very descriptive word
   Ⓓ a word that contains a sound

2. Which verbals function as adjectives?

   Ⓐ infinitives
   Ⓑ participles
   Ⓒ gerunds
   Ⓓ nouns

3. Which verbals function as nouns?

   Ⓐ infinitives
   Ⓑ gerunds
   Ⓒ participles
   Ⓓ verbs

4. Which verbals function as nouns, adjectives, or adverbials?

   Ⓐ gerunds
   Ⓑ infinitives
   Ⓒ participles
   Ⓓ verbs

5. Which of the following sentences uses the verbal known as an infinitive?

   Ⓐ Looking back through the photo albums gives me fond memories of the time I spent in Italy with my grandparents.
   Ⓑ My cousins like to visit the beach when they come to our house, since they live in the mountains.
   Ⓒ She was terminated from her job because she was never on time.
   Ⓓ Kelsey received the best present for her birthday

6. Which of the following sentences uses the verbal known as a gerund?

   Ⓐ Sarah enjoys hiking on the local trails.
   Ⓑ My older sister is going to go off to college at the end of summer.
   Ⓒ I really enjoy giving special gifts to my friends and family members on their birthdays.
   Ⓓ My favorite time of the year is summer vacation.

7. Which of the following sentences uses the verbal known as a participle?

(A) After school, my friends and I are going to go to the mall.
(B) The soup boiling on the stove smells delicious.
(C) I walked my dog around the block.
(D) My friends are coming over after school today.

8. What part of speech is the verbal taking in the following sentence?

The sparkling ring is beautiful.

(A) noun
(B) adjective
(C) verb
(D) adverb

9. What part of speech is the verbal taking in the following sentence?

The bird was sleeping in its nest.

(A) noun
(B) adjective
(C) verb
(D) adverb

10. What part of speech is the verbal taking in the following sentence?

The sound of running water became louder and louder.

(A) noun
(B) adjective
(C) verb
(D) adverb

11. What part of speech is the verbal taking in the following sentence?

Jogging is my least favorite cardio activity.

Circle the correct answer choice.

    Ⓐ noun
    Ⓑ adjective
    Ⓒ adverbial

12. What part of speech is the verbal taking in the following sentence?

The laughing children were having a fabulous time on the Ferris wheel.

Circle the correct answer choice.

    Ⓐ noun
    Ⓑ adjective
    Ⓒ verb

Chapter 4

Lesson 6: Capitalization

You can scan the QR code given below or use the url to access additional EdSearch resources including videos and mobile apps related to *Capitalization*.

ed)Search

Capitalization

URL	QR Code
http://www.lumoslearning.com/a/l82	

1. Which of the following words should always be capitalized?

Ⓐ Grandmother
Ⓑ the first word of every sentence
Ⓒ names of subjects, such as Science
Ⓓ all of the above

2. What is the correct way to capitalize "grandmother" in the below sentences?

a. We should go visit (grandmother/ Grandmother) today.
b. This weekend we went to see my (grandmother/ Grandmother).

Ⓐ grandmother, grandmother
Ⓑ Grandmother, grandmother
Ⓒ grandmother, Grandmother
Ⓓ None of the above

3. Which words need to be capitalized in the following sentences?

next week, my report on wwll is due. I have an awful lot of studying and research to complete; it looks like I will be spending a lot of time at the Joann Darcy public library.

Ⓐ next
Ⓑ wwll
Ⓒ public library
Ⓓ all of the above

4. How many capitalization errors are in the following passage?

Every morning I have the same routine. First, i make my bed and fluff my pillows. Next, i head to the shower. I always pick my clothes out the night before so that I don't spend too much time on deciding what to wear. Then, I run downstairs to eat cheerios, my favorite cereal, and finally, I brush my teeth. On the way out of the door, I grab my backpack, which hangs on a hook by the front door, and hug my mom goodbye before I rush off to meet the bus.

Ⓐ 2
Ⓑ 3
Ⓒ 4
Ⓓ none

5. Which of the following must always be capitalized?

Ⓐ names of states
Ⓑ names of seasons
Ⓒ every word in the title of a work of literature
Ⓓ none of the above

6. Which of the following are always capitalized?

Ⓐ names of holidays
Ⓑ languages
Ⓒ days of the week
Ⓓ all of the above

7. Which of the following sentences contains a capitalization error?

Ⓐ I can't wait for Spring!
Ⓑ Spring has finally arrived.
Ⓒ I titled my narrative, The Best Spring Break Ever.
Ⓓ None of the above.

8. Which is the correct way to capitalize the word, "mayor" in a sentence?

Ⓐ This weekend, I had the opportunity to meet Mayor Sandburg of Gantsville.
Ⓑ This weekend, I had the opportunity to meet Carl Sandburg, the mayor of Gantsville.
Ⓒ Both of the above.
Ⓓ None of the above.

9. Which is correct way to capitalize the abbreviation for the state of California?

Ⓐ Ca
Ⓑ Calif
Ⓒ CA
Ⓓ Cali

10. Is it correct to capitalize the first letter of a quote when it is in the middle of a sentence, as in the following example?

Samuel Montgomery once said, "Every once in a while we must evaluate ourselves, for only with self reflection can we reach perfection."

Ⓐ Yes
Ⓑ No

11. Which word should be capitalized in the following sentence?

Betty and I are going to france for spring break.
Write your answer in the box given below.

```
┌────────────────────────────────────────────┐
│                                            │
│                                            │
└────────────────────────────────────────────┘
```

12. What should be capitalized in the following sentence?

One of my favorite plays is romeo and juliet.
Write your answer in the box given below.

```
┌────────────────────────────────────────────┐
│                                            │
│                                            │
└────────────────────────────────────────────┘
```

Chapter 4

Lesson 7: Punctuation

You can scan the QR code given below or use the url to access additional EdSearch resources including videos and mobile apps related to *Punctuation*.

ed Search	**Punctuation**	
URL		**QR Code**
http://www.lumoslearning.com/a/l82		

1. Determine which sentence shows the correct usage of the comma.

Ⓐ Please pick up glue, scissors, and construction paper.
Ⓑ The names of my pets are, Max, Goldie, and Emily.
Ⓒ I looked everywhere for my keys, including the trash and under the couch and in the kitchen.
Ⓓ My father Jim and my mother Martha enjoy camping dancing and jogging together.

2. The following sentences is missing one or more commas. Determine which example shows the correct comma placement.

Ⓐ My uncle, who is an incredibly talented actor encouraged me to try out in the talent show.
Ⓑ My uncle who is an incredibly talented actor, encouraged me to try out in the talent show.
Ⓒ My uncle, who is an incredibly talented actor, encouraged me to try out for the talent show.
Ⓓ My uncle who, is an incredibly talented actor, encouraged me to try out for the talent show.

3. How would you fix the following sentence?

After you have finished taking out the trash you may watch your favorite show.

Ⓐ After you have finished, taking out the trash you may watch your favorite show.
Ⓑ After you have finished taking out the trash, you may watch your favorite show.
Ⓒ After, you have finished taking out the trash you may watch your favorite show.
Ⓓ After you have finished taking out the trash you may watch your favorite show.

4. Select the sentence that shows the correct usage of the semicolon.

Ⓐ Her uncle is coming to visit; and he is traveling from far away.
Ⓑ This summer we went camping; always fun.
Ⓒ I enjoy the arts; I especially love to paint with watercolors.
Ⓓ I enjoy the arts and; I especially love to paint with watercolors.

5. Determine which sentence shows the correct usage of the apostrophe.

Ⓐ That girl is Mrs. Jones's daughter.
Ⓑ That girl is Mrs. Jones' daughter.
Ⓒ That girl is Mrs. Jones daughter.
Ⓓ That girl is Mrs'. Jones' daughter.

6. Which of the following is the plural possessive form of "mice"?

Ⓐ mices
Ⓑ mices'
Ⓒ mice's
Ⓓ mouse's

7. Determine which sentence shows the correct usage of the apostrophe and comma.

Ⓐ I couldn't wait to see Katie's new dog, Alfie.
Ⓑ I couldn't wait to see Katies new dog, Alfie.
Ⓒ I couldn't wait to see Katie new dog Alfie.
Ⓓ I couldn't wait to see Katie's new dog Alfie.

8. Which of the following does the contraction "would've" take the place of?

Ⓐ would of
Ⓑ would have
Ⓒ will of
Ⓓ will have

9. What is the best way to fix the following sentence?

Yvettes invitation for Brendas surprise party said to bring the following things to the party cupcakes soda and a gag gift

10. Where would you include a dash in the following sentence?

Kasey had not taken the time to read the directions no wonder the bookcase fell apart after an hour!

Lesson 8: Ellipsis

You can scan the QR code given below or use the url to access additional EdSearch resources including videos and mobile apps related to *Ellipsis*.

URL	QR Code
http://www.lumoslearning.com/a/l82	

1. Which of the following symbols is an ellipsis?

Ⓐ ...
Ⓑ ;
Ⓒ :
Ⓓ --

2. What is the purpose of an ellipsis?

Ⓐ To indicate text has been omitted
Ⓑ To add extra significance to sentence
Ⓒ To end sentence powerfully
Ⓓ Both A and B

3. An ellipsis can be used to create suspense.

Ⓐ True
Ⓑ False

4. You cannot use an ellipsis at the beginning of a sentence.

Ⓐ True
Ⓑ False

5. If an ellipsis comes at the end of the sentence, add it after the period for a total of 4 dots, so it looks like this....
Mark "True" or "False"

Ⓐ True
Ⓑ False

6. The following is the correct use of an ellipsis.
I don't know...I'm not sure...What do you think?
Mark "True" or "False"

Ⓐ True
Ⓑ False

7. When is it appropriate to use an ellipsis?

Ⓐ when citing evidence from a text that is long
Ⓑ when researching and information is at the beginning and end of a paragraph
Ⓒ when trying to be concise and only use necessary facts
Ⓓ all of the above

8. What is the appropriate way to cite the following information?

58 million Americans are overweight (getfitamerica.com). This number is and has been on a steady rise. More and more Americans are exercising less and less. The Center for Disease Control recommends 2.5 hours of moderate aerobic activity each week, along with 2 days of strength training. Americans are clearly not abiding by these minimum recommendations as the numbers prove. It is necessary for Americans to get more exercise in order to lead a healthy life. There is no good reason for healthy people not to exercise but there are many benefits including maintaining a healthy weight, relieving everyday stress and lowering one's chances for certain diseases.

Ⓐ After examining the facts, it is evident that Americans need exercise. A recent article explained, "58 million Americans are overweight-- It is necessary for Americans to get more exercise in order to lead a healthy life."

Ⓑ After examining the facts, it is evident that Americans need exercise. A recent article explained, "58 million Americans are overweight: It is necessary for Americans to get more exercise in order to lead a healthy life."

Ⓒ After examining the facts, it is evident that Americans need exercise. A recent article explained, "58 million Americans are overweight… It is necessary for Americans to get more exercise in order to lead a healthy life."

Ⓓ None of the above

9. The following sentence properly uses an ellipsis?

"…[T]here are many benefits including maintaining a healthy weight, relieving everyday stress and lowering one's chances for certain diseases."

Ⓐ True
Ⓑ False

10. What is the appropriate way to cite the following information?

It was a dark and stormy night. The people of Cape Hatteras hid indoors. Mrs. Peabody shivered, hoping the hurricane would not visit and wondering whether she would be able to fall asleep. Across the street, Mr. Greer kept watch from the high tower of his attic, certain that the hurricane would strike soon.

Ⓐ The newspaper reported on the hurricane. The writer explained, "The people of Cape Hatteras hid indoors. … Mr. Greer kept watch from the high tower of his attic…."

Ⓑ The newspaper reported on the hurricane. The writer explained, "The people of Cape Hatteras hid indoors; Mr. Greer kept watch from the high tower of his attic…."

Ⓒ The newspaper reported on the hurricane. The writer explained, "The people of Cape Hatteras hid indoors. Mr. Greer kept watch from the high tower of his attic…."

Ⓓ None of the above

Chapter 4

Lesson 9: Spelling

You can scan the QR code given below or use the url to access additional EdSearch resources including videos and mobile apps related to *Spelling*.

ed Search

Spelling

URL	QR Code
http://www.lumoslearning.com/a/l82	

1. **What are homophones or homonyms?**

   Ⓐ the scientific name for humans
   Ⓑ two or more words that are pronounced the same but have different meanings
   Ⓒ two or more words that mean the opposite
   Ⓓ none of the above

2. **Choose the words that correctly complete the following sentence. Make sure that you pick the answer that shows the words in the correct sequence, as they would appear in the sentence.**

   I accidentally _____ the ball _____ the living room window.

   Ⓐ through/ threw
   Ⓑ threw/ though
   Ⓒ threw/ through
   Ⓓ through/through

3. **Choose the words that correctly complete the following sentence. Make sure that you pick the answer that shows the words in the correct sequence, as they would appear in the sentence.**

   My cousins are so silly. _____ always running late because _____ are no alarm clocks in _____ house to wake them up in the morning.

   Ⓐ There, they're, their
   Ⓑ They're, there, their
   Ⓒ Their, there, they're
   Ⓓ There, there, there

4. **Which word(s) in the following passage are misspelled?**

   I was trying to acommodate all of my friends. They were all coming to my birthday party, and I wanted to insure that I had the coolest prizes for the winners of the games; I made sure their were enough prizes for everyone.

   Ⓐ acommodate
   Ⓑ insure
   Ⓒ their
   Ⓓ all of the above

5. Which word(s) in the following passage are misspelled?

The night of the dance was amazing. My parents rented a limousine for my friends and me. When it pulled up, the chaufer held the door open for us and we climbed in, one after the other. We wore the fanciest dresses that we could find and wore the sparkliest accessories.

- (A) limousine
- (B) chaufer
- (C) sparkliest
- (D) accessories

6. What is the correct spelling for the misspelled or misused word in the sentence below?

I couldn't weight to go to the movies.

- (A) wait
- (B) wieght
- (C) moovies
- (D) moveis

7. What is the correct spelling for the misspelled word in the sentence below?

I had to write a buisness letter for English class.

- (A) right
- (B) business
- (C) bisness
- (D) english

8. What is the correct spelling for the misspelled word in the sentence below?

Usually, I like to read on the beach; however, occationally I will swim.

- (A) usualy
- (B) beech
- (C) occasionally
- (D) how ever

9. What is the correct spelling for the misspelled word in the sentence below?

I am going to perswade my mother to buy me a dog.

[ ]

10. What is the correct spelling for the misspelled word in the sentence below?

It is unclear whether or not I will go on vacation with my family.

- Ⓐ weather
- Ⓑ knot
- Ⓒ vacetion
- Ⓓ none of the above

11. What is the correct spelling for the misspelled word in the sentence below?

My little brother can be such a nusssance when he is hungry for dinner.

Write the correct spelling in the box given below.

[ ]

12. What is the correct spelling for the misspelled word in the sentence below?

Their is a loose dog in the neighborhood.

Write the correct spelling in the box given below.

[ ]

Chapter 4

Lesson 10: Mood in Verbs

You can scan the QR code given below or use the url to access additional EdSearch resources including videos and mobile apps related to *Mood in Verbs*.

URL	QR Code
http://www.lumoslearning.com/a/l83	

1. All verbs in the English language have which of the following?

Ⓐ mood
Ⓑ tense
Ⓒ voice
Ⓓ all of the above

2. What of the following is NOT a mood in verbs?

Ⓐ active
Ⓑ subjunctive
Ⓒ indicative
Ⓓ imperative

3. In which of the following instances would the subjunctive mood be necessary?

Ⓐ writing about a hypothetical situation
Ⓑ making a wish
Ⓒ making a suggestion
Ⓓ all of the above

4. What is the mood of a verb?

Ⓐ how the author feels before writing
Ⓑ what state of mind the author is in when writing
Ⓒ the author's attitude about what he is writing
Ⓓ none of the above

5. The indicative mood of a verb does what?

Ⓐ gives a command
Ⓑ states a fact
Ⓒ expresses a wish
Ⓓ states a condition

6. The imperative mood of a verb does what?

Ⓐ gives a command
Ⓑ states a fact
Ⓒ expresses a wish
Ⓓ states a condition

7. The subjunctive mood of a verb does what?

Ⓐ gives a command
Ⓑ states a fact
Ⓒ expresses a wish
Ⓓ states a condition

8. Part A
Which of the following sentences is written in the subjunctive mood?

Ⓐ It will rain tomorrow.
Ⓑ It might rain tomorrow.
Ⓒ Prepare for the rain tomorrow.
Ⓓ None of the above

8. Part B
Which of the following sentences is written in the imperative mood?

Ⓐ It will rain tomorrow.
Ⓑ It might rain tomorrow.
Ⓒ Prepare for the rain tomorrow.
Ⓓ None of the above

9. Which of the following sentences is written in the indicative mood? Circle the correct answer choice.

Ⓐ It will rain tomorrow.
Ⓑ It might rain tomorrow.
Ⓒ Prepare for the rain tomorrow.
Ⓓ None of the above

Lesson 11: Active and Passive Voice

You can scan the QR code given below or use the url to access additional EdSearch resources including videos and mobile apps related to *Active and Passive Voice.*

URL	QR Code
http://www.lumoslearning.com/a/l83	

1. **What comes first in active voice?**

   Ⓐ subject
   Ⓑ object
   Ⓒ action
   Ⓓ fall

2. **What is passive voice?**

   Ⓐ When the writer uses a very nice tone of voice
   Ⓑ When the writer says nice things
   Ⓒ A sentence that is not a question or command
   Ⓓ A sentence in which the subject is acted upon instead of doing the action

3. **What is active voice?**

   Ⓐ When somebody talks a lot
   Ⓑ A sentence with a lot of action
   Ⓒ A sentence in which the subject is performing the action
   Ⓓ When someone talks and performs an activity at the same time

4. **Is the following sentence written in active or passive voice?**

   Margaret is loved by Brian.

   Ⓐ active
   Ⓑ passive
   Ⓒ neither
   Ⓓ both

5. **Is the following sentence written in active or passive voice?**

   The stray dog was being taken care of by Matthew.

   Ⓐ active
   Ⓑ passive
   Ⓒ neither
   Ⓓ both

6. Is the following sentence written in active or passive voice?

Samantha sewed the hem of her sister's wedding dress when it ripped.

Ⓐ active
Ⓑ passive
Ⓒ neither
Ⓓ both

7. Which of the following sentences is written in active voice?

a) One day that dress will be handed down to me by my mother.
b) My father always changes the oil in our vehicles by himself.
c) I made chocolate chip cookies for the birthday party.
d) That cabinet was made by my grandfather.

Ⓐ a and b
Ⓑ b and c
Ⓒ d and c
Ⓓ a and d

8. Which of the following sentences are written in active voice?

a) This house was built by my uncle.
b) This wonderful dessert was baked by my mother.

Ⓐ a
Ⓑ b
Ⓒ both a and b
Ⓓ none of the above

9. Which of the following sentences is written in active voice?

a) Everybody should eat vegetables.
b) At the concert, one audience member will be selected to participate.
c) Everyone should learn how to swim as early as possible.

Ⓐ a
Ⓑ b
Ⓒ c
Ⓓ all of the above
Ⓔ none of the above

10. Which of the following sentences is written in passive voice.

a) One day, that dress will be handed down to me by my mother.
b) My father always changes the oil in our vehicles by himself.
c) I made chocolate chip cookies for the birthday party.
d) My grandfather made that cabinet.

Ⓐ a
Ⓑ b
Ⓒ c
Ⓓ d

11. Identify whether the following sentence is written in the active or passive voice.

Much to her mother's dismay, Chloe colored on the dining room table.

Write your answer in the box given below.

12. Identify whether the following sentence is written in the active or passive voice.

Camille was going to make dinner for everyone before she went to bed.

Write your answer in the box given below.

Lesson 12: Context Clues

You can scan the QR code given below or use the url to access additional EdSearch resources including videos and mobile apps related to *Context Clues*.

ed Search	**Context Clues**	
URL		**QR Code**
http://www.lumoslearning.com/a/l84		

1. The context of a word means _____.

(A) the words that surround it
(B) words that don't mean the same as they say
(C) using detail
(D) finding facts to support

2. What should you do when using context clues?

(A) Read the sentence containing the unfamiliar word, leaving that word out.
(B) Look closely at the words around the unfamiliar word to help guess its meaning.
(C) Substitute a possible meaning for the word and read the sentence to see if it makes sense.
(D) all of the above

3. Brian appeared infallible on the basketball court because he never missed a shot.

What is the best meaning of infallible?

(A) incapable of making an error
(B) imperfect
(C) faulty
(D) unsure of what he's doing

4. After the police broke up a skirmish between opposing groups, everyone went their separate ways.

What is the best meaning of skirmish?

(A) peace protest
(B) fight
(C) theft
(D) agreement

5. What is the best meaning of excruciating?

(A) bearable
(B) extremely pleasant
(C) unbearable
(D) soon went away

6. Michael's overt flirting with Michelle during lunch drew the attention of Larry, her boyfriend.

What is the best meaning of overt?

Ⓐ concealed
Ⓑ hidden
Ⓒ obvious
Ⓓ secret

7. Vanity got the best of Sarah as she ran into the wall while checking her hair in the mirror at the end of the hallway.

What is the best meaning of vanity?

Ⓐ modestly
Ⓑ pride in one's qualities
Ⓒ lack of real value
Ⓓ tried things in vain

8. Becca's rude and pithy response to her teacher only took a second, but it landed her a week in after school detention.

What is the best meaning of pithy?

Ⓐ brief
Ⓑ long winded
Ⓒ sweet
Ⓓ impolite

9. His emotions were difficult to articulate, but Fredrick knew it was now or never. He had to tell Francie how much he loved her before she got on the bus and left him and his heart forever.

What is the best meaning for the word articulate?

Ⓐ unclear
Ⓑ clearly spoken
Ⓒ hidden
Ⓓ move in segments

10. The pungent odor of my mom's shower cleaning fluid burned my nostrils and made it hard for me to breathe.
What is the best meaning of pungent?

Ⓐ pleasant
Ⓑ bland
Ⓒ sharp or acidy
Ⓓ odorless

Bailey had a sense of foreboding as she walked into the classroom. She noticed that all the bulletin boards were covered up and the privacy folders were lying on the desks. Had she forgotten a test?

11. What is the best definition of foreboding? Circle the correct answer choice.

Ⓐ good fortune
Ⓑ bad feeling
Ⓒ fortune
Ⓓ anticipation

Bruce proved his incredible stamina as he jumped rope for twenty minutes without a break.

12. Which is the best definition of stamina? Circle the correct answer choice.

Ⓐ laziness
Ⓑ strength, vigor
Ⓒ weakness
Ⓓ fatigue

Chapter 4

Lesson 13: Multiple Meaning Words

You can scan the QR code given below or use the url to access additional EdSearch resources including videos and mobile apps related to *Multiple Meaning Words*.

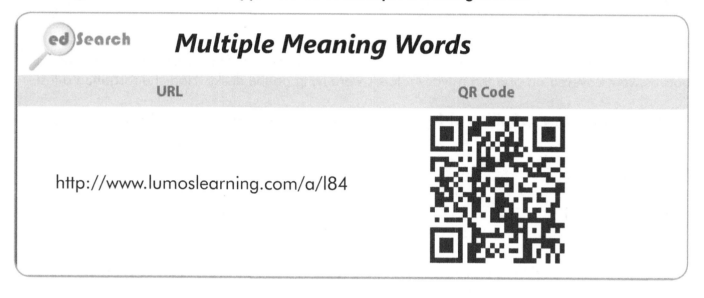

ed Search	**Multiple Meaning Words**	
URL	QR Code	
http://www.lumoslearning.com/a/l84		

1. What is a homonym?

Ⓐ words that sound the same but have different meanings and spellings.
Ⓑ words that sound the same and have the same spelling but different meaning.
Ⓒ words that do not sound the same or have the same spelling or meaning.
Ⓓ words that neither sound or look alike.

2. What is the correct definition of a homophone?

Ⓐ words that sound and look alike.
Ⓑ words that sound alike but are spelled differently.
Ⓒ words that sound different but mean the same thing.
Ⓓ none of the above.

3. Which meaning of the word "address" is used in the following sentence?

One should always address the president as, "Mr. President".

Ⓐ a formal communication
Ⓑ a place where a person or organization can be contacted
Ⓒ to direct a speech
Ⓓ the place you live

4. Which of the homophones, "complement" and "compliment," will correctly fit into the following sentence?

I like to wear my blue, flowered dress. Whenever I wear it I receive a lot of _____ (s).

Ⓐ compliment
Ⓑ complement

5. Which meaning of the word "strike" is used in the following sentence?

If the two sides cannot come to an agreement, there will be a strike.

Ⓐ to aim and deliver a blow
Ⓑ to lower a flag, as in surrender
Ⓒ to knock all the pins down in bowling
Ⓓ to stop work in an attempt to force an employer to comply with demands

6. Choose the word that is a synonym for the underlined word in the following sentence.

Amanda has not been feeling well lately. She went to visit her doctor today to <u>determine</u> why she has been under the weather.

- Ⓐ settle
- Ⓑ decline
- Ⓒ abstain
- Ⓓ study

7. What is the correct definition of the word "suit" as it is used in the sentence below?

When I decided not to go to the prom, my girlfriend said, "Suit yourself. I'll find someone else to dance with."

- Ⓐ formal attire
- Ⓑ legal action
- Ⓒ benefit
- Ⓓ request

8. What is the correct definition of the word "band" as it is used in the sentence below?

Let's band together to stamp out hunger!

- Ⓐ encircle
- Ⓑ a group of people with the same interest
- Ⓒ to come together
- Ⓓ a musical group

9. What is the correct definition of the word "fair" as it is used in the sentence below?

I couldn't wait for the fair to come to town. Nothing beats a funnel cake from the fair!

- Ⓐ impartial
- Ⓑ a carnival
- Ⓒ equal
- Ⓓ a charge for transportation

10. What are the two possible definitions for the word stalk?

Ⓐ a part of a plant
Ⓑ a part of a human
Ⓒ to follow someone
Ⓓ to be the leader

11. Which are the synonyms of graduation. More than one answer may be correct. Select all the correct ones.

Ⓐ completion
Ⓑ confidence
Ⓒ realize
Ⓓ concentration
Ⓔ culmination
Ⓕ close

Lesson 14: Roots, Affixes, and Syllables

You can scan the QR code given below or use the url to access additional EdSearch resources including videos and mobile apps related to *Roots, Affixes, and Syllables*.

ed Search	**Roots, Affixes, and Syllables**
URL	QR Code
http://www.lumoslearning.com/a/l84	

1. Where does the prefix go in a word?

- (A) at the end
- (B) at the beginning
- (C) in the middle
- (D) none of the above

2. Where does a suffix go in a word?

- (A) at the end
- (B) at the beginning
- (C) in the middle
- (D) none of the above

3. What is an affix?

- (A) a repair for something
- (B) a prefix or suffix attached to a root to form a new word
- (C) a sound made by blends of letters
- (D) the phonetic understanding of words

4. What is the best definition of a "root" of a word?

- (A) the beginning of a word
- (B) the end of a word
- (C) the base of a word
- (D) the middle of the word

5. What is a syllable?

- (A) the sound of a vowel when pronouncing a word
- (B) what a teacher gives students that outlines what will be studied in class
- (C) the sound of a consonant when pronouncing a word
- (D) a prefix or suffix attached to a root to form a new word

6. An omnivore is an animal that eats both plants and meat. What does the prefix omni mean?

- (A) everywhere or everything
- (B) animal
- (C) to eat
- (D) starvation

7. Identify the affixes in the following words?

mislead, unrestricted, reiterate

Ⓐ mis, un, re
Ⓑ lead, ed, ate
Ⓒ lead, stricted, rate
Ⓓ lead, restricted, iterate

8. The root word, cede means, "to go". With this knowledge, determine the meaning of the word, "precede".

Ⓐ to go after
Ⓑ to go away
Ⓒ to go before
Ⓓ to go never

9. Dynamic means physical force or energy. What does the root word "dyna" mean?

Ⓐ to be weak
Ⓑ power
Ⓒ to be little
Ⓓ to be tired

10. The prefix "un" means not. What does "unable" mean?

Ⓐ ready
Ⓑ not able
Ⓒ unclear
Ⓓ not unable

11. Match the word to its meaning based on the suffix

	full of care	someone who applies for something	a person who specializes in studying the history of the earth, including rocks
The suffix "ist" means a skilled person in. a geologist is			
The suffix "ful" means full of. Therefore the word "careful" means:			
The suffix "ant" means a person who. Applicant means			

12. The suffix "er" means a person who does an action. What does "announcer" mean? Circle the correct answer choice.

Ⓐ someone who announces
Ⓑ someone who works on automobiles
Ⓒ someone who works for a news station
Ⓓ all of the above

Lesson 15: Reference Materials

You can scan the QR code given below or use the url to access additional EdSearch resources including videos and mobile apps related to *Reference Materials*.

URL	QR Code
http://www.lumoslearning.com/a/l84	

1. **Which of the following are acceptable reference materials to use for a research assignment?**

   Ⓐ questionnaires
   Ⓑ experiments
   Ⓒ field studies
   Ⓓ scholarly articles
   Ⓔ all of the above

2. **Part A**
   What are primary sources?

   Ⓐ materials that come directly from the source
   Ⓑ materials that have been copied from the source
   Ⓒ materials that are found only in encyclopedias
   Ⓓ materials that are over 100 years old

   Part B
   Which of the following are examples of secondary sources?

   Ⓐ biographies
   Ⓑ encyclopedias
   Ⓒ textbooks
   Ⓓ documentaries
   Ⓔ all of the above

3. **How can you determine whether a source is reliable?**

   Ⓐ If you obtained your information from the Internet, it is always reliable.
   Ⓑ You should consider who wrote the source and why.
   Ⓒ If you obtained your information from an actual article, it will be reliable.
   Ⓓ answer choices B & C

4. **Why must you be very careful about obtaining information from websites?**

   Ⓐ It can be difficult to find reputable sources.
   Ⓑ Some sites can be edited by anyone.
   Ⓒ It is too easy to find what may look like good information but sources are often unverifiable.
   Ⓓ All of the above

5. Part A
What are the benefits of using primary sources?

Ⓐ They are first-hand accounts from those who witnessed or experienced the event being researched.
Ⓑ They offer a limited perspective.
Ⓒ They haven't been very well researched.
Ⓓ They are reposted hundreds of times.

Part B
What are the benefits of using secondary sources?

Ⓐ They have been analyzed and interpreted.
Ⓑ They have not often used a variety of primary sources to come to their conclusions.
Ⓒ They are straight from the source.
Ⓓ They have been reposted hundreds of times.

6. What do the following items have in common?

diary
journal
letter
official letters

Ⓐ They are secondary sources.
Ⓑ They are primary sources.
Ⓒ They are neither primary nor secondary sources.

7. What do the following items have in common?

books
journal articles
textbooks
reference sources

Ⓐ They are primary sources.
Ⓑ They are secondary sources.
Ⓒ Some are secondary sources.
Ⓓ None of the above

8. **If you were researching Anne Frank, which of the following would be your choice for a primary source?**

Ⓐ your teacher
Ⓑ an encyclopedia
Ⓒ a website about Anne Frank
Ⓓ Anne Frank's diary

Chapter 4

Lesson 16: Using Context to Verify Meaning

You can scan the QR code given below or use the url to access additional EdSearch resources including videos and mobile apps related to *Using Context to Verify Meaning.*

---

ed Search   ***Using Context to Verify Meaning***

URL	QR Code
http://www.lumoslearning.com/a/l84	

Question 1-9 are based on the passage below.

Marathon

Training for a marathon takes hard work and **perseverance**. It is not something you can do on the **spur** of the moment. Preparing for a marathon takes months, particularly if you have never run a marathon before. The official distance of a full marathon is 26.2 miles. In 2005, the average time to complete a marathon in the United States was 4 hours 32 minutes 8 seconds for men and 5 hours 6 minutes 8 seconds for women.

Most people who run marathons are not trying to win. Many runners try to beat their own best time. Some compare their time to other runners in the same gender and age group. Some people set time-oriented goals, such as finishing under four hours, while others try to complete the race without slowing to a walk. Many beginners simply hope to finish the marathon.

Trainers recommend that beginners maintain a **consistent** running schedule for six weeks prior to even starting a marathon training program. The purpose of this is to allow the body to adapt to the **various** physical demands of long-distance running. First-time marathon runners should train by running four days a week for at least four months, increasing distance by no more than ten percent weekly. As race day approaches, runners should **taper** their runs, reducing the strain on their bodies and resting before the marathon. It is important not to over**exert** yourself during training because that can lead to a lot of injuries. Most common injuries are spraining of the knees and ankles. These sprains can **hinder** the training.

Before the race, it is important to stretch in order to keep muscles **limber**. Staying hydrated is also important, but there is a danger in drinking too much water. If a runner drinks too much water, they may experience a dangerous condition called **hyponatremia**, a drop of sodium levels in the blood. During the race, trainers recommend maintaining a steady pace. It is normal to feel sore after a marathon. Light exercise will help sore muscles heal faster.

Some people run marathons in pairs or groups. Training for and running a marathon with another person or group of people can make the experience more enjoyable and more rewarding. A running partner might be just the motivation you need to show up for an early morning run instead of rolling over to hit the snooze button. And, when you cross the finish line together, you can share the satisfaction of reaching your common goal.

Usually, thousands of people sign up and run a marathon. Most people finish the race. The thrill of running a marathon for the first time is unbelievable. The training sessions are harder if you have never run before. But it is unbelievable what ones' body can do when one puts his/her mind to it. Having a good coach to support you makes all the difference in training for a marathon.

The daily runs are very important. Strength training and core training are also very important.

Using context clues in the story, determine the meaning of the *bold* words.

1. perseverance

- Ⓐ determination
- Ⓑ routine
- Ⓒ flexibility
- Ⓓ practice

2. spur

- Ⓐ after long planning
- Ⓑ without planning
- Ⓒ with much discussion
- Ⓓ with significant thought

3. consistent

- Ⓐ varying
- Ⓑ changing
- Ⓒ regular
- Ⓓ dynamic

4. various

- Ⓐ many
- Ⓑ few
- Ⓒ hard
- Ⓓ simple

5. taper

- Ⓐ add more
- Ⓑ pick and choose
- Ⓒ scale back
- Ⓓ candle

6. exert

- Ⓐ sleep
- Ⓑ utilize
- Ⓒ rest
- Ⓓ run

7. hinder

- Ⓐ delay
- Ⓑ speed up
- Ⓒ help
- Ⓓ assist

8. Part A
limber

- Ⓐ tone
- Ⓑ tight
- Ⓒ loose
- Ⓓ wavy

8. Part B

hyponatremia

- Ⓐ a drop of sodium levels in the blood
- Ⓑ dehydration
- Ⓒ a pulled muscle
- Ⓓ easily able to swim

9. If you cannot determine a word's meaning in context, where can you look? From among the 4 choices given below, select the correct answer and enter it in the box given below.

- Ⓐ thesaurus
- Ⓑ dictionary
- Ⓒ encyclopedia
- Ⓓ journal

Chapter 4

Lesson 17: Interpreting Figures of Speech

You can scan the QR code given below or use the url to access additional EdSearch resources including videos and mobile apps related to *Interpreting Figures of Speech*.

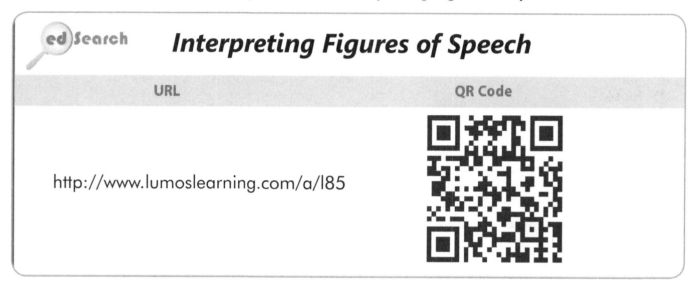

Interpreting Figures of Speech

URL	QR Code
http://www.lumoslearning.com/a/l85	

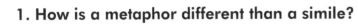

1. **How is a metaphor different than a simile?**

   Ⓐ A metaphor is the same as a simile.
   Ⓑ A metaphor does not use like or as in the comparison of two unlike things.
   Ⓒ A metaphor is not at all similar to a simile.
   Ⓓ A metaphor uses like or as in the comparison of two unlike things.

2. **What two figures of speech listed below have to do with word sounds?**

   Ⓐ metaphor and simile
   Ⓑ personification and idiom
   Ⓒ alliteration and onomatopoeia
   Ⓓ noun and verb

3. **Which of the following is a metaphor?**

   Ⓐ It is as hot as the surface of the sun out there.
   Ⓑ She sold seashells by the seashore.
   Ⓒ I stayed up too late last night studying and now my mind is foggy.
   Ⓓ She plopped on the sofa after babysitting nine hours.

4. **What does the idiom "burning the candle at both ends" mean?**

   Ⓐ You are wasting wax.
   Ⓑ You are doing too much.
   Ⓒ You are preparing for an emergency.
   Ⓓ You have a great need for a lot of light.

5. **What is the meaning of the following simile?**

   Her eyes are like fiery diamonds.

   Ⓐ sparkly and bright
   Ⓑ hard and hot
   Ⓒ warm and light
   Ⓓ expensive and desirable

6. Today, my brother and I went to the batting cages. I was in awe of him as I watched him hit ball after ball; he was a machine.

Why is the brother being compared to a machine?

Ⓐ He seemed to be under the control of a robot.
Ⓑ He hit every ball with accuracy and efficiency.
Ⓒ He was rigid and metal-like.
Ⓓ He didn't show much emotion as he hit the balls.

7. What is the meaning of the following metaphor?

He has the heart of a lion.

Ⓐ The people on the street.
Ⓑ He is hairy.
Ⓒ He has a large heart.
Ⓓ He is courageous.

8. What figure of speech is used in the following sentence?

The leaves of the tree danced in the breeze.

Ⓐ personification
Ⓑ metaphor
Ⓒ simile
Ⓓ idiom

9. Donna's brother said, "you're selling yourself short." What does she mean by this?

Ⓐ you need to grow a little taller
Ⓑ you are not giving yourself enough credit
Ⓒ you are a little short
Ⓓ you do not need to worry about being tall

10. What figure of speech is used in the following sentence?

I saw the coolest concert last night.

Ⓐ personification
Ⓑ alliteration
Ⓒ metaphor
Ⓓ simile

11. What figure of speech is used in the following sentence:

Sarah was like a toddler hungry for food; I was ready to get out of the car with her.
Write your answer in the box given below.

> [   ]

12. What figure of speech is used in the sentence below:

I heard the pop of the kernels in the microwave and knew my snack was almost ready.
Write your answer in the box given below.

> [   ]

13. The teacher told us the test would be a piece of cake, but I disagree.
What does the idiom ""a piece of cake"" mean? Write your answer in the box given below.

> [   ]

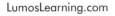

Chapter 4

Lesson 18: Relationships Between Words

You can scan the QR code given below or use the url to access additional EdSearch resources including videos and mobile apps related to *Relationships Between Words*.

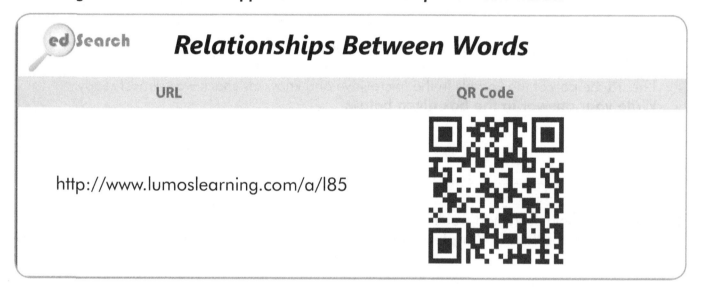

ed Search

Relationships Between Words

URL	QR Code
http://www.lumoslearning.com/a/l85	

1. What is an analogy?

  Ⓐ words that mean the opposite
  Ⓑ a comparison of two words
  Ⓒ a short story
  Ⓓ the study of ants

2. Select the best choice to explain the relationship of the words in the following analogy.

branch is to tree as fingers are to hand

  Ⓐ antonyms
  Ⓑ synonyms
  Ⓒ part to whole
  Ⓓ whole to part

3. Select the best choice to finish the following analogy.

repel is to attract as _____ is to lead

  Ⓐ follow
  Ⓑ guide
  Ⓒ direct
  Ⓓ head

4. Select the best choice to finish the following analogy.

I is to mine as they is to _____

  Ⓐ there's
  Ⓑ theirs
  Ⓒ they'res
  Ⓓ theirses

5. Select the best choice to finish the following analogy.

ostracism is to acceptance as _____ is to charitable

  Ⓐ deliberate
  Ⓑ rejection
  Ⓒ greedy
  Ⓓ giving

6. Study the analogy below to determine the relationship between the words that are presented.

won is to one as rode is to road

  (A) homonyms
  (B) synonyms
  (C) homophones
  (D) homographs

7. Study the analogy below to determine the relationship between the words that are presented.

woman is to women as mouse is to mice

  (A) present tense to past tense
  (B) singular to plural
  (C) plural to singular
  (D) antonyms

8. Finish the following analogy.

tiny is to small as enormous is to

  (A) minute
  (B) monstrous
  (C) large
  (D) petite

9. Complete the following analogy.

television is to view as _____ is to listen

  (A) radio
  (B) movie
  (C) computer
  (D) people

10. Finish the following analogy.

woman is to girl as man is to _____

  (A) son
  (B) boy
  (C) father
  (D) dad

11. Match the word to it's definition.

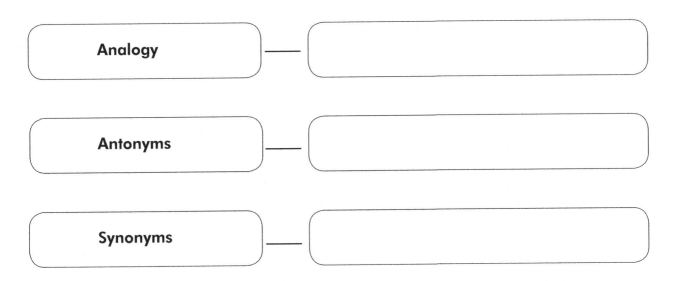

words that mean the same thing
words with opposite meanings
a comparison of two words

12. Match the word sets to its correct category.

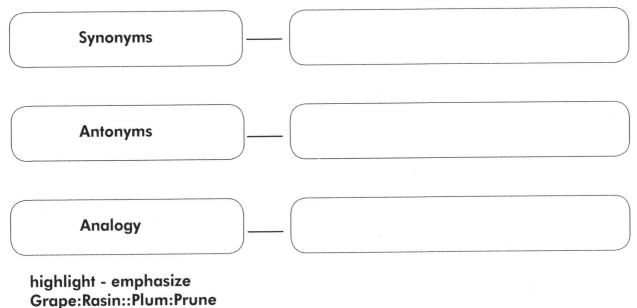

highlight - emphasize
Grape:Rasin::Plum:Prune
detached - interested

13. Words that express extreme exaggeration are called as _____

Identify the figure of speech defined by above sentence.

Chapter 4

Lesson 19: Denotations and Connotations

You can scan the QR code given below or use the url to access additional EdSearch resources including videos and mobile apps related to *Denotations and Connotations*.

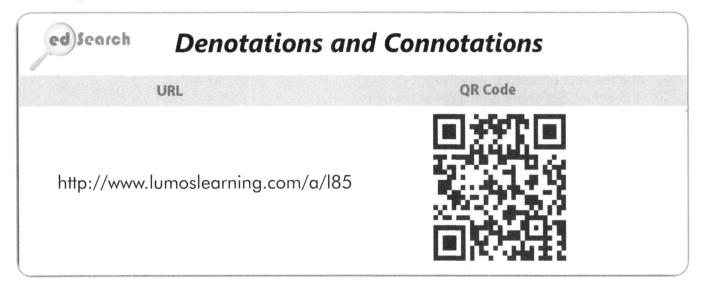

ed Search	**Denotations and Connotations**	
URL		**QR Code**
http://www.lumoslearning.com/a/l85		

1. Part A
What is the definition of <u>denotation</u>?

Ⓐ the feelings or ideas a word suggests
Ⓑ the actual dictionary definition of a word
Ⓒ a word that is a symbol of the opposite word
Ⓓ words that have the same meanings

1. Part B
What is the definition of <u>connotation</u>?

Ⓐ the feelings or ideas a word suggests
Ⓑ the actual dictionary definition of a word
Ⓒ a word that is a symbol of the opposite word
Ⓓ a word that means the same thing

2. The denotation of a word is the literal dictionary definition. The connotation of a word is the idea or feeling associated with the word.

Is the underlined word used denotatively or connotatively?

That girl is <u>immature</u> and impossible to be around because she is always goofing around and is a huge disruption in class.

Ⓐ denotatively
Ⓑ connotatively
Ⓒ both

3. Which of the following words has the most positive connotation?

dwelling, house, home, residence

Ⓐ dwelling
Ⓑ house
Ⓒ home
Ⓓ residence

4. Which of the following words has the most negative connotation?

cheap, frugal, thrifty

Ⓐ cheap
Ⓑ frugal
Ⓒ thrifty

5. Which of the following has the most positive connotation?

- Ⓐ plain
- Ⓑ dull
- Ⓒ ugly
- Ⓓ unattractive

6. Which word has the most neutral connotation?

assertive, pushy, aggressive

- Ⓐ assertive
- Ⓑ pushy
- Ⓒ aggressive

7. What is a negative connotation for funny?

- Ⓐ absurd
- Ⓑ uncommon
- Ⓒ comical
- Ⓓ amusing

8. What would a negative connotation for the word "quick" be?

- Ⓐ prompt
- Ⓑ rapid
- Ⓒ hasty
- Ⓓ responsive

9. What is a neutral connotation for small?

- Ⓐ short
- Ⓑ paltry
- Ⓒ insignificant
- Ⓓ trivial

10. My mom screamed when she realized she won first place in the pie baking contest.

Does the word "screamed" in the above sentence have a positive, negative, or neutral connotation?

11. My mom screamed as she fell off the ladder into the bushes.

Does the word "screamed" in the above sentence have a positive, negative, or neutral connotation?

Chapter 4

Lesson 20: Domain Specific Words

You can scan the QR code given below or use the url to access additional EdSearch resources including videos and mobile apps related to *Domain Specific Words*.

ed Search

Domain Specific Words

URL	QR Code
http://www.lumoslearning.com/a/l86	

1. What is jargon?

Ⓐ words that are silly
Ⓑ words that are specific to an area a study
Ⓒ words that are slang
Ⓓ words that describe nouns

2. Given the task to write an essay about literature, what would be a good domain specific vocabulary word to use?

Ⓐ plot
Ⓑ characterization
Ⓒ dialogue
Ⓓ all of the above

3. Read the sentence below; identify a domain specific vocabulary word in it.

After reading the novel, it is clear that the author's use of setting is meant a symbol for bravery.

Ⓐ symbol
Ⓑ bravery
Ⓒ use
Ⓓ author's

4. Which of the following words would best fit in the following sentence?

Samuel felt _____ by his teachers consistent nagging about his grades. He knew he needed to bring them up, and her constant reminders increased his anxiety.

Ⓐ angry
Ⓑ annoyed
Ⓒ frustrated
Ⓓ mad

5. What word in the following sentence is a domain specific vocabulary word?

An animal's predatory instincts are what helps it survive when it needs food or protection.

Ⓐ instinct
Ⓑ animal
Ⓒ food
Ⓓ protection

6. What word in the following sentence is a domain specific vocabulary word?

The slope of the line is calculated using slope intercept form. It is important to understand this formula if you want to be a successful math student.

Ⓐ student
Ⓑ successful
Ⓒ calculated
Ⓓ important

7. What word in the following sentence is a domain specific vocabulary word?

The economy is governed by supply and demand. The market is what drives the economy and the economy is what capitalism is based upon.

Ⓐ market
Ⓑ economy
Ⓒ capitalism
Ⓓ all of the above

8. What words in the following sentences is a domain specific vocabulary words?

The poem can be interpreted in many ways. Readers can begin their interpretation by looking at a poem's meter, and then by closely examining its rhyme scheme and its rhythm. The overall interpretation should include the many nuances of the poem.

9. What word in the following sentence is a domain specific vocabulary word?

Look closely to see that the plugs and plug wires are all in good shape. Do this simple check before taking your car to the mechanic and it might save you a few bucks. Keep your money in your pocket if you can.

10. What word in the following sentence is a domain specific vocabulary word?

Check the motherboard first. If the motherboard is fried, you might as well just go to the store and get a new computer. There is no sense in spending that much time and energy to fix your machine if the brain of it is broken.

```
┌─────────────────────────────────────────────────┐
│                                                 │
│                                                 │
└─────────────────────────────────────────────────┘
```

End of Language

Answer Key and Detailed Explanations

Chapter 4: Language

Lesson 1: Adjectives and Adverbs

Question No.	Answer	Detailed Explanations
1.	B	Answer choice B is correct. An adjective describes or modifies a noun in a sentence.
2.	D	Answer choice D is correct. An adverb can modify an adjective, verb, or another adverb in a sentence.
3.	D	Answer choice D is correct. The word "good" is an adjective that is used to describe a person, place, thing, or idea. The word "well" is an adverb that is used to explain how something is done.
4.	C	Answer choice C is correct. In the first sentence, the word "bad" is an adverb describing how the narrator felt. In the second sentence, the word "well" is an adverb describing how the narrator did on a test. In the third sentence, the word "honestly" is an adverb describing how a question was answered.
5.	A	Answer choice A is correct. The word "patiently" is an adverb describing how Miss Jenkins teaches.
6.	D	Answer choice D is correct. The words "very" and "carefully" are both adverbs which describe how the baby was picked up.
7.	D	Answer choice D is correct. The adjectives "tired, dirty, and hungry" describe how the narrator feels after a long afternoon at practice.
8.	A	Answer choice A is correct. The word "pretty" is used to describe the girl. The adjective is describing the noun in this sentence.
9.	A	Answer choice A is correct. The adverb is "slowly." It describes how the man walked.
10.	A	Answer choice A is correct. The word "sadly" describes how the narrator walked after a tough baseball game.
11	new	The word "new" describes the slide.
12	happily	The word "happily" describes the very playing.
13	blonde	The word "blonde" describes the son's hair color.
14	lazily	The word "lazily" describes the way her son is lounging in the pool.
15	smartest	The word "smartest" is a superlative adjective describing the breed.
16	fairly	The word "fairly" describes how certain Caroline is.

Lesson 2: Subject-Verb Agreement

Question No.	Answer	Detailed Explanations
1.	B	Answer choice B is correct. When subjects are connected by "or", the subject closest to the verb determines whether the verb is plural or singular.
2.	A	Answer choice A is correct. When there is more than one subject, where one is singular and the other is plural (cat and dogs), the verb (have) will match the subject that is closest to it. So, if the sentence was written as, "Neither the dogs nor the cat...", the verb would be "has" because the subject "cat" is singular. The sentence would read like this, "Neither the dogs nor the cat has been fed".
3.	A	Answer choice A is correct. When subjects are connected by "or", the subject closest to the verb determines whether the verb is plural or singular.
4.	B	Answer choice B is the correct answer because it is in agreement with the subject, some. (Prepositional phrases such as of the answers, can NEVER be the subject of a sentence.)
5.	B	Answer choice B is correct. When the subject has two or more nouns connected by "and", use a plural verb.
6.	A	Answer choice A is correct. When two or more singular nouns are connected with "or" or "nor" use a singular verb.
7.	A	Answer choice A is correct. The subject of this sentence is "the student," which is singular, so the verb must also be singular. Be careful with sentences that put a phrase in between the subject and the verb.
8.	A	Answer choice A is correct. When there is more than one subject, one being singular and one being plural, the verb matches the subject closest to it.
9.	B	A complete subject includes the simple subject and any details supporting it. Answer B is correct. Answer A is not correct because it does not include all the complete subject, only the noun and adjective. Answer C is not correct as it is part of the complete predicate. Answer D is a part of the subject and a part of the predicate.
10.	C	Answer C is correct because it includes all the complete subject and details. Answer A is incorrect as it does not include the complete subject. Answer B is not correct as it is a part of the predicate. Answer D is also a part of the predicate and incorrect.

Question No.	Answer	Detailed Explanations
11	are	The nouns in the subject are plural; therefore the verb must also be plural.
12	are	The subject in this sentence is plural because the word "and" compounds the subject.

Lesson 3: Pronouns

Question No.	Answer	Detailed Explanations
1.	B	Answer choice B is correct. When a pronoun and a noun are used together, choose the pronoun that would fit best if the noun were not there. Answer choice A is incorrect because "we" would not fit without the noun students.
2.	A	Answer choice A is correct. "I" is the correct answer. One way to test whether you have the correct answer is to write the sentence out using only the pronoun you are testing and the object. For example, to test the word, "I", you would write, "I enjoyed spending the day at the fair". In contrast, if you were to test the word, "me" you would write, "Me enjoyed spending the day at the fair". This is not correct.
3.	D	Answer choice D is correct. When a pronoun and a noun are combined (which will happen with the plural first- and secondperson pronouns), choose the case of the pronoun that would be appropriate if the noun were not there.
4.	A	Answer choice A is correct. That, this, these, those, and such are demonstrative pronouns which means they identify or point to nouns. They can even convey emotion.
5.	A	Answer choice A is correct. The correct answer is "who". Who is a subject pronoun and Whom is an object pronoun. The subject of the sentence above is, "The woman" therefore, you use the pronoun, "who" when referring to her. A test to determine which pronoun to use is to substitute the words "who" and "whom", with "she" and "her". Whenever the word "she" is appropriate, the pronoun "who" can be used. Whenever the word "her" is appropriate, the word "whom" can be used. You would apply this to the above sentence, by asking the question, "Who would like to make a reservation?" The answer is, "she would." According to the test, we would use the pronoun "who".
6.	B	Answer choice B is correct. "Who" is a subject pronoun and "whom" is an object pronoun. In the sentence above, the word "you" is the subject, and "whom" is the direct object. A test to determine which pronoun to use is to substitute the words "who" and "whom" with "she" and "her". Whenever the word "she" is appropriate, the pronoun "who" can be used. Whenever the word "her" is appropriate, the word "whom" can be used. You would apply this test to the sentence by asking the question, "Who am I speaking with?" To which the answer would be, "I am speaking with her". According to the test, we would use the pronoun, "whom".

Question No.	Answer	Detailed Explanations
7.	B	Answer choice B is correct. Who is a subject pronoun and whom is an object pronoun. The subject of the sentence above is you, so we know that the answer is whom because it is the direct object. A test to determine which pronoun to use is to substitute the words who and whom with she and her. Whenever the word she is appropriate, the pronoun who can be used. Whenever the word her can be used, the pronoun whom can be used. You would apply this to the sentence above by answering the question which is being asked. The answer would be, "They are sending her to help us". According to the test we would use the pronoun, whom.
8.	D	Answer choice D is correct. The pronoun "her" is used three times and refers to Martha.
9.	B	Answer choice B is correct. The demonstrative pronoun "those" conveys disdain for the choice of shoes.
10.	C	Answer choice C is correct. The pronoun "him" refers to Mike. If the noun, Mike, were repeated, the sentence would read: Mike's mother told Mike that the trash needed to be taken out sooner rather than later. Using pronouns makes our writing clearer and less repetitive.
11	her, her	The pronoun "her" is used twice and refers to Julie.
12	his, him	This sentence requires the use of two different pronouns, "his" and "him." Both pronouns, however, refer to Michael.

Lesson 4: Phrases and Clauses

Question No.	Answer	Detailed Explanations
1.	A	Answer choice A is correct. An infinitive phrase always begins with the word "to" followed by a verb. In this case, the infinitive phrase in the sentence is "To make my birthday special."
2.	independent	It is an independent clause because it can stand alone.
3.	B	Answer choice B is correct. A subordinate, also called a dependent, clause depends on more words in the sentence. It cannot stand alone and always begins with a subordinate conjunction or a relative pronoun.
4.	A	Answer choice A is correct. It is an independent clause because it can stand alone.
5.	B	Answer choice B is correct. A subordinate, also called a dependent, clause depends on more words in the sentence. It cannot stand alone and always begins with a subordinate conjunction or a relative pronoun.
6.	A	Answer choice A is correct. An independent clause has a subject and a verb and can stand by itself.
7.	B	Answer choice B is correct. A subordinate clause, also known as a dependent clause, has a subject and a verb but cannot stand by itself as a complete sentence.
8.	C	Answer choice C is correct. An adjective phrase modifies a noun and tells "what kind" or "which one."
9.	B	Answer choice B is correct. The adjective phrase is "with the bright blue collar." It describes (tells which one) the dog.
10.	B	Answer choice B is correct. The adverb clause is "because she did not clean her room." Adverb phrases are dependent, meaning they cannot stand alone.
11	subordinate	The clause is "an accomplished fisherman." It cannot stand alone; therefore, it is subordinate (or dependent).

Lesson 5: Verbals

Question No.	Answer	Detailed Explanations
1.	B	Answer choice B is correct. A verbal is a verb that acts as another part of speech, such as an adjective or verb. If the question asked for a definition of "verbal" (instead of "a verbal"), then A would be the correct answer.
2.	B	Answer choice B is correct. A participle is a verbal that functions as an adjective and will end with either an -ing, -en, or -ed.
3.	B	Answer choice B is correct. Gerunds take the place of nouns in a sentence, and they are made by adding -ing to the original verb.
4.	B	Answer choice B is correct. Infinitives are usually marked with the word "to" followed by a verb.
5.	B	Answer choice B is correct. Infinitives use the word "to" followed by a verb; in this case, the infinitive is "to visit."
6.	A	Answer choice A is correct. While there are two sentences that include a verbal ending in -ing, the gerund is the one that takes the place of a noun.
7.	B	Answer choice B is correct. The participle, "boiling on the stove," describes the soup.
8.	B	Answer choice B is correct. The word "sparkling" describes the ring; therefore, it works as an adjective in this sentence.
9.	C	Answer choice C is correct. The word "sleeping" functions as a verb in the sentence.
10.	B	Answer choice B is correct. The word "running" describes the water; therefore, it is functioning as an adjective.
11.	A	Answer choice A is correct. The word "jogging" functions as a noun in this sentence.
12.	B	Answer choice B is correct. The word "laughing" describes the children on the Ferris wheel.

Lesson 6: Capitalization

Question No.	Answer	Detailed Explanations
1.	B	Answer choice B is correct. The first word of every sentence should ALWAYS be capitalized. Answer choice A, grandmother, would be capitalized when it is used as a proper noun. Proper nouns should always be capitalized.
2.	B	Answer choice B is correct. In the first sentence, the word "grandmother" is used as a proper noun.
3.	D	Answer choice D is correct. Always capitalize historical events, the first letter of a sentence, and all words in the title or name of an organization.
4.	B	Answer choice B is correct. There are three mistakes. The paragraph should be capitalized like this: Every morning I have the same routine. First, I make my bed and fluff my pillows. Next, I head to the shower. I always pick my clothes out the night before so that I don't spend too much time on deciding what to wear. Then, I run downstairs to eat Cheerios, my favorite cereal, and finally, I brush my teeth. On the way out of the door, I grab my backpack, which hangs on a hook by the front door, and hug my mom goodbye before I rush off to meet the bus. The pronoun "I" is ALWAYS capitalized and Cheerios is the name brand of a cereal. Name brands are always capitalized.
5.	A	Answer choice A is correct. The names of states will ALWAYS be capitalized, there are no exceptions to this rule. Answer choice B is incorrect because the names of the seasons are not capitalized unless they are being used in a title. Answer choice C is incorrect. The main words in titles are capitalized, but words such as "of" or articles such as "the" "a" or "an" are not capitalized if they are not the first word in the title.
6.	D	Answer choice D is correct. Holidays, languages (such as French, English, Spanish) and the days of the week are always capitalized.
7.	A	Answer choice A is correct. The word "spring" is incorrectly capitalized. The seasons should not be capitalized unless they are included in a title or start a sentence.
8.	C	Answer choice C is correct. Both sentences are correct. Titles, such as mayor, are capitalized when they come before a name but not when they come after a name.
9.	C	Answer choice C is correct. Both letters in all state abbreviations are capitalized.

Question No.	Answer	Detailed Explanations
10.	A	Answer choice A is correct. The first letter of a direct quote is always capitalized when the quote is a complete sentence. A capital letter is not used if the quote is a fragment or portion of the quote.
11	France	Only the proper noun, France, should be capitalized. Remember seasons are not capitalized.
12	Romeo, Juliet	The words that has to be capitalized are Romeo, Juliet

Lesson 7: Punctuation

Question No.	Answer	Detailed Explanations
1.	A	Answer choice A is correct. Commas are used to separate three or more items in a list.
2.	C	Answer choice C is correct. When an appositive is in the middle of a sentence, it must be set off by commas. An appositive is a noun phrase that renames or clarifies the noun.
3.	B	Answer choice B is correct. In complex sentences, a subordinating clause is set off with a comma. "After you have finished taking out the trash" is the subordinating clause in the sentence.
4.	C	Answer choice C is correct. A semicolon can separate two closely related independent clauses that are not joined by a coordinating conjunction.
5.	A	Answer choice A is correct. When a singular noun ends in "s" an apostrophe "s" is added to the word. For example, Mrs. Jones's.
6.	C	Answer choice C is correct. In order to make a plural noun possessive, add an apostrophe to the word. If the plural noun does not end with an s, add an apostrophe then an s. Examples include women's, children's and men's.
7.	A	Answer choice A is correct. Commas should be used to separate a series of words or word groups, between two independent clauses joined by a coordinating conjunction (and, or, but, for, nor), and in a date between the day and year. These are not all the comma rules, but they are the rules that are mostly commonly broken.
8.	B	Answer choice B is correct. The missing, or omitted, letters are "h" and "a". The word "would've" is a contraction for the words "would have".
9.	-	Correct Answer- Yvette's invitation for Brenda's surprise party said to bring the following things to the party: cupcakes, soda, and a gag gift. Both names are possessive; a colon is used because a list follows, and commas separate the list.
10.	-	Correct Answer- Kasey had not taken the time to read the directions - no wonder the bookcase fell apart after an hour! The dash takes the place of a semicolon in this example. Remember to use dashes sparingly and not in formal writing.

Lesson 8: Ellipsis

Question No.	Answer	Detailed Explanations
1.	A	Answer choice A is correct. An ellipsis is ...
2.	D	Answer choice D is correct. An ellipsis is used to: * Indicating omissions in quoted material * Indicating hesitation or trailing off in spoken words * Imparting extra significance to a sentence
3.	A	Answer choice A is correct. An ellipsis can be used to create suspense.
4.	B	Answer choice B is correct. You can use an ellipsis at any point in a sentence.
5.	A	Answer choice A is correct. The statement above is true.
6.	A	Answer choice A is correct. An ellipsis in dialogue can indicate a pause.
7.	D	Answer choice D is correct. In all of the above examples, an ellipsis would be used.
8.	C	Answer choice C is correct. The ellipsis indicates that information has been omitted.
9.	A	Answer choice A is correct. When you omit the beginning of a sentence: you have to put anything you change in brackets.
10.	A	Answer choice A is correct. The ellipsis indicates that areas of the text have been omitted.

Lesson 9: Spelling

Question No.	Answer	Detailed Explanations
1.	B	Answer choice B is correct. Homophones, also known as homonyms, are words that are pronounced the same, but have different meanings. Often they are spelled differently, and it is important to learn to use the correct spelling of the word. An example is: threw, through
2.	C	Answer choice C is correct. The word "threw" means to propel or hurl an object. The word "through" means to go in one end and out another.
3.	B	Answer choice B is correct. The first "they're" is a contraction for "they are." The second "there" refers to a location and the third "their" shows possession.
4.	D	Answer choice D is correct. Answer choice A is spelled accommodate. Answer choice B is a homophone; the correct word is ensure. Answer choice C is also a homophone and should be spelled there.
5.	B	Answer choice B is correct. The correct spelling of this word is chauffeur.
6.	A	Answer choice A is correct. Weight and wait are homophones. Weight is a unit of heaviness. Wait means to stop for a bit. Notice that weight does not follow the rule, "i before e except after c." This is why it is important to use a dictionary when unsure of word spellings.
7.	B	Answer choice B is correct. The correct spelling is business.
8.	C	Answer choice C is correct. The correct spelling is occasionally.
9.	persuade	The correct spelling is persuade.
10.	D	Answer choice D is correct. No words are misused or misspelled.
11.	nuisance	The correct spelling is nuisance.
12.	there	The correct word is there.

Lesson 10: Mood in Verbs

Question No.	Answer	Detailed Explanations
1.	D	Answer choice D is correct. Verbs have mood, tense, and voice.
2.	A	Answer choice A is correct. Active is a voice, not a mood.
3.	A	Answer choice A is correct. Subjunctive mood suggests an unreal situation.
4.	C	Answer choice C is correct. Mood is an author's attitude about his topic.
5.	B	Answer choice B is correct. The indicative mood of a verb indicates some sort of fact.
6.	A	Answer choice A is correct. The imperative tone of a verb gives a command.
7.	C	Answer choice C is correct. The subjunctive form of a verb expresses anything uncertain. Since a wish is uncertain, it is in a subjunctive mood.
8. Part A	B	Answer choice B is correct because it expresses an uncertainty.
8. Part B	C	Answer choice C is correct. An imperative tone gives a command, and answer choice C is giving a command.
9.	A	Answer choice A is correct because an indicative tone indicates a fact.

Lesson 11: Active and Passive Voice

Question No.	Answer	Detailed Explanations
1.	A	Answer choice A is correct. The subject comes before the action in active voice.
2.	D	Answer choice D is correct. A sentence written in the passive voice means the subject is acted upon instead of doing the action.
3.	C	Answer choice C is correct. A sentence written in active voice means the subject of the sentence is performing the action.
4.	B	Answer choice B is correct. The correct answer is passive. When the voice is active, the subject is doing the action. When the voice is passive, the target or object is treated like the subject of the sentence. In the sentence above, the subject is Brian, but Margaret is being treated like the subject.
5.	B	Answer choice B is correct. The correct answer is passive because the subject of the sentence, which is Matthew, is being treated as the object. We know that Matthew is the subject because he is doing the action.
6.	A	Answer choice A is correct. The correct answer is active. The subject of the sentence is Samantha, as she is doing the action, and she is treated as the subject. If this sentence were passive it would read, "The wedding dress was sewn by Samantha." The answer could not be neither, because a sentence is ALWAYS either active or passive.
7.	B	Answer choice B is correct. Both B and C are written in active voice. The sentences show that the subjects are doing the action.
8.	D	Answer choice D is correct. Both of the above sentences are written in passive voice. In both examples, the objects are being treated as the subject.
9.	D	Answer choice D is correct. In each of the three sentences, the subject is doing the action, which classifies them as active.
10.	A	The correct answer is A. The subject is being acted upon, instead of doing the action.
11	Active	The subject is doing the action.
12	Active	The subject is doing the action.

Lesson 12: Context Clues

Question No.	Answer	Detailed Explanations
1.	A	Answer choice A is correct. Context clues are the words that surround the unknown word. Context clues help the reader determine the meaning of the word.
2.	D	Answer choice D is correct. When faced with an unfamiliar word in a story or passage, it is helpful to go back and reread the surrounding text, both before and after the unfamiliar word. The words and phrases that help the reader determine the meaning of the word are called context clues.
3.	A	Answer choice A is correct. Context clues can be found at the end of the sentence, "...because he never missed a shot." This means he never made a mistake or error.
4.	B	Answer choice B is correct. After the police broke up a skirmish between opposing groups, everyone went their separate ways.
5.	C	Answer choice C is correct. After running into a parked car and then falling off my bike, the pain in my thumb was excruciating.
6.	C	Answer choice C is correct. Michael's overt flirting with Michelle during lunch drew the attention of Larry, her boyfriend.
7.	B	Answer choice B is correct. Vanity got the best of Sarah as she ran into the wall while checking her hair in the mirror at the end of the hallway.
8.	A	Answer choice A is correct. Becca's rude and pithy response to her teacher only took a second, but it landed her a week in after school detention.
9.	B	Answer choice B is correct. His emotions were difficult to articulate, but Fredrick knew it was now or never. He had to tell Francie how much he loved her before she got on the bus and left him and his heart forever.
10.	C	Answer choice C is correct. The pungent odor of my mom's shower cleaning fluid burned my nostrils and made it hard for me to breathe.
11.	B	Answer choice B is correct. Context clues are underlined in the sentences: Bailey had a sense of foreboding as she walked into the classroom. She noticed that all the bulletin boards were covered up and the privacy folders were lying on the desks. Had she forgotten a test?
12.	B	Answer choice B is correct. Context clues are underlined in the sentence: Bruce proved his incredible stamina as he jumped rope for twenty minutes without a break.

Lesson 13: Multiple Meaning Words

Question No.	Answer	Detailed Explanations
1.	B	Answer choice B is correct. Homonyms are words that are considered multiple-meaning words. They are words that share the same spelling and pronunciation but have a different meaning.
2.	B	Answer choice B is correct. Homophones are words that sound the same but are spelled differently and have different meanings.
3.	C	Answer choice C is correct. Address is a homonym meaning it is a multiple-meaning word.
4.	A	Answer choice A is correct. The definition of compliment is: praise. The definition of complement is: add to in a way that enhances or improves a thing.
5.	D	Answer choice D is correct. Strike is a homonym meaning it is a multiple-meaning word. All the definitions are correct, but in the context of the sentence, only D is correct.
6.	A	Answer choice A is correct. Determine has many meanings, but within the context of the sentence, only A is correct.
7.	C	Answer choice C is correct. Suit, in this case, means benefit, as in benefit or be happy with your own decision.
8.	C	Answer choice C is correct. While all the definitions for band are correct, within the context of this sentence, only answer choice C is correct.
9.	B	Answer choice B is correct. Fair, in the context of this sentence, means a carnival.
10.	A, C	Stalk is a homonym meaning it is a multiple-meaning word. The meaning depends upon the context in which it is used. Homonyms are spelled the same and sound the same. Choice A and C are the 2 different meanings of Stalk based on the context in which it is used.
11.	A,E,F	Graduation refers to completion, culmination and closure. Hence, answer choices A, E and F are correct.

Lesson 14: Roots, Affixes, and Syllables

Question No.	Answer	Detailed Explanations
1.	B	Answer B is correct. The prefix "pre" means before; therefore, a prefix goes at the beginning of a word.
2.	A	Answer choice A is correct. A suffix is the letter blend that goes at the end of a word.
3.	B	Answer choice B is correct. An affix is the prefix or suffix that is attached to a root to create a new word.
4.	C	Answer choice C is correct. The root of a word is the base. It is what a prefix or suffix is attached to.
5.	A	Answer choice A is correct. Syllables are the sounds of vowels when you pronounce a word. The word "cheese" has one syllable. The word "chicken" has two syllables. Answer choice B is incorrect. An outline of the school year that a teacher provides is actually called a syllabus.
6.	A	Answer choice A is correct. The prefix omni means everywhere or everything. An omnivore eats everything (meaning plants and meats). Other words with the prefix omni are omniscient (knowing everything) and omnipotent (having unlimited power).
7.	A	Answer choice A is correct. Mis, un, and re are prefixes. Prefixes are also known as affixes. Suffixes are also affixes.
8.	C	Answer choice C is correct. The prefix "pre" means before. If cede means to, then when combined, the word prefix means to go before.
9.	B	Answer choice B is correct. The root word "dyna" means power. Other words that include the root word dyna are: dynamite and dynamo.
10.	B	Answer choice B is correct. Un, meaning not, plus able means not able to. I am unable to attend the party on Friday.
11.	-	Geologist - a person who specializes in studying the history of the earth, including rocks careful - full of care applicant - someone who applies for something
12.	A	someone who announces

Lesson 15: Reference Materials

Question No.	Answer	Detailed Explanations
1.	E	Answer choice E is correct. Questionnaires, experiments, field studies, and scholarly articles are all acceptable references for research. Using a variety of these resources makes for the most reliable research.
2. Part A	A	Answer choice A is correct. Primary sources are those that come directly from the source.
2. Part B	E	Answer choice E is correct. Secondary sources interpret and analyze primary sources.
3.	B	Answer choice B is correct. It is difficult to determine the reliability of one or two sources. When doing research, it is important to constantly ask yourself who wrote the resources you are using and why were they written? Using several sources for research will prove to be most reliable.
4.	D	Answer choice D is correct. Use caution when using Internet resources. Make sure the author is reliable and the information is current.
5. Part A	A	Answer choice A. The benefit of using a primary source is that the account from the source actually witnessed or experienced the event being researched.
5. Part B	A	Answer choice A is correct. Using secondary sources for research is beneficial because the primary sources have already been analyzed and interpreted.
6.	B	Answer choice B is correct. Although not a complete list of primary sources, these items are generally considered to be primary sources. The researcher, however, must ensure the validity of the documents.
7.	B	Answer choice B is correct. All four items are considered secondary sources. Secondary sources are those items that are not first-hand accounts of events.
8.	D	Answer choice D is correct. Anne Frank's diary was written by her; therefore it is a primary source.

Lesson 16: Using Context to Verify Meaning

Question No.	Answer	Detailed Explanations
1.	A	Answer A is correct. The context clue is a synonym, "hard work" helps determine the meaning.
2.	B	Answer B is correct. The context clues are antonyms, "preparing takes months".
3.	C	Answer choice C is correct. The context clue "maintain" shows it must stay the same.
4.	A	Answer choice A is correct. Because the context says "demands" not "demand" readers know there are many.
5.	C	Answer choice C is correct. Some of the words in context like "reducing" and "relaxing" show readers that "taper" means to scale back.
6.	B	Answer choice B is correct. The context of "leading to injuries" helps reader understand not to push too hard; hence, utilize.
7.	A	Answer choice A is correct. The word is used in the context of an injury which talks about what it can do to hurt training; therefore, the context indicates the word means "delay".
8. Part A	C	Answer choice C is correct. Stretching loosens things; therefore, the context indicates "limber" means loose.
8. Part B	A	Answer choice A is correct. The definition is given following the word's use.
9.	B	Answer choice B is correct. A dictionary is the right choice.

Lesson 17: Interpreting Figures of Speech

Question No.	Answer	Detailed Explanations
1.	B	Answer choice B is correct. Like a simile, a metaphor compares two unlike things; however, it does not use like or as in the comparison. Instead, it just makes the statement. For example: The treacherous road snaked wildly through the canyons. In this sentence, the curves of a dangerous (treacherous) road are being compared to the curves of a snake as it slithers across the ground. You could make this sentence say something similar by using a simile instead of a metaphor: The treacherous road curved like a snake through the canyons. Answer choices A, C, and D are incorrect.
2.	C	Answer choice C is correct. Alliteration is the repetition of same letter sounds at the beginning of words or stressed syllables. Onomatopoeia is a sound word like splash, squirt, and plop. Both figures of speech have to do with the sounds of words. Answer choices A, B, and D are incorrect.
3.	C	Answer choice C is correct. Remember a metaphor is like a simile, but doesn't use "like" or "as" in the comparison. In this metaphor, the speaker is comparing his blurry thinking to fog. Answer choice A is a simile. Answer choice B is alliteration. Answer choice D is onomatopoeia.
4.	B	Answer choice B is correct. The phrase "burning the candle at both ends" is an idiom that means a person is doing too much and not getting enough rest, which will eventually exhaust them. If you were to burn a candle at both ends, it would burn out much more quickly than if you had burned it from one end. Answer choices A, C, and D are incorrect.
5.	A	Answer choice A is correct. A fire is bright and diamonds sparkle in the light. Answer choices B, C, and D are incorrect.
6.	B	Answer choice B is correct. This sentence uses a simile to compare the speaker's brother to a machine. Because of the simile, the reader can determine the brother hit the ball flawlessly, like a machine designed to hit balls would. Answer choices A, C, and D are incorrect.
7.	D	Answer choice D is correct. Lions are thought to be courageous, so someone with a lion's heart is courageous. Answer choices A, B, and C are incorrect.
8.	A	Answer choice A is correct. The ability to dance is a human characteristic; therefore, the leaves dancing are an example of personification. Answer choices B, C, and D are incorrect.

Question No.	Answer	Detailed Explanations
9.	B	Answer choice B is correct. When someone sells himself or herself short, he/she is not giving himself/herself enough credit for an accomplishment. Answer choices A, C, and D are incorrect.
10.	B	Answer choice B is correct. I saw the coolest concert last night uses alliteration. Coolest and concert both have the same beginning consonant sound giving the sentence more interest. Answer choices A, C, and D are incorrect.
11.	simile	Sarah is being compared to a hungry toddler. When toddlers are hungry, they are cranky and generally cry and carry on.
12.	onomatopoeia	"Pop," the sound a popcorn kernel makes when it pops, is a sound word.
13.	easy	The idiom "a piece of cake" means something is easy.

Lesson 18: Relationships Between Words

Question No.	Answer	Detailed Explanations
1.	B	Answer choice B is correct. An analogy compares two words, specifically two words which can somehow be compared. For example, a heart and a pump. Answer choices A, C, and D are incorrect.
2.	C	Answer choice C is correct. This analogy is comparing a part of a tree (branch) to the whole tree. The second half of the analogy compares part of a hand (fingers) to the whole hand. Answer choices A, B, and D are incorrect.
3.	A	Answer choice A is correct. The first set of words in the analogy are antonyms, repel and attract are opposite in meaning. Therefore, the second half of the analogy should also have a word set which are antonyms. "Follow" is an antonym to "lead". Answer choices B, C and D are not antonyms to the word lead, therefore are incorrect.
4.	B	Answer choice B is correct. Mine is the possessive case of I. The second set in the analogy must, therefore, be the possessive case of "they" which is "theirs". Answer choices A, C, and D are incorrect. Answer choices C and D are not even words.
5.	C	Answer choice C is correct. The first set of words in the analogy, "ostracism" and "acceptance", are antonyms; therefore, the second set of words must also be antonyms. The only antonym to "charitable" is "greedy". Answer choices A, B, and D are incorrect.
6.	C	Answer choice C is correct. The word pairs are homophones meaning each pair sounds the same but are spelled differently and have different meanings. Answer choices A, B, and D are incorrect.
7.	B	Answer choice B is correct. The analogy includes pairs of words are singular and plural. Answer choices A, C, and D are incorrect.
8.	C	Answer choice C is correct. "Tiny" and "small" are synonyms so the word pair must also be synonyms. While "enormous" and "monstrous" could be considered synonyms, the word "large" is a better choice. You must look more at the analogy and notice that the first words in the pair are antonyms: "tiny" and "enormous". Keeping that in mind, the best antonym pair for the second set of words is "small" and "large". Answer choices A and D are incorrect.

Question No.	Answer	Detailed Explanations
9.	A	Answer choice A is correct. In looking at the analogy, students must first look at the relationship of the word pair and then look at the part of speech. In this case, people watch a television, so it stands to reason that the missing word should be something that people listen to. Students must be very careful, though, to select the matching part of speech - a noun in this case. A radio is a noun and one does listen to a radio. Answer choices B, C, and D are incorrect.
10.	B	Answer choice B is correct. A female adult is a woman, and a female child is a girl. The same relationship must be completed in the analogy. A male adult is a man and a male child is a boy. Answer choices A, C, and D are incorrect.
11	-	Analogy - a comparison of two words Antonyms - words with opposite meanings Synonyms - words that mean the same thing
12	-	Synonyms are words that mean the same thing Antonyms are words with opposite meanings Analogy is a comparison of two words Hence, highlight - emphasize are Synonyms detached - interested are antonyms and Grape:Rasin::Plum:Prune - Analogy
13	-	Hyperbole

Lesson 19: Denotations and Connotations

Question No.	Answer	Detailed Explanations
1. Part A	B	Answer choice B is correct. One way to remember that denotation refers to the dictionary definition of a word is to remember that they both begin with the letter "d". Answer choices A is incorrect. Connotation means the feelings or ideas a word suggests. Answer choices C and D are incorrect.
1. Part B	A	Answer choice A is correct. The connotation (suggested meaning) of a word can change, depending on how it is used in a sentence. Connotations are usually described as positive or negative. Answer choice B is the definition of denotation. Answer choices C and D are incorrect.
2.	B	Answer choice B is correct. This word is used connotatively to describe that the girl doesn't act her age. Immature is a word in which the connotation can vary depending on the words around it. If it were used to describe a very young child, the connotation would be neutral as young children are immature, or the opposite of mature. In this sentence, immature is used to convey a negative idea. Answer choices A and C are incorrect.
3.	C	Answer choice C is correct. While none of the words have a negative connotation, home conveys to the reader a place where a family lives and is loved. Answer choices A, B, and D have neutral connotations.
4.	A	Answer choice A is correct. In this case, all three words are adjectives used to describe the spending habits of an individual. Being described as cheap has a negative connotation. If you are frugal or thrifty, that means you are careful with your money.
5.	A	Answer choice A is correct. All of the words are adjectives describing something. Plain has the most positive connotation of these words. Dull, ugly, and unattractive all have negative connotations.
6.	A	Answer choice A is correct. Depending upon the text surrounding the word "assertive," the connotation can change. Pushy and aggressive could also be considered somewhat neutral depending upon the surrounding text, but they are generally considered negative.

Question No.	Answer	Detailed Explanations
7.	A	Answer choice A is correct. The word "absurd" is a synonym for funny, but means something unreasonably funny. Answer choices B, C, and D are incorrect because they are all words with positive connotations.
8.	C	Answer choice C is correct. The word "hasty" is used when a decision is made quickly without much thought. Answer choices A, B, and D are incorrect because they are words with positive connotations.
9	A	Answer choice A is correct. The word "short" has a neutral connotation and generally stays neutral within surrounding text. Answer choices B, C, and D all carry negative connotations.
10.	Positive	As used in the sentence, the word "screamed" has a positive connotation. The narrator's mom was happy she won first place and, as a result, her scream was happy.
11.	Negative	The narrator's mom was falling from a ladder, something bad that can result in injury. Her scream was from fear; therefore, the connotation is negative.

Lesson 20: Domain Specific Words

Question No.	Answer	Detailed Explanations
1.	B	Answer choice B is correct. Jargon is words that are specific to an area of study.
2.	D	Answer choice D is correct. All of the examples are specific to literature.
3.	A	Answer choice A is correct. A symbol is specific to literature; therefore, it is domain specific.
4.	C	Answer C is the correct answer. The context clues in the sentence "increased his anxiety" shows that he was frustrated, not angry, annoyed or mad.
5.	A	Answer choice A is correct. Instincts are specific to animals so it is domain specific.
6.	C	Answer choice C is correct. A calculation is specific to math; therefore, it is domain specific.
7.	D	Answer choice D is correct. All of the choices relate to economics; therefore, they are all domain specific.
8.	-	Meter is specific to poetry; therefore, it is domain specific.
9.	-	Plugs are specific to cars; therefore, it is domain specific.
10.	-	A motherboard is specific to a computer; therefore, it is domain specific.

Notes

SBAC FAQ

What will SBAC English Language Assessments Look Like?

In many ways, the SBAC assessments will be unlike anything many students have ever seen. The tests will be conducted online, requiring students complete tasks to assess a deeper understanding of the CCSS. The students will be assessed once 75% of the year has been completed in two different assessments - a Computer Adaptive Testing (CAT) and a Performance Task (PT).

The time for each ELA portion is described below:

Estimated Time on Task in Minutes		
Grade	CAT	PT
3	90	120
4	90	120
5	90	120
6	90	120
7	90	120
8	90	120

Because the assessment is online, the test will consist of a combination of new types of questions:

1. Drag and Drop
2. Drop Down
3. Essay Response
4. Extended Constructed Response
5. Hot Text Select and Drag
6. Hot Text Selective Highlight
7. Matching Table In-line
8. Matching Table Single Response
9. Multiple Choice – Single Correct Response, radial buttons
10. Multiple Choice – Multiple Response, check boxes
11. Numeric Response
12. Short Text
13. Table Fill-in

For more information on 2022-23 Assessment year, visit
www.lumoslearning.com/a/sbac-2022-faqs   OR
Scan the **QR Code**

What is this SBAC Test Practice Book?

Inside this book, you will find practice sections aligned to each CCSS. Students will have the ability to review questions on each standard, one section at a time, in the order presented, or they can choose to study the sections where they need the most practice.

In addition to the practice sections, you will have access to two full-length CAT and PT practice tests online. Completing these tests will help students master the different areas that are included in newly aligned SBAC tests and practice test taking skills. The results will help the students and educators get insights into students' strengths and weaknesses in specific content areas. These insights could be used to help students strengthen their skills in difficult topics and to improve speed and accuracy while taking the test.

Because the SBAC assessment includes newly created, technology-enhanced questions, it is necessary for students to be able to regularly practice these questions. The Lumos online StepUp program includes thirteen technology enhanced questions that mimic the types students will see during the assessments.

Why Practice with Repeated Reading Passages?

Throughout the Lumos Learning Common Core Practice workbooks, students and educators will notice many passages repeat. This is done intentionally. The goal of these workbooks is to help students practice skills necessary to be successful in class and on standardized tests. One of the most critical components to that success is the ability to read and comprehend passages. To that end, reading fluency must be strengthened. According to Hasbrouck and Tindal (2006), "Helping our students become fluent readers is absolutely critical for proficient and motivated reading" (p. 642). And, Nichols et al. indicate, (2009), "fluency is a gateway to comprehension that enables students to move from being word decoders to passage comprehenders" (p. 11).

Lumos Learning recognizes there is no one-size-fits-all approach to build fluency in readers; however, the repeated reading of passages, where students read the same passages at least two or more times, is one of the most widely recognized strategies to improve fluency (Nichols et al., 2009). Repeated reading allows students the opportunity to read passages with familiar words several times until the passage becomes familiar and they no longer have to decode word by word. As students reread, the decoding barrier falls away allowing for an increase in reading comprehension.

The goal of the Lumos Learning workbooks is to increase student achievement and preparation for any standardized test. Using some passages multiple times in a book offers struggling readers an opportunity to do just that.

References
Hasbrouck, J., and Tindal, G. (2006). Oral reading fluency norms: A valuable assessment tool for reading teachers. Reading Teacher, 59(7), 636644. doi:10.1598/RT.59.7.3.
Nichols, W., Rupley, W., and Rasinski, T. (2009). Fluency in learning to read for meaning: going beyond repeated readings. Literacy Research & Instruction, 48(1). doi:10.1080/19388070802161906.

Discover Engaging and Relevant Learning Resources

Lumos EdSearch is a safe search engine specifically designed for teachers and students. Using EdSearch, you can easily find thousands of standards-aligned learning resources such as questions, videos, lessons, worksheets and apps. Teachers can use EdSearch to create custom resource kits to perfectly match their lesson objective and assign them to one or more students in their classroom.

To access the EdSearch tool, use the search box after you log into Lumos StepUp or use the link provided below.

www.lumoslearning.com/a/edsearchb	

The Lumos Standards Coherence map provides information about previous level, next level and related standards. It helps educators and students visually explore learning standards. It's an effective tool to help students progress through the learning objectives. Teachers can use this tool to develop their own pacing charts and lesson plans. Educators can also use the coherence map to get deep insights into why a student is struggling in a specific learning objective.

Teachers can access the Coherence maps after logging into the StepUp Teacher Portal or use the link provided below.

www.lumoslearning.com/a/coherence-map	

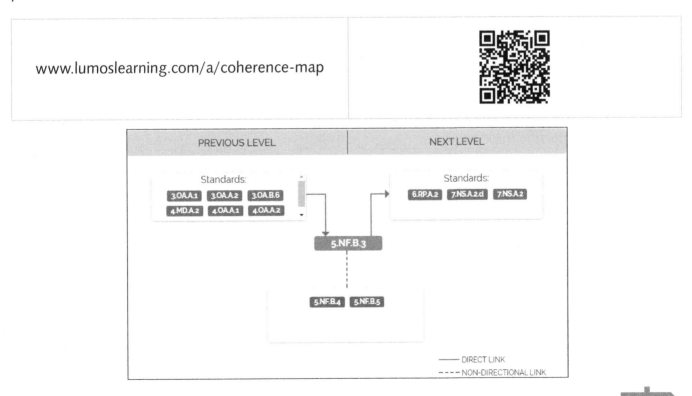

Progress Chart

Standard	Lesson	Page No.	Practice		Mastered	Re-practice /Reteach
CCSS			Date	Score		
RL.8.1	Textual Evidence	10				
RL.8.1	Inferences	19				
RL.8.2	Theme	28				
RL.8.2	Objective Summary	37				
RL.8.2	Plot	47				
RL.8.2	Setting	52				
RL.8.2	Character	58				
RL 8.3	Analyzing Literature	64				
RL.8.4	Meaning and Tone	71				
RL.8.5	Compare and Contrast	81				
RL.8.6	Producing Suspense and Humor	88				
RL.8.7	Media and Literature	93				
RL 8.9	Modern Fictions and Traditional Stories	100				
RI.8.1	Making Inferences Based on Textual Evidence	131				
RI.8.2	Central Idea	138				
RI 8.3	Connections and Distinctions	146				
RI.8.4	Determining Meaning of Words	152				
RI 8.5	Analyzing Structures in Text	158				
RI.8.6	Author's Point of View	167				
RI.8.7	Publishing Mediums	173				
RI.8.8	Evaluating Authors Claims	179				
RI.8.9	Conflicting Information	184				

Standard	Lesson	Page No.	Practice		Mastered	Re-practice /Reteach
CCSS			Date	Score		
L.8.1.A	Adjectives and Adverbs	203				
L.8.1.B	Subject-Verb Agreement	208				
L.8.1.C	Pronouns	212				
L.8.1.C	Phrases and Clauses	216				
L.8.1.D	Verbals	219				
L.8.2	Capitalization	223				
L.8.2.A	Punctuation	227				
L.8.2.B	Ellipsis	230				
L.8.2.C	Spelling	233				
L.8.3.A	Mood in Verbs	237				
L.8.3.A	Active and Passive Voice	240				
L.8.4.A	Context Clues	244				
L.8.4.B	Multiple Meaning Words	248				
L.8.4.B	Roots, Affixes, and Syllables	252				
L.8.4.C	Reference Materials	256				
L.8.4.D	Using Context to Verify Meaning	260				
L.8.5.A	Interpreting Figures of Speech	264				
L.8.5.B	Relationships Between Words	268				
L.8.5.C	Denotations and Connotations	273				
L.8.6	Domain Specific Words	277				

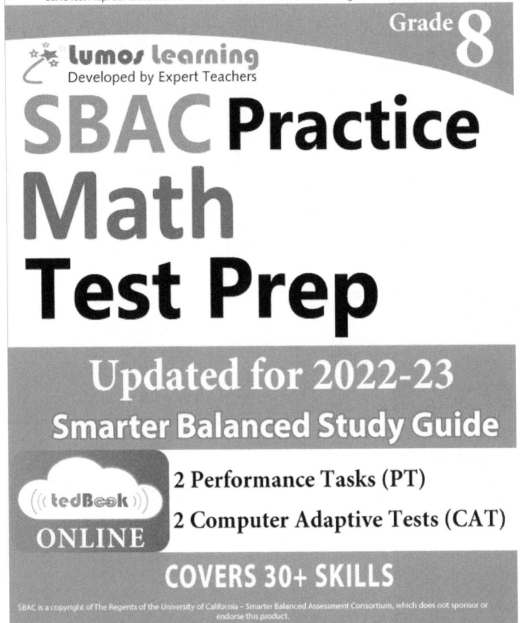

Grade 8

Lumos Learning
Developed by Expert Teachers

SBAC Practice Math Test Prep

UPDATED for 2022-23
Smarter Balanced Study Guide

(((tedBook)))
ONLINE

2 Performance Tasks (PT)

2 Computer Adaptive Tests (CAT)

COVERS 30+ SKILLS

SBAC is a copyright of The Regents of the University of California – Smarter Balanced Assessment Consortium, which does not sponsor or endorse this product.

Available

• At Leading book stores

• Online www.LumosLearning.com